MANAGING GLOBAL SUPPLY AND RISK

Best Practices, Concepts, and Strategies

Robert J. Trent ▪ **Llewellyn R. Roberts**

Copyright ©2010 by Robert J. Trent and Llewellyn R. Roberts

ISBN-13: 978-1-60427-014-3

Printed and bound in the U.S.A. Printed on acid-free paper
10 9 8 7 6 5 4 3 2 1

Library of Congress Cataloging-in-Publication Data
Trent, Robert J.
 Managing global supply and risk : best practices, concepts, and strategies
/ by Robert J. Trent and Llewellyn R. Roberts.
    p. cm.
 Includes index.
 ISBN 978-1-60427-014-3 (hardcover : alk. paper)
 1. Business logistics. 2. Risk management. 3. International trade. 4.
International business enterprises--Management. I. Roberts, Llewellyn R.,
1955- II. Title.
 HD38.5.T739

                                                    2009026694

Phone: (954) 727-9333
Fax: (561) 892-0700
Web: www.jrosspub.com

To Jan, Ellen, Jack, Natalie, and Sophia

Bob Trent

To my wonderful wife Nancy and dearest daughter Donnalee, with love

Llewellyn Roberts

CONTENTS

PART IV. PURSUING GLOBAL SUPPLY MANAGEMENT EXCELLENCE

FOREWORD

We live in a world where globalization is an inherent part of what we do. Globalization supports the very necessities of life such as food, clothing, and shelter. Regardless of where you are personally or professionally, you are most likely connected to the tangible effects of globalization. And regardless of where you are, you are living in a world where risk seems to be increasing rather than decreasing.

The globalization of world markets has reconfigured supply networks and supply chains across the globe, causing increasing complexities and challenges in sourcing and risk management. Consider for a moment the profound growth in international trade within the U.S. Since 1980 the total value of goods and services exported from the U.S. has increased almost 600% (from $271.8 billion in 1980 to $1.844 trillion in 2008). The value of services imported into the U.S. for this same period increased over 750% (from $291.3 billion in 1980 to almost $2.52 trillion in 2008). Clearly, the need to pursue global supply and to ensure that risk management is in place has never been greater.

Relentless pressure to improve constantly challenges corporate leaders with a diversity of questions:

- How do we grow our business?
- How do we improve customer satisfaction?
- How do we maintain a competitive advantage?
- How do we increase profitability?
- How do we improve cash flow?
- How do we make sense of the many laws and regulations we face daily?
- How do we deliver a reasonable return to our shareowners?
- How do we stay connected to our community and promote social responsibility?

- How do we maintain employee satisfaction?
- And ultimately, how do we win in the marketplace?

The role of procurement and supply chain professionals in ensuring business success has never been as important as it is now.

Supply management leadership has evolved over the years from a supply order taker to that of a key senior management leader involved with the most strategic corporate initiatives. It is therefore imperative that today's supply leader has the education, skill set, and experience to match the importance of, and reliance on, the position. That's what makes this book extremely timely and worthwhile as it walks the reader through the critical dependencies, education, learning, and practical experience required to be a best in class supply organization for the twenty-first century. Global supply management and global risk management are topics that every supply leader must understand.

Companies throughout the world are experiencing the effects of an ever-changing global economy. Consider some of the challenges that companies face daily as they expand their buying and selling operations around the world:

- The search for new markets and revenue channels
- Constant pressure to innovate and develop new products and services
- Constant pressure to reduce costs
- The need to manage a wide variety of global risks
- Understanding how to reduce the time to market for new products and services
- How to achieve continuous quality improvements
- How to manage volatile currencies
- Ensuring access to raw materials and supplies
- Managing fluctuations between supply and demand
- Balancing all the trade-offs associated with transportation, logistics, and inventory management
- Understanding customs, brokerage, duty, tax, and trade laws
- Dealing with trade quotas
- Responding to political and governmental unrest
- Dealing with the effects of financial market concerns
- Concerns about supplier solvency

The list could go on and on. Going global is certainly easier said than done. There are many complex components to consider when expanding into global markets, whether you are buying or selling. These are just a few of the many elements that the current and future supply professional must master. We must not merely be content with executing the day-to-day tasks at hand, but more importantly, we must focus on the future and vision of our organizations, ensuring that supply management is strategically placed at the forefront. To coin a phrase, we shouldn't just focus on where the puck is, but rather where the puck is going.

In closing, I am pleased that this book is highly educational but, most importantly, also practical. It captures many lessons learned and best practices, including business cases from companies that have a great deal to share from their globalization journey. Change is the one constant we all face. Learning and adapting should be as well. Enjoy the book!

— **James E. Mallard**
Vice President, Global Procurement,
UPS Procurement Services

PREFACE

A survey several years ago by the Foundation for the Malcolm Baldrige National Quality Award revealed almost unanimous agreement among CEOs that becoming more global was a major challenge as they looked toward the future. Furthermore, almost 80% of CEOs indicated that reducing costs and improving global supply chain performance was a top priority. Given the importance that executives placed on globalization, understanding this subject becomes a strategic necessity.

Part of the reason that globalization is or will become an integral part of the corporate business model is because most executive leaders have globalization on their minds. A challenge when thinking about globalization is that relatively few individuals understand this topic or agree about what it means. In some ways the words *global* and *quality* share a similarity: although almost everyone is familiar with these words, few can define them precisely—they're broad domains.

As a concept, globalization can evoke some raw emotions, making this discussion even more challenging. During a recent global economic summit, a masked street protester was observed smashing the windows of a Starbucks. When a reporter asked this individual why he was so angry about globalization, his responded, "Globalization is bad." To say that globalization is good or bad reveals the serious lack of understanding about a complex, multidimensional topic. On the one hand, globalization can be a way to grow markets, reduce costs, manage risks, and elevate the standard of living of people that formerly lived in poverty. On the other hand, when performed poorly, globalization can create a whole new set of complications at the company, country, and environmental level.

It is not unusual to see the word *global* tossed about too freely. Executives at all kinds of companies talk about a global footprint, global mergers, global acquisitions, global marketing, global engineering, global finance, global product design, and global manufacturing. We even hear about a push to develop global accounting standards. One area that is rarely talked about, however, is something we call global supply management. But what is global supply management, and why should we care about this topic?

The condensed view is that *global supply management* is the pinnacle of supply management played out at a worldwide level. Much more than international purchasing, the longer version views global supply management as a process that proactively integrates and coordinates common items and materials, processes, designs, technologies, and suppliers across worldwide purchasing, engineering, and operating locations. Increasingly, this coordination occurs with finance and marketing groups. Global supply management is supply management performed at the highest organizational and geographic levels. It is a process that could very well provide your company with its next quantum leap in performance. And it is a process this book will explain in detail.

When evolving from domestic purchasing to international purchasing, and then from international purchasing to global supply management, risk is a subject that must unquestionably become part of the discussion. Although risk is a complex construct with different definitions, our interpretation views risk as "the probability or likelihood of realizing an unintended or unwanted consequence." In some regards increased international purchasing and global supply management should help reduce certain kinds of risk. In other ways these activities will increase risk, particularly logistical and time risks. Risk is a broad concept with many dimensions.

A growing emphasis on international purchasing over the years has made us aware of a relatively long list of risks that link directly to the practice. A small subset from this list includes shifting currency values; pirating of intellectual property; pirates with guns; tainted products; lengthened cycle times that make planning difficult; and cost elements that chip away at those marvelously low prices. If we really think about risk hard enough, we might just become depressed. Or, if we think about risk hard enough, we might just figure out ways to assess, manage, and even prevent those nasty outcomes from occurring. Welcome to the inevitable merger of risk management and supply management. And this merger is increasingly taking place at the global level.

International purchasing, global risk management, and global supply management are not mutually exclusive topics. Anything that is purchased overseas requires suppliers and a supply chain to get to its destination. And, increasingly, these supply chains face a multitude of risks. These three areas are becoming so intertwined (or should be) that failing to recognize this interrelationship can lead to some serious surprises. It is becoming difficult to talk about international purchasing and global supply management without also including risk management as part of the discussion. We need to understand these three topics as well as their interrelationships. Let's see how this book approaches these topics.

Organization of the Book

This book blends three distinct but interrelated topics: international purchasing, global risk management, and global supply management. It is divided into five sections that present a story that is relevant today. These sections are not only loaded with the critical concepts that supply managers must understand, but they also include company examples, cases, best practices, and strategies that offer prescriptions for success.

Section I. Setting the Stage

The first section includes a single chapter that starts our journey through the world of international purchasing, global supply risk, and global supply management. Chapter 1 examines the dramatic growth in international trade; explains how macroeconomic topics affect companies at the micro level; highlights the growth in international purchasing; and explains the reasons behind this growth. Perhaps most importantly, Chapter 1 presents a continuum that highlights the progression from basic international purchasing to sophisticated global supply management. The chapter concludes by introducing how the concept of global risk fits into a discussion of international purchasing and global supply management.

Section II. Understanding International Purchasing

Section II presents the essential elements of international purchasing. For our purposes, international purchasing relates to a commercial purchase transaction between a buyer and supplier located in different countries. This type of purchase is typically more complex than a domestic purchase and presents an abundance of opportunities to expose your company to unintended consequences. We have no intention of minimizing or downplaying the complexities of international purchasing as we evolve toward global supply management.

The chapters in Section II cover some important topics that relate to international purchasing. These topics include the many issues that arise with international logistics, sourcing in emerging and low-cost countries, and the essential elements of developing total cost of ownership models. Section II also includes a chapter that addresses international purchasing for buying services internationally and the importance of cultural differences.

Section III. Managing Global Supply Risk

Although the topic of risk management appears throughout this book, it is so central to our discussion that it warrants its own section and set of chapters. The three chapters in Section III provide a comprehensive overview of global supply risk, including a thorough understanding of global risk, how to prevent and manage global supply risk, and how to leverage supply market intelligence.

Although risk is present throughout a supply chain, this book focuses primarily on that part of the supply chain that links upstream suppliers and buyers. Risks that relate to downstream distribution channels will not receive the same attention—not because that part of the supply chain is unimportant, but because it simply is not the primary focus of this book. At times the terms *supply risk* and *supply chain risk* will be used interchangeably.

Section IV. Pursuing Global Supply Management Excellence

Section IV moves beyond international purchasing by looking at supply management as part of a cohesive and coordinated worldwide strategy. At some point, supply organizations recognize they are leaving some value unrealized unless they take a more coordinated view of their worldwide supply organization.

Section IV will describe in detail what it takes to pursue supply management at a global level. This section includes five chapters that cover every aspect of global supply management. These chapters show how to make the business case for global supply management; present the critical differences between companies that pursue international purchasing and those that have evolved toward a sophisticated global supply management model; explain how to develop global supply strategies; identify the factors that are critical to global success; and present the characteristics of a world class global supply organization. Section IV concludes with three detailed cases that show how leading companies are gaining a competitive advantage from their global efforts.

The authors of a recent *Harvard Business Review* article maintain that companies of almost every size feel the strategic need to go global in one form or another (see M. Alexander and H. Kordine. When You Shouldn't Go Global. *Harvard Business Review* 2008 Dec; 70–77). This article also points out that far too often global initiatives are ill advised. And why might that be? Executives often fail to ask three fundamental questions about their global ambitions: are there potential benefits for our company; do we have the necessary management skills; and will the benefits outweigh the costs? The primary objective of Section IV is to elevate your knowledge and awareness to the point where the answer to each of these questions, at least as it pertains to your global supply management efforts, is a resounding "yes!"

Section V. Looking Toward the Future

The last section contains a single chapter that examines where we're heading in the future. What might happen within international purchasing, global risk management, and global supply management over the next 3, 5, or even 10 years? Even companies that are experienced with a global supply model know the journey is always evolving and changing. These companies never discount the need for continuous improvement. If you think that improvement is complete, it is time to step aside and let someone else lead the charge.

It's Time to Begin

Leading companies know that the improvement pressures they face from competitors and customers are relentless and severe. They also know they can never become complacent or satisfied with the status quo. It is a safe bet that what is leading edge or unique today will only define tomorrow's performance baseline. At one time, companies achieved competitive advantage from their international purchasing efforts. Then, a few companies pursued a more coordinated view of their global supply requirements and captured a whole new level of benefits. And along the way, these companies came to appreciate the important relationship between global supply management and global risk management. Slowly but surely some companies will define what the next level of global excellence looks like. The objective of this book is to make sure your company is part of that next level. Let's get to it!

ABOUT THE AUTHORS

Robert J. Trent (Bob) is the supply chain management program director, associate director of the Manufacturing Systems Engineering Program, and George N. Beckwith professor of management at Lehigh University, where he teaches at the undergraduate and graduate levels. He holds a B.S. degree in materials logistics management from Michigan State University, an M.B.A. degree from Wayne State University, and a Ph.D. in operations management from Michigan State University.

Prior to returning to academia, Bob worked for Chrysler Corporation. His industrial experience includes assignments in production scheduling; package engineering with responsibility for new part packaging setup and the purchase of nonproductive materials; distribution planning; and operations management at the Boston regional parts distribution center. He also worked on numerous special projects.

He has authored or coauthored over 30 articles appearing in the *International Journal of Purchasing and Materials Management*; the *Journal of Supply Chain Management*; the *International Journal of Physical Distribution and Logistics Management*; *Total Quality Management*; *Supply Chain Management Review*; *Inside Supply Management*; *The Purchasing Handbook; Academy of Management Executive*; *Business Horizons*; *Team Performance Management*; *Supply Chain Forum: An International Journal*; and *Sloan Management Review*.

His coauthored study on cross-functional sourcing team effectiveness was published through the Center for Advanced Purchasing Studies (CAPS) in 1993. A research report on purchasing and sourcing trends was also published through CAPS in 1995. He completed a third CAPS project in 1999 that investigated how organizations reduce the effort and transactions required to purchase low-value goods and services. A fourth CAPS project on global sourcing was published in 2006. Bob has coauthored a textbook titled *Purchasing and Supply Chain Management*. He authored *Strategic Supply Management—Creating the Next Source of Competitive Advantage*, which was published in 2007. Another book, *End-to-End Lean Management—A Guide to Complete Supply Chain Improvement*, was published in 2008.

Bob is a recipient of a National Association of Purchasing Management (now ISM) research grant for the study of cross-functional sourcing team effectiveness. Over his career at Lehigh University he has also been awarded the Class of 1961 Professorship, the Eugene Mercy Professorship, and the George N. Beckwith Professorship. Bob is also active with ISM, serving for many years as the Professional Development Director of the National Association of Purchasing Management (NAPM) of the Lehigh Valley and, at the national level, as a member of the ISM Educational Resources Committee. He and his family reside in Lopatcong Township, New Jersey. He can be reached at rjt2@lehigh.edu.

Llewellyn R. Roberts (Lew) is an industrial engineer specializing in the fields of business performance improvement and supply chain management. He has studied under Dr. Richard Schonberger, who is recognized as one of the world's leading authorities in the fields of JIT and business performance improvement.

His consulting and management development career over the last twenty years includes working with Ryder, Caliber Logistics, Exel/DHL, Menlo Worldwide, BAX Global, Owens Corning, Coca-Cola, Georgia-Pacific, Baxter, Mercedes Benz, Nissan, and many other major firms worldwide. He has developed and delivered training in strategic sourcing for major firms around the world, including firms such as UPS and De Beers.

Lew has spoken at many conferences and universities in his chosen field, including the Colorado School of Mines (by invitation of Professor Gene Woolsey), Cleveland State University, the University of Toledo, Pretoria University, the National University of Singapore, and Macquarie University. Lew has also lectured on the Executive Masters in International Logistics program (EMIL) at the Georgia Institute of Technology (Georgia Tech) in Atlanta. In addition he has written many articles on the subject of business performance improvement and supply chain management.

Lew is president and founder of L. Roberts & Associates Inc., a firm that provides a wide range of professional consulting and management development services aimed at improving business performance, with an emphasis in the field of supply chain management. Among its services, Roberts & Associates provides training in warehouse design and layout and warehouse management under license to Supply Chain Planning Limited, Cranfield University (U.K.). Lew resides with his wife in Toledo, Ohio. He can be reached at robertsasc@aol.com.

Web
Added
Value™

Free value-added materials available from
the Download Resource Center at www.jrosspub.com

At J. Ross Publishing we are committed to providing today's professional with practical, hands-on tools that enhance the learning experience and give readers an opportunity to apply what they have learned. That is why we offer free ancillary materials available for download on this book and all participating Web Added Value™ publications. These online resources may include interactive versions of material that appears in the book or supplemental templates, worksheets, models, plans, case studies, proposals, spreadsheets and assessment tools, among other things. Whenever you see the WAV™ symbol in any of our publications it means bonus materials accompany the book and are available from the Web Added Value™ Download Resource Center at www.jrosspub.com.

Downloads available for *Managing Global Supply and Risk: Best Practices, Concepts, and Strategies* consist of global sourcing and supply management assessment tools, a comprehensive process for developing and using supply management teams, and white papers describing how to measure, audit, and evaluate supply chain performance.

PART I.
SETTING THE STAGE

Chapter 1. The Changing Global Landscape

THE CHANGING
GLOBAL LANDSCAPE

To say that the search for new sources of competitive advantage is a relentless challenge grossly understates the reality of today's competitive world. Whether we are talking about marketing, finance, operations, logistics, or supply management, the need to do something better, faster, and cheaper is never ending. And nowhere is the need to show year-after-year progress greater than within the supply group.

The need to show constant improvements, particularly cost reductions, has resulted in a search for lower-cost sources of supply that has become a central part of most supply strategies. Sometimes, however, the best of intentions results in some less-than-desirable outcomes, creating a new-found awareness and appreciation of supply chain risk. Consider the following example.

In an effort to remain competitive across its product line, a U.S. producer of power tools outsourced its lower-end tools to a contract manufacturer in Asia. The plan was to allow the U.S. producer to focus on higher-margin products while still offering customers a full range of tools. Unfortunately, a seemingly sound business strategy did not lead to the best of results. The Asian supplier not only sold the excess tools it produced to other companies across Asia, but the contract manufacturer also shared the product's design among a close circle of friends. Before long the U.S. producer found itself competing in the marketplace against its own products! How could a supply strategy that was designed to help create a competitive advantage go so wrong? How could a plan that was supposed to reduce risk actually increase risk?

This chapter begins our journey through the world of international purchasing, global risk, and global supply management. It starts at a very high level by looking at the phenomenal growth in international trade. The second section examines some macroeconomic topics and discusses how they affect supply managers at the micro level. The third and fourth sections discuss the growth in international purchasing and explore the reasons behind this growth. We next present a model that underlies the framework that supports this book's progression and introduces a best-practice supply organization. The chapter concludes by introducing the important concept of global risk.

THE GROWTH IN INTERNATIONAL TRADE

Any discussion of international purchasing or global supply management would be incomplete without first stepping back and taking a look at the broader picture. The growth in worldwide commerce over the last 30 years, which includes buying and selling across borders, has been nothing short of astounding. Since the late 1980s, the level of international trade has accelerated rapidly, and the U.S. has played a major role in this growth. Starting with a discussion of the growth in worldwide trade, a broad starting point by any standard, will help lay the foundation for where we want to proceed within this book.

International trade is made up of the goods and services that enter (imports) and exit (exports) a country. For reporting purposes, the U.S. government divides imports and exports into six primary categories—foods, feeds, and beverages; industrial supplies, including petroleum and petroleum-based products; capital goods; automotive vehicles and related items; consumer goods; and other goods. Other countries also segment their trade statistics in some logical manner.

To give some idea of the magnitude of just a portion of these categories, when oil is $140 a barrel, the U.S. imports about a $1 billion a day just in petroleum. The U.S also imports several hundred billion dollars a year in automotive vehicles and parts. So it's not hard to see what makes up a major part of the U.S. trade deficit.

We hear a great deal about the trade deficit that the U.S. maintains with the rest of the world, and this roughly $700 billion annual deficit is not trivial. Often overlooked, however, is the dramatic increase in exports over the last several decades (although the economic downturn of 2008 and beyond quickly curtailed exports and import figures). Table 1.1 shows the increase in imports and exports since 1980 for goods and services. Table 1.1 also provides yearly U.S. trade balances for goods and services. Since 1980 the total value of goods exported from the U.S. has increased over 475% (from $224 billion in 1980 to almost $1.3 trillion in 2008). The value of services exported from the U.S. for this same period increased over 1000% (from $47.5 billion in 1980 to almost $552 billion in 2008).[1] Although manufacturing is still a major part of the U.S. economy, the growth

Table 1.1 U.S. Exports, Imports, and Trade Balances

Year	Exported Goods	Imported Goods	Goods Balance	Exported Services	Imported Services	Services Balance
1980	224.2	249.8	−25.5	47.6	41.5	+6.1
1981	237.0	265.1	−28.0	57.4	45.5	+11.9
1982	211.2	247.6	−36.5	64.1	51.7	+12.3
1983	201.8	268.9	−67.1	64.3	55.0	+9.3
1984	219.9	332.4	−112.5	71.2	67.7	+3.4
1985	215.9	338.1	−122.1	73.2	72.9	+0.3
1986	223.3	368.4	−145.1	86.7	80.1	+6.5
1987	250.2	409.8	−159.6	98.7	90.8	+7.9
1988	320.2	447.2	−127.0	110.9	98.5	+12.4
1989	359.9	477.7	−117.7	127.1	102.5	+24.6
1990	387.4	498.4	−111.0	147.8	117.7	+30.2
1991	414.0	491.0	−76.9	164.3	118.5	+45.8
1992	439.6	536.5	−96.9	177.3	119.6	+57.7
1993	456.9	589.4	−132.5	185.9	123.8	+62.1
1994	502.9	668.7	−165.8	200.4	133.0	+67.3
1995	575.2	749.4	−174.2	219.2	141.4	+77.8
1996	612.2	803.1	−191.0	239.5	152.6	+86.9
1997	678.4	876.8	−198.4	256.1	165.9	+90.1
1998	670.4	918.6	−248.2	262.8	180.7	+82.1
1999	684.0	1031.8	−347.8	281.9	199.2	+82.7
2000	772.0	1226.7	−454.7	298.6	223.7	+74.9
2001	718.7	1148.2	−429.5	286.2	221.8	+64.4
2002	682.4	1167.4	−484.9	292.3	231.1	+61.2
2003	713.4	1264.3	−550.9	304.3	250.4	+53.8
2004	807.5	1477.1	−669.6	349.7	292.2	+57.5
2005	894.6	1681.8	−787.1	388.4	315.7	+72.8
2006	1023.1	1861.4	−838.3	422.6	342.8	+79.7
2007	1149.2	1964.6	−815.4	479.1	372.3	+106.9
2008	1291.0	2112.0	−821.0	551.6	407.6	+144.0

Note: Numbers are in billions of dollars and are rounded.

Source: http://www.census.gov.

in services supports the contention that the U.S. is becoming a services- and knowledge-based economy.

Is it not possible that these figures have increased simply because prices have also increased? After all, higher prices will inflate the value of the goods and services that move across borders. While inflation explains some of the changes in these trade figures, the consumer price index (CPI) in 1980 averaged 82.4 and the index averaged 215.3 in 2008,representing an increase of 161%.[2] The producer price index (PPI) also showed similar restraint over this period. Factors besides price increases were clearly responsible for the dramatic export and import growth.

What other reasons might explain this phenomenal growth? Perhaps first and foremost is the overall growth in the world economy. In 1980, the U.S. gross domestic product, which represents the total value of goods and services produced in the country, was $2.8 trillion. By 2008 this figure climbed to $14.3 trillion, or an increase of over 410%.[3] The percentage growth in GDP coincided with the percentage growth in imports and exports. In fact, faster economic growth in the U.S. compared with other industrialized countries, particularly during the latter 1990s and early 2000s, combined with a strong dollar that made imports relatively cheap, were largely responsible for the widening gap between exports and imports. Imports and exports grew as the economy grew.

Other factors affect the amount and pattern of global trade. The end of the Cold War resulted in increased trade in emerging markets in Eastern Europe and Russia (although a sometimes tenuous relationship with Russia could cause a reversal of this trend). And of course, the formerly closed country known as China became receptive to international commerce and the money that came along with it. The 1990s also witnessed a growth in trade agreements that lessened import and export restrictions. World Trade Organization (WTO) rules, the General Agreement on Tariffs and Trade (GATT), and the North American Free Trade Agreement (NAFTA) all promoted a dramatic increase in worldwide trade. Various other free-trade agreements between countries, too numerous to review here, also helped to reduce trade restrictions.

The last 20 years clearly favored the dismantling of trade barriers between countries, although some will argue this dismantling was not always equitable. Interestingly, we appear to be entering a period in which free trade is not as welcomed as it was during the 1990s. The bottom line is that the world has generally become a more open place for business, at least for now.

Something that most observers probably do not realize is that a large part of international trade consists of transactions between subsidiaries or units of the same company. The U.S government calls this "related-party trade," which includes trade by U.S. companies with their subsidiaries abroad as well as trade by U.S. subsidiaries of foreign companies with their parent companies. Although related-party trade fluctuates year to year, it accounts for almost 50% of imports and almost 30% of exports.[4] Related-party trade currently comprises around 40% of the dollar value of all exports and imports in the U.S., a percentage that has remained fairly consistent over the years. As companies become more global in their operations, we should expect to see an increase in international trade in the form of related-party trade.

THE MICRO EFFECTS FROM MACRO EVENTS

It would be easy for supply managers to look at macro economic data and events, including trade data, shrug their shoulders, and wonder what this means to supply chain risk and global supply management. After all, aren't we all just little cogs in this global economic machine that seems to have a mind of its own? How much do we really control? Although the global economic system does seem to have a mind of its own, astute managers must do their best to understand this thing called the "bigger picture."

We should not even debate that what goes on at the macro or worldwide level affects supply conditions at the micro or company level, particularly because we witnessed the great financial meltdown of 2008. Furthermore, the effects of fluctuating exchange rates; surging demand in emerging countries; new trade agreements or restrictions; geographic conflict and terrorist activities; national- ization of companies (think of Venezuela); the free flow of capital as it seeks its highest return; government budget deficits; and global supply and demand that determines the price of commodities and services are all areas that impact supply managers. Let's look at some macroeconomic examples to illustrate how global changes, a constant that will always be present, affect virtually all companies.

Trade Imbalances

Economists will tell us that it is not healthy over the longer term for trade to be predominantly one way or unbalanced. World trade works best when there is some semblance of equilibrium between trading partners. We know this equi- librium is not always present because imports and exports between countries are often widely divergent in terms of volume and value. Trade imbalances such as the one between the U.S. and China, and to a lesser extent between European countries and China, have effects that may not be obvious at first glance.

One tangible area that showed the effect of trade imbalances during the last several years involved returnable shipping containers. It may be hard to believe, but in the U.S. during 2008 there was actually a widespread shortage of shipping containers for exports. With all the freight that arrives in containers from China and other parts of the world, one would think that getting a container for exporting goods would be easy. In this case that would be wrong. And trade imbalances are the reason.[5]

It was not that shipping containers did not exist. It was the *placement* of the containers that created the dilemma. Incoming containers brought tons of consumer goods to the U.S., such as electronics and clothing, largely to the U.S. west coast from Asia, where many of the containers were also unpacked. Not nearly enough goods, however, went back to those countries in the form of U.S. exports. The result: thousands and thousands of containers sat idly in California enjoying the sunny weather.

Another issue was that the exporters that needed the containers, particularly in the Midwest, were far from where the containers were being unpacked. And the places where U.S. exporters wanted to send these containers were not necessarily the Asian countries where the containers had originated (remember the trade imbalance?). As a result, the containers did not flow back and forth fully loaded or to the places that were responsible for the most U.S. exports. Compounding the problem was a shortage of chassis (the truck wheels and frames that a container sits on as it moves over the road). This shortage made it difficult to get empty containers to the places where they were needed. Additionally some big shipping lines had shifted container capacity away from the U.S. to support other worldwide trade routes just when the containers were needed the most. All these things resulted in delays, lost orders, and at times crops rotting in the fields because they had nowhere to go.

In a dramatic change of events, the great economic meltdown of 2008 rapidly changed the demand for containers as imports and exports declined rapidly throughout the world. Suddenly the major container shipping carriers were talking about taking entire ships out of service because the world was awash with unused shipping capacity. To the average exporter this situation might be painful, but it emphasizes that the connection between trade balances, the pattern of trade (what goods are going where), and supply chain infrastructure is very real.

Changing Supply and Demand Markets

Commodity markets such as rubber, corn, gold, copper, and oil are a real source of concern for many supply organizations. A primary characteristic of most commodity markets is that no single industrial buyer affects or controls prices within these markets, although cartels of producers might attempt to manipulate world markets. Many commodities operate in markets that economists call *pure competition.* This means prices are dictated by the market forces of supply and demand, although some will argue that speculators have skewed the behavior of some markets. An increase in copper demand in China means higher prices for copper buyers in Des Moines, Iowa. At the other extreme is the situation in which commodity markets, such as oil and cocoa, are controlled by cartels that affect prices through their coordinated (and some would call coercive) actions. For industrial buyers neither scenario is much fun.

Consider an example that shows how shifting commodity markets can affect innocent bystanders. For years automakers used platinum in catalytic converters for emission control. However, in anticipation of tougher rules by the U.S. government, automotive engineers designed palladium into pollution control equipment, suddenly comprising over half of the world's demand for this previously minor element. Besides being more effective at cleaning vehicle exhaust, palladium was also less expensive (at the time) than platinum, the previous element of choice for catalytic converters.[6]

At the end of the Cold War, there was a large stockpile of inexpensive palladium, particularly in Russia. Yet as engineers created designs that replaced platinum with palladium, the worldwide price of palladium became very volatile. As demand skyrocketed, palladium peaked at almost $1000 an ounce with each vehicle requiring almost an ounce of palladium. At this point, higher prices should have encouraged suppliers to provide more output, moving supply and demand closer to equilibrium—something that did not happen for two reasons. First, the two primary supply sources of palladium, Russia and Africa, were not known for supply stability. In Russia, the size of the palladium stockpile left over from the Cold War was treated as a state secret (and we know what happens to those in Russia who divulge state secrets). The Russian government also showed a willingness to "delay" releases from its stockpile, thereby creating major supply and price disruptions. Second, palladium was mined with platinum in Russia and with nickel in Africa, and the amount of palladium present was less, proportionally, than platinum or nickel. A producer would have to increase the production of platinum and nickel to increase the output of palladium. That would drive down the price of nickel and platinum as new supply flooded the market with no change in demand. Switching to palladium in pollution control equipment was a classic example in which the desire to pursue an improvement resulted in some serious unintended consequences.

Interestingly, palladium was also widely used in dental implants. Palladium had become the material of choice for some dental implant producers because it was cheaper than gold, another material used in implants. Now, put yourself in the shoes of an implant producer as he watched helplessly as automotive producers consumed most of the world's palladium, driving prices to levels that would become his worst nightmare. Fortunately, the implant producer was able to switch back to gold, which at the time was cheaper than palladium! Of course, in 2009 gold had increased to nearly $1000 per troy ounce. The dental implant producer probably looked to the heavens and asked, "Why me?"

As expected, the implosion of global industry has since brought most commodity prices back to earth, but what about the costs of moving these commodities and goods around the globe? International shipping rates that had soared during the boom times were suddenly looking much more "down to earth." In fact, a glut of shipping capacity resulting from the launch of massive new container ships had reduced shipping costs on some routes to a tenth of their previous level. Some carriers even offered to ship loaded containers for free if the shipper would cover fuel and transit fees of around $500.[7]

Changing Exchange Rates

Another macro area that affects industrial buyers and sellers is changing exchange rates. It was not that long ago that the financial headlines boldly stated, and with fairly good reason, that the U.S. would unquestionably be in a recession if it were not for the boost in GDP growth from manufactured exports; and those exports were boosted by a dollar whose value was weak relative to many U.S. trading partners. (A weaker dollar makes exports from the U.S. less expensive to foreign buyers.) The *Wall Street Journal* even published an impressive story chronicling the export-driven resurgence of Manitowoc, Wisconsin, an old industrial town that has seen its share of bad times.[8] Suddenly, the dollar began to strengthen, mainly due to the economic weaknesses of global trading partners. In the blink of an eye the headlines began to proclaim the dangers to U.S. exports because of the strengthening dollar. Are these fluctuations making you dizzy? As a side note, one of the first acts of the Obama administration was to accuse China of manipulating the Chinese currency value, something that signaled a possible change in trade relations.

A point to take away from this discussion is that events and changes that occur around the world do not happen in isolation. These events have direct and indirect effects that cannot be ignored by global risk and supply managers. For example, Hurricane Katrina directly affected a relatively small portion of the U.S. population. The hurricane's affect on government spending, logistical networks, building supplies, and energy prices, however, was not quite so limited. Supply chain risk and global supply management demand a thorough understanding of the macro events that affect supply organizations at the micro level. An important point to remember is that we need to approach supply chains and supply markets with an explicit understanding that we are all part of a much larger system that we do not control. But not being in control does not mean having to remain passive or uninformed. Constantly being reactive or caught off guard is not the best way to go through life.

THE GROWTH IN INTERNATIONAL PURCHASING

The preceding sections looked at international trade and other topics at a macro level, but don't forget that macro-level trade statistics represent the aggregation of all the micro-level transactions that occur daily. Now let's move to international purchasing, an activity that has demonstrated steady growth over the last three decades.

The number of U.S. companies that source internationally has increased dramatically over the last 35 years. Although precise data are hard to come by, between 1973 and 1975 the percentage of U.S. companies purchasing internationally doubled from around 20 to 45%. The oil embargo of the 1970s coupled with shortages of other basic materials forced purchasers to search worldwide for sources of supply. During this time many foreign producers were beginning their ascent as quality, cost, and even technology leaders. In the mid-1970s the most sought after import items by U.S. companies were production machinery and equipment followed by chemicals and mechanical and electrical components.

By 1982 the percentage of U.S. companies that engaged in international purchasing increased to just less than 60%. This growth reflected the continuing inability of domestic suppliers (and original equipment manufacturers) to compete in terms of price, quality, and even delivery performance. The early 1980s were also a difficult time economically for many U.S. companies as they adjusted to the onslaught of worldwide competition. Foreign suppliers, particularly from Japan, often provided higher-quality goods at a lower total cost compared with their U.S. counterparts. The survival of many U.S. companies demanded that they source from the same suppliers that supported their foreign competitors.

The early to late 1980s witnessed a sharp increase in the number of companies that pursued international purchasing. One study concluded that just over 70% of U.S. companies engaged in foreign sourcing by 1987. Part of this growth was attributable to a dramatic increase in the value of the U.S. dollar against other major currencies. Imports became less expensive while exports from the U.S. became more costly to foreign trading partners. U.S producers found competing in world markets difficult, leading to (then) unheard of trade imbalances. A stronger dollar coupled with a relative lack of competitiveness made life difficult for many in the U.S.

Another way to look at the growth in international purchasing, and probably a better way, is to look at the percentage of total purchases that are sourced from outside the U.S. Again, although precise numbers are hard to come by, total purchases from non-U.S. sources by U.S. companies have increased from under 10% of total purchases on average in the early 1990s to over 25% in 2000. The current figure most likely averages around 30%.[9]

A Center for Advanced Purchasing Studies (CAPS) report noted that the percentage of total direct purchases sourced on a worldwide basis has increased dramatically since 2000, growing from between 21 and 30% of total purchases to between 31 and 40% currently. Furthermore, companies expect to eventually increase direct purchases sourced offshore to between 41 and 50% of total purchases by 2010.[10] Since this CAPS report was published, dramatic economic changes have prompted some companies to look closer to home to fulfill their needs. The economic meltdown of 2008 has also altered the amount of activity and the patterns of trade. We will have to wait to see the net effect of what is occurring across world markets. What was expected to happen just a few years ago might radically change.

The rapid growth in foreign sourcing has surely been a contributing factor in the large trade deficits the U.S. maintains with much of the world. Although currency adjustments and other cost factors, such as labor and transportation, will constantly tweak the volume of goods and services that are sourced worldwide, the emphasis that U.S. producers place on international purchasing will not go away. It is safe to say that international purchasing, even with its associated risks and uncertainties, is a permanent part of the sourcing landscape. This point is the primary motivation behind this book. If we are going to do something, let's understand what we are doing, why we are doing it, and how to do it right. And let's understand how to take worldwide sourcing to the next level.

Why Do We Engage in International Purchasing?

Why do supply organizations engage in international purchasing? After all, it is probably easier to work with a supplier down the street than one located around the world. Long distances make planning and logistics more difficult; currencies fluctuations can change the economics of a transaction; different business cultures and languages can lead to misunderstandings; and the paperwork that comes with international transactions can be cumbersome. Oftentimes bad things happen with long distances. Why go through this hassle?

Industry participants consistently say the number one pressure they face day to day is a relentless pressure to reduce costs, which largely explains the motivation behind international purchasing. Regardless of the study or survey conducted, the primary reason to source on a worldwide basis is to obtain lower prices. In fact, one could say that supply managers have a solid reputation for chasing lower labor costs and goods around the globe. As a cost-cutting move, Dell Computer Corporation has announced that it is moving its European manufacturing from Ireland to Poland, no small undertaking that will affect almost 2000 employees. The move is part of a $3 billion company-wide cost reduction initiative.[11] But how long will it be before Poland is no longer cost competitive?

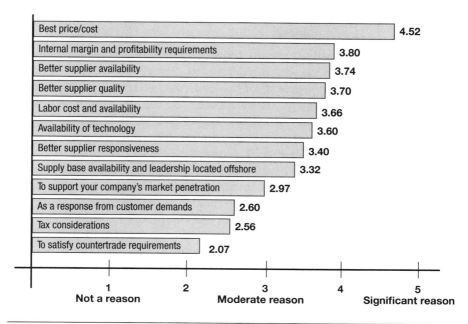

Figure 1.1. Reasons for Buying Internationally. (Adapted from R.M. Monczka, R.J. Trent, and K.J. Petersen. *Effective Global Sourcing and Supply for Superior Results*. Tempe, AZ: CAPS Research; 2006, 14.)

The next highest-rated reasons to look internationally, which may differ depending on who is being asked, sometimes hardly register on the scale. For most supply managers international purchasing is about price, price, and then price. Once in a while the decision might be about gaining access to new sources of technology, higher quality, or introducing competition to the domestic supply base, but by and large, however, price reduction is the driver.

Figure 1.1 presents data concerning the reasons why companies buy internationally. Consistent with just about any other study of international purchasing, the pursuit of lower prices is, and will likely remain, the primary motivation for buying internationally. Interestingly, research conducted in 2000 revealed that access to technology was the second most important reason for buying internationally. While access to technology still appears in Figure 1.1, cost-related reasons have moved up the list relative to technology. In all likelihood this reflects a growing emphasis over the last 8 years on sourcing from emerging countries such as China. As will be discussed in Chapter 3, the allure of sourcing from China is beginning to fade for many supply managers. At least for now, sourcing from emerging markets is primarily a function of price rather than technology needs.[12] It is important to note that this data set does not include retailers, a group that is forced to buy overseas because domestic sources are no longer competitive or even available (think of clothes and toys).

Although cost reductions usually result from the crafting of international agreements, there is also the risk of hidden costs, particularly for those who are less experienced. At least a quarter of the unit cost savings, if not more, from international purchasing disappears when estimating the total cost of ownership. This is due to hidden costs associated with longer cycle times, lengthened supply chains, and increased administrative and budget costs incurred during global strategy development and execution. The time required to analyze and execute a global agreement usually takes months longer than the time required for domestic or regional agreements. Although international purchasing can offer attractive cost-saving opportunities, the process also requires supply managers to address a wider range of issues in terms of cost, time, and complexity.

The total cost of buying internationally is called the total landed cost. Total landed cost includes many elements beyond unit price, including transportation, tariffs, third-party fees, and inventory carrying charges. Chapter 4 will show how to develop a total landed cost model, something that should routinely occur when evaluating sourcing options domestically and abroad.

An obvious but often overlooked reason why supply organizations buy internationally is because some simply do not have a choice in the matter. Some commodities are only available from certain regions, such as central Africa, Australia, or South America, making worldwide sourcing a necessity when those items are required. Also, the supply base to support certain industries, particularly in the U.S. and Europe, is gone and is not coming back anytime soon. Companies such as Intel and Apple know that electronics components and contract manufacturers are located almost exclusively in Asia today. The few shoemakers that still operate in the U.S. (primarily Allen-Edmonds and Red Wing) know that U.S. suppliers to that industry are an endangered species bordering on extinction.

Companies can have their own unique reasons for sourcing internationally to support the organization's growth strategy. These reasons can differ dramatically from Figure 1.1. Boeing, for example, actively searches for suppliers in countries where it has a major sales presence or wants to develop a major presence. The company, particularly on the defense side of its business, also faces countertrade demands, something most producers never experience. Although sourcing to help a selling position and responding to countertrade requirements are usually not primary drivers for foreign sourcing, they can be important reasons at Boeing.

CHS, once a collection of farm co-operatives that marketed U.S. farm products around the world, is now a global powerhouse that, besides representing its U.S. farmer-owners, also purchases crops from other countries to offer for sale. CHS has prospered by partnering with farmers and brokers in South America,

Eastern Europe, Australia, and Canada. These international buying partnerships allow CHS to offer grain and soybeans to customers 12 months a year rather than being constrained by the growing season within the U.S. CHS farmer-shareholders in the U.S. who once worried about letting foreign growers get a piece of their action now view things a bit differently after receiving annual dividend checks that are well into the six-figure range.

The reasons to source internationally are varied, although most studies conclude lower price is the primary driver. One thing is certain, however. Jumping on the international bandwagon because everyone else is doing it is not a sound argument. Pursuing international purchasing because it is a well-thought-out part of your supply strategy makes a better argument.

EVOLVING TOWARD GLOBAL SUPPLY MANAGEMENT

At some point supply organizations mature beyond basic international purchasing and pursue a more coordinated view of their worldwide supply operations. Central to this book, including its flow and structure, is the distinction between international purchasing and global supply management, or what some also call global sourcing. Technically speaking, we view global sourcing, which focuses more on global buying and contracting, as a subset of the broader process called global supply management. Although many in academia and in industry interchange the terms, as they are presented throughout this book, meaningful differences exist between international purchasing and global supply management. To show how confusing this can become, various terms that describe the international domain include worldwide sourcing, international sourcing, international buying, international purchasing, offshoring, foreign sourcing, worldwide buying, foreign buying, and global sourcing. We think you get the idea that many terms are used somewhat interchangeably to describe essentially the same concept. Yet few sources attempt to provide any meaningful differences between the terms. A primary objective of this book is to provide a framework that provides some differentiation between terms:

International purchasing. For our purposes, international purchasing relates to a commercial purchase transaction between a buyer and supplier located in different countries. This type of purchase is typically more complex than a domestic purchase. Organizations must contend with lengthened material pipelines, increased rules and regulations, currency fluctuations, customs requirements, increased supply chain risk, and a host of other variables such as language and time differences. Chapters 2 through 5 address the many topics that are unique to international purchasing. Chapters 6 through 8 will address the topic of supply chain risk, a topic area that is increasingly a part of the international purchasing

Figure 1.2. International Purchasing and Global Supply Management Levels.

equation. We have absolutely no intention of minimizing or downplaying the complexities of international purchasing.

Global supply management. Global supply management, which differs from international buying in its scope and complexity, is not just about buying or contracting on a worldwide basis—although that clearly is part of this construct. Global supply management is a process that proactively integrates and coordinates common items and materials, processes, designs, technologies, and suppliers across worldwide purchasing, engineering, and operating locations. It is supply management performed at the highest worldwide level. Even within global supply management we often see various levels of sophistication and progress. A supply group may be effective at developing global contracts, but is less effective at developing process consistency across its worldwide buying centers. Another may be proficient at developing process consistency, but has done little to coordinate its indirect purchase requirements. A third may be effective at managing direct items globally, but has done an incomplete job of managing capital investment items. Improvement opportunities always exist somewhere within global supply management.

It is difficult to discuss an evolution from international purchasing to global supply management without some framework underlying this progression. Figure 1.2 presents international purchasing and global supply management as a series of evolving levels or steps. An internationalization of the sourcing process takes place as companies evolve or progress from domestic purchasing to the global coordination and integration of common items (including services), processes, designs, technologies, and suppliers across worldwide locations. As will become clear, global supply management involves more than simply buying goods or services from foreign suppliers. In many ways it represents the pinnacle of supply strategy.

As defined in Figure 1.2, companies that operate at Levels II and III practice or exhibit behaviors that are characteristic of international purchasing, while companies that operate at Levels IV and V practice global supply management. As we progress through the book, this distinction will become quite meaningful. The framework presented here underlies a major part of this book, making it essential to understand the various levels that make up this model.

Although becoming harder to find, there are companies that do not engage directly in any international purchasing. This does not mean, however, that Level I companies do not use goods produced in countries other than their own. Many of these companies, for example, will use distributors that provide items that are sourced internationally. The key point is that someone else is responsible for managing the international transaction. At a personal level, all of us have purchased clothes and shoes manufactured outside our home country. However, the international supply chain issues that surround the purchase and movement of those goods across borders were not our concern.

Supply organizations progress, usually reactively, toward a basic level of international purchasing (Level II) because they are confronted by some scenario, such as a lack of suitable domestic suppliers, or because competitors are gaining an advantage (usually cost advantages) from their international practices. Level I participants may also find themselves being driven toward Level II because of various events in the supply market. Such events could be a supply disruption, rapidly changing currency exchange rates, a declining domestic supply base, or the sudden emergence of worldwide competitors. International purchasing in this level is usually limited or performed on an ad hoc or reactive basis. Most supply organizations begin to learn the fundamentals of international purchasing as they evolve to Level II.

Strategies and approaches developed in Level III begin to recognize that properly executed worldwide buying strategies can result in major improvements. In fact, and as will be demonstrated later, most of the price reductions that often drive a search for international sources are gained in Level III. However, strategies at Level III are not well coordinated across worldwide buying locations, operating centers, functional groups, or business units. Each unit is operating essentially as a stand alone or decentralized buying center. Many of the benefits that are available from global supply management are not as readily available to those that practice international purchasing. (Chapters 2 through 5 address a range of topics that are associated with international purchasing.)

At some point supply organizations begin to realize that it might be in their best interests to begin integrating and coordinating their sourcing activities on a worldwide basis. Chapter 9 will present very compelling evidence that successfully practicing global supply management (Levels IV and V) results in a range of benefits that are simply not available when operating at Levels I to III. Chapters

9 through 13 focus specifically on achieving excellence in global supply management.

Level IV, which is the first of two global supply management levels in this model, represents the integration and coordination of sourcing strategies across worldwide buying locations. Operating at this level requires worldwide information systems; personnel with sophisticated knowledge and skills; extensive coordination and communication mechanisms; an organizational structure that promotes central coordination of global activities; and executive leadership that endorses a global approach to sourcing. Although worldwide integration occurs in Level IV, which is not the case with Level III, the integration is primarily cross-locational rather than cross-functional. Level IV also features an extensive focus on global contracting.

Organizations that operate at Level V have achieved the cross-locational integration that those operating at Level IV have achieved. The primary distinction is that Level V participants integrate and coordinate common items, processes, designs, technologies, and suppliers across worldwide purchasing centers *and with other functional groups*, particularly engineering. This integration occurs during new product development as well as during the sourcing of items or services to fulfill continuous demand or aftermarket requirements. Furthermore, design, build, and sourcing responsibilities are often assigned to the most capable units around the world.

A major distinction between Level IV and V participants is that the highest-level companies do not view global supply management so much in terms of global contracting or buying. Although global contracting is important (just as all the international purchasing issues that lower-level companies face do not go away as a company progresses toward higher levels), the most sophisticated companies look to global supply management as a means to develop a consistency across buying locations that less sophisticated organizations lack. This theme will emerge repeatedly in Chapters 9 through 13.

Only those companies that have worldwide design, development, production, logistics, and procurement capabilities can progress to Level V. Data presented in Chapter 9 will show that most supply managers expect their organization to advance toward the more sophisticated levels presented in this model. The reality is that many supply organizations will lack the understanding or the willingness to achieve this level of sophistication. Some will not even have the necessity to advance much past Level IV. This reality is one of the reasons underlying the development of this book.

Taking a global supply perspective demands a solid understanding and blueprint concerning how to make this transition. Chapters 11 and 12 will identify the attributes of an advanced Level V organization as defined by quantitative research and detailed executive interviews. (In reality, no supply organization in our experience demonstrates all the features that will be presented within those chapters.) A framework presented in Chapter 12 will serve as a useful guide when developing internal improvement plans.

When looking at the five-level model in Figure 1.2, supply professionals should view global supply management as a process rather than as a set of discrete activities or approaches—and it is a global process that is about as far from being reactive or passive as one can get. Global supply management should become an integral and imbedded part of supply planning and execution. (Developing a leading-edge global supply management process makes sense for some sound reasons, which Chapter 9 will present in detail.)

Looking across most industries leads to an unmistakable conclusion: competitive and customer pressure to improve is severe—and this pressure is not going away in our lifetime. The winners will be those companies that understand how to leverage and coordinate their activities on a global basis. For many, global supply management offers an attractive and largely untapped opportunity to achieve the performance breakthroughs required to compete in intensely competitive markets. It is our job in this book to provide the blueprint that helps make this a reality.

A Global Supply Management Success Story

Throughout this book we will present cases and best practices that highlight the ideas we are presenting. Let's start with Air Products, a U.S.-based company that designs and operates industrial gas facilities in over 30 countries. Air Products has attained some serious cost benefits from its global supply efforts.

Several years ago, executives at Air Products were surprised when an internal study concluded that the company must lower its operating costs by 30% to remain competitive globally. This was due to the emergence of low-cost competitors in Asia/Pacific along with industrial buyers increasingly viewing the company's products as commodity items, both of which, at the time, created extensive downward pricing pressures.

In their search for improved performance, managers concluded that globalization offered extensive and untapped improvement opportunities. Air Products had historically operated in an engineer-to-order environment using regional design and procurement centers, which resulted in highly customized design and procurement efforts for each new project as well as a lack of coordination between the company's North American and European units. Remaining competitive demanded that Air Products better coordinate design and sourcing activities across its worldwide locations.

A major action taken was to first define what globalization meant. (It's surprising: for a term that almost everyone has heard of, most people either have a different perspective of its meaning—some outside of industry will simply describe globalization as a bad thing—while others cannot even begin to describe its meaning.) At Air Products globalization referred to a process that brought together global engineering and procurement to capture worldwide design and sourcing synergies.

Recall that a differentiating feature between Level IV and Level V is a willingness of supply managers to integrate and coordinate activities with other functional groups. Each newly designed facility at Air Products now involves an extensive analysis between U.S. and European centers to identify areas of commonality, standardization, and synergy in procurement and design. Cross-functional teams, with members from the U.S. and Europe working jointly, develop common design specifications and contracts that satisfy each center's needs while supporting future replacement and maintenance requirements.

After years of experience and over 100 global agreements in place, Air Products averages 20% in cost savings compared with its previous sourcing and design practices. Furthermore, worldwide design and procurement centers have better aligned their sourcing philosophies and strategies between themselves and with the corporate business strategy. What makes this process add additional value is the fact that procurement managers now work with marketing to include expected savings from in-process global projects when responding to customer proposals. Global supply management is providing a new source of competitiveness to a company that operates in a mature industry. Chapter 13 will build on this example and show how Air Products has moved beyond a focus on global contracts to one of developing consistency across its worldwide sourcing processes and locations.

DON'T FORGET ABOUT SUPPLY CHAIN RISK

As companies search the world over to find lower cost sources of supply, a topic that has sometimes been lost in the shuffle concerns supply chain risk. In some ways, increased globalization should reduce some forms of risk. Yet in other ways, globalization will increase certain kinds of risk, particularly logistical risk. Risk is a broad concept with many dimensions.

Although risk is a construct that has different interpretations, one interpretation that captures the concept well views risk as the probability or likelihood of realizing an unintended or unwanted consequence. As individuals we face risk every day, whether we are walking down a set of stairs, driving a car, using products that we hope will perform safely, or trusting that others will not do something that harms our well being. At the supply and supply chain level, we face risks associated with shifting currency values; suppliers failing to deliver on time;

on time; quality defects; price increases for purchased materials that make our products no longer profitable; material shortages; labor disputes that lead to dockworkers slowing down the unloading of ships; and 1001 other scenarios that keep managers up at night. If we really think about risk hard enough, we might just become downright discouraged. Or, if we think about this topic long enough, we might just figure out ways to assess, manage, and even prevent those nasty risk outcomes from occurring in the first place.

Supply managers should not risk ignoring the topic of risk. In fact, one could make a convincing argument that at a higher level the three primary objectives of supply chain managers today are to manage risk, relationships, and trade-offs. The topic of risk prevention and management is that important. On the supply side it is becoming difficult to talk about global supply management without also including risk management as part of the discussion.

Global supply management and supply risk are not mutually exclusive topics. Anything that is purchased oversees requires suppliers and a supply chain to get to its destination; and, increasingly, these suppliers and supply chains face a multitude of risks. Although risk as a topic has earned the right to have its own set of chapters, other chapters will show how global supply management can help alleviate supply chain risk. These two areas, supply chain risk management and global supply management, are becoming so intertwined (or should be) that failing to recognize this interrelationship can lead to some serious surprises. More and more supply organizations are requiring commodity teams to develop risk management plans when developing their supply management strategies.

Although risk is present at any point along a supply chain, this book focuses primarily on the link between upstream suppliers and buyers. Risk issues that relate to downstream distribution channels will not receive the same attention. This is not because the downstream portion of the supply chain is not important. It is simply not the primary focus of this book.

CONCLUDING THOUGHTS

This chapter began by talking about the growth in international trade, a broad topic by anyone's measure, and ended with discussions about the need to think about global supply management and supply chain risk. So, where do we go from here? The next four chapters provide much more detail about the operational topic called international purchasing. After that we present three chapters that address the important topic of risk. A series of five chapters will next explain the logic behind global supply management as well as how to pursue it correctly. The book concludes with a look toward the future.

REFERENCES

1. From www.census.gov.

2. From www.bls.gov.

3. From www.bea.gov.

4. From www.census.gov foreign trade statistics.

5. T. Aeppel. Container Shortage Puts U.S. Export Boom in a Box. *The Wall Street Journal* 2008 April 10; B1.

6. G.L. White. Unruly Element: Russian Maneuvers Are Making Palladium More Precious than Ever. *Wall Street Journal* 2000 March 6; A1.

7. J.W. Miller. The Mega Containers Invade. *The Wall Street Journal* 2009 January 26; B1.

8. T. Aeppel. Export Boom Fuels Factory Town's Revival. *The Wall Street Journal* 2008 July 18; A1.

9. R.M. Monczka and R.J. Trent. Purchasing and Supply Management: Key Trends and Changes Throughout the 1990s. *International Journal of Purchasing and Materials Management* 1998 Fall; 34(4): 2–11.

10. R.M. Monczka, R.J. Trent, and K.J. Petersen. *Effective Global Sourcing and Supply for Superior Results.* Tempe, AZ: CAPS Research; 2006, 13.

11. Q. Fottrell and J. Scheck. Dell Moving Irish Operations to Poland. *The Wall Street Journal* 2009 January 9; B4.

12. R.M. Monczka, R.J. Trent, and K.J. Petersen. *Effective Global Sourcing and Supply for Superior Results.* Tempe, AZ: CAPS Research; 2006, 14.

PART II. UNDERSTANDING INTERNATIONAL PURCHASING

2

MANAGING INTERNATIONAL LOGISTICS ISSUES

It is no secret that the global business market is changing. And it is also no secret that companies that are ill-prepared to make the necessary changes to compete globally stand a good chance of losing their competitive advantage. Logistics plays a vital role in the global market. Therefore, logistics, or the means whereby we obtain products from foreign countries, is of prime importance to supply managers. Because international carriers transport goods, either by air, road, rail, or sea and "grease the wheels" of global commerce, we cannot do one (purchasing) without the other (logistics).

Demographics combined with economic forces and changing geopolitical events are changing the global market. In the not too distant future, various experts predict that Asia's GDP will be greater than that of North America. Within Asia, China and India are predicted to remain among the world's fastest growing economies.[1] As a result, leading companies are formulating sourcing strategies on a global basis. This includes strategically sourcing materials worldwide; selecting global locations for key supply and distribution centers; using existing and potential new logistics networks when sourcing and distributing products; transferring existing technologies to emerging markets; and learning from best practitioners in supply management worldwide.

The growth in international purchasing and trade has had a major impact on logistics. The complexity of logistics and transportation has increased because of greater distances, different modes of transportation, and an increase in the number of carriers and parties involved. Domestic transportation and distribution networks must link with global transportation and distribution networks. For those companies distributing and sourcing globally, transportation and distribution systems are the thread that ties geographically dispersed regions together.[2] It almost goes without saying that companies doing business around the globe must rely on a transportation and distribution network that is reliable and capable.

The need to blend international purchasing and international logistics topics reflects the early placement of this topic in this book. In Chapter 2 we examine the various international logistical issues that must be confronted.

INTERNATIONAL LOGISTICS COMPLEXITIES

Increased speed and improvements in transportation and communication have facilitated the growth of the global economy. The total value of world merchandise imports in 2002 was $7.9 trillion. By 2008 this figure had grown to over $19 trillion—evidence of the strong growth in world trade.[3] With this growth came an increase in material movement, handling, and storage.

Although Canada and the U.S. remain important trading partners, there has been a growth in imports to North America from other parts of the world. Figure 2.1 shows the top 15 trading partners of the U.S. and their volume of import and export trade with the U.S. The expansion of global markets has resulted in increasing supply chain logistics complexity.

It is not surprising that logistics presents some of the biggest concerns for supply managers. The desire to move toward integrated logistics domestically is also occurring globally. A requirement for integrated services has led many companies to outsource their logistics activities to third-party logistics (3PL) providers that have the required expertise and global reach. Deregulation and globalization have resulted in a series of mergers and alliances in the 3PL industry, as service providers attempt to provide a global presence for their major customers. In this section we will outline the key logistics challenges that modern supply managers face, including:

- Longer material pipelines
- Increase in total supply chain costs
- Increased supply chain risk
- Poor and differing logistics infrastructures
- Different shipping terms, laws, and acts
- Reverse logistics requirements
- Increased use of agents and third parties
- Environmental issues and concerns
- Supply chain security and post 9-11 requirements

The nuances of managing currencies internationally are presented in Chapter 7.

Rank	Country	Total Trade (billions of $)
1	Canada	562.0
2	China	386.7
3	Mexico	347.3
4	Japan	208.1
5	Germany	144.0
6	U.K.	107.2
7	South Korea	82.3
8	France	69.0
9	Taiwan	64.7
10	Netherlands	51.4
11	Brazil	50.3
12	Venezuela	50.0
13	Italy	49.2
14	Saudi Arabia	46.0
15	Singapore	44.7

Figure 2.1. Top 15 Trading Partners of the U.S. (Adapted from World Trade's 2008 Top U.S. Trading Partners and Trade Gateways. *World Trade Magazine* 2008 Aug 7.)

Longer Material Pipelines

Longer material supply pipelines pose a variety of challenges and concerns for supply managers. Lead times and delivery times are naturally extended when sourcing internationally. Although improvements in the quality of transportation and the ability to track and trace shipments electronically have helped to reduce uncertainty, a buyer can still experience additional lead time in several areas. Delays can occur when working with countries where the transportation infrastructure is poor, resulting in delays within that country and at the point of embarkation for the goods. In addition, delays can occur in processing goods between countries through customs—especially in third world or less-developed countries. Delays can also occur at the transfer points for goods due to congestion at these points or simply due to the need for multiple handling.

Longer supply pipelines mean that the lead time to obtain goods is extended, and worse, any changes to scheduled delivery compound this extra lead time, rippling throughout the entire supply chain. Therefore, a supply manager's concerns are magnified: he or she must engage in much longer-range planning, must have in place early warning systems for potential late deliveries, and must have backup resources planned and available. Additionally, in order to compensate for potential shortages, it is often necessary to hold additional inventory as safety stock.

As supply chains stretch across greater distances and across international borders, we become more susceptible to delays and problems caused by transportation disruptions. Recent examples of this include Hurricane Katrina, which disrupted the ocean-borne supply of polyethylene foam used in furniture and mattresses, causing polyethylene prices to jump 60% the day after the hurricane hit land. A labor strike at U.S. West Coast ports in 2003 caused a disruption for computer manufacturers that were waiting for electronic parts from Asia. A related example involves the introduction of the Nintendo Wii game console in 2006. Nintendo wasn't able to keep up with demand and an extended supply pipeline resulted in widespread stock-outs and lost sales.

Increase in Total Supply Chain Costs

With longer supply pipelines comes the need for more inventories to "fill" the pipeline, an added cost that can represent as much as 30 to 40% of the cost of the goods. These inventory carrying charges consist of all of the major components of inventory, including the cost of capital, labor, storage, or damages that are often unaccounted for when companies weigh the total cost of sourcing from other countries. It is the additional costs of purchasing internationally that may make a potential decision to source in other countries less attractive or even marginal. Other cost elements that can increase the total cost of doing business around the world include:

- Freight forwarding and customs clearance and services
- Additional touch points and handling that leads to additional labor costs as well as potential damages
- Loss-of-goods costs including losses from natural disasters, spoilage, or theft
- Costs required to protect the environment from the goods or to protect the goods from the environment
- Costs of fuel that increase with greater distances
- Costs related to additional staff in the supply chain, including additional staff needed to manage the inevitable problems of extended supply chains

Costs associated with delivery-window variability also play a role here. As supply distances increase, delivery-window variability also increases. This has the added effect of increasing inventory costs, expediting costs, and planning costs that are incurred to ensure customers receive their goods on time.[4] A lack of coordination between domestic and international transportation networks can also add to the stress.

Once the major supply chain-related costs are taken into account, it may not be worthwhile to outsource to low-cost countries or to outsource at all. Recent studies have shown that costs are increasing, sometimes rapidly in certain countries. Food prices and wages, for example, have recently increased sharply in China, a favorite sourcing location for many Western companies. This situation certainly has an affect on total supply chain costs.

Many companies continue to view outsourcing as necessary in order to remain competitive. However, many companies that have made the decision to outsource to China and other parts of the world from the U.S. are reconsidering this strategy as they begin to understand the true supply chain costs. Some companies are considering *nearshoring*, a term that refers to the sourcing of manufacturing or service activities to a foreign, lower-wage country that is relatively close in distance. By doing this the customer expects to benefit from closer proximity: geography, time, culture, language, economy, politics, and/or historical linkages. Research has shown that products are more likely to be manufactured on a near-shore basis when they:[5]

- Require automated processes to produce them
- Are of a size or weight that will incur high transportation charges via air or ocean
- Need inherent scheduling flexibility
- Have intellectual or patent rights that lend themselves to being easily copied and marketed

Consider an example of increased global supply chain costs that influenced sourcing decision making for a U.S. producer of office furniture. The office furniture company carried out a detailed cost exercise to determine where the company should have office furniture components manufactured and assembled. Management commissioned a study to determine the total landed cost of manufacture and assembly from various Asian and European countries. The study concluded that from a labor cost perspective, it was cheaper to produce the subassemblies in China with final assembly in China and Japan. However, once the carrying charges for the inventory in the supply pipeline were accounted for, it was actually less expensive to have subassemblies produced in Europe with final assembly in the U.S.

Whether offshoring or nearshoring, best practice companies need to ensure they have analyzed all supply chain costs before sourcing globally. In addition, best practice companies revisit these supply chain costs on a regular basis because costs can change due to micro- and macroeconomic events. (Chapter 4 covers total cost analysis in greater detail.)

Increased Supply Chain Risk

Although the world is full of opportunities for supply managers, it is also full of risk. It would be hard to argue with the notion that the risks that are present when sourcing locally are often magnified when sourcing globally. Supply and logistics managers must understand what these risk elements are and then manage them by having plans in place that ensure continuity of supply. The following are but a few examples of undesirable outcomes that potentially may occur when sourcing globally.

Damages. For several reasons the risk of damages to goods sourced overseas increases dramatically. The first key factor has to do with the increased handling that goods must undergo in transit from distant points. Each time goods are handled the chances of damages to products in transit increase. Although many shipments are packed in overseas containers, significant handling of the goods within these shipments can take place prior to the goods being placed into a container. In addition, goods can be damaged even within the containers due to long transit times and rough seas. Goods might also be transported through countries where the logistics infrastructure is not particularly good and where roads are poor and less-suitable vehicles are used. Untrained or careless operators might also handle the goods in a manner leading to damage to the goods.

Theft. Theft is highly prevalent in certain countries, especially underdeveloped nations. Most companies do not want to publicize the extent to which they experience international supply chain theft. This theft is often carried out by highly organized groups in countries with poor security and policing. Newspapers are full of accounts of such theft, ranging from the recent cases of piracy of goods on container ships off the East coast of Africa to the case of a major 3PL provider doing business through a distribution center in Mexico. In the case in Mexico, a vehicle displaying the logo of a third party arrived at a distribution center to pick up a shipment of CDs. The men in the vehicle presented the necessary paperwork, loaded up the CDs, and left the premises. Soon after, the real truck arrived to pick up the CDs only to discover—to everyone's surprise—that a truck with a fake logo had been used to steal the highly valuable shipment of CDs. Later the truck was found abandoned on a stretch of dirt road. The CDs were never recovered. In addition to physical theft of goods, we often hear of the theft of intellectual capital. Examples abound of companies that sent samples of products overseas to be manufactured. Within a relatively short time, the designs were copied, manufactured, and sold without permission. (Chapter 3 addresses intellectual property theft in greater detail.) Whether physical or intellectual, the time and cost required to recover from supply chain theft is surely substantial.

Delays. The chance that a shipment will be delayed increases when the shipment originates overseas. Longer transportation routes combined with the potential need to merge goods with other shipments in transit, along with the necessary customs clearances, can cause considerable delays. The use of poorer-quality logistics infrastructures can also contribute to delays through inherent inefficiencies of distribution networks.

Loss. A very real danger in transporting or storing goods in international supply chains is the risk of loss of goods due to man-made or natural disasters. Even though insurance is available for this purpose, the loss of a key shipment of goods can be substantial: a company might have to expedite additional shipments of goods; temporarily seek other more expensive sources of supply; or temporarily idle a plant while awaiting replenishment. A worst-case scenario features customers who become dissatisfied and terminate their business.

Best practice companies understand that risk is inherent in sourcing globally and they institute structured risk-assessment and management practices. Chapters 6 and 7 cover risk management in greater detail.

Poor and Differing Logistical Infrastructures

Significant challenges exist within developing nations in terms of their infrastructures, including roadways, rail and air systems, and ports and waterways. This situation is more prevalent in some countries than in others as well as in certain parts of the same country. For example, in China the infrastructure closer to the main ports and coastal regions might be acceptable. However, these roadways deteriorate the further inland one travels, resulting in delays and problems for shipments. Although major plans are underway to expand the total size of the highway network in China, the current situation is that poor road networks still exist.

Increased road travel and the increased use of motor vehicles for the transportation of people and goods have meant an increase in traffic accidents. The growth in the number of drivers on China's expanding network of roads has not come without a cost: China's roadways are some of the most dangerous on the planet. According to estimates from the World Health Organization, more than 600 people die each day in China due to vehicle accidents. Beyond China, road accidents in general are a major public health problem in Asia and the Pacific, with some 10 million people severely injured or killed annually on the region's roads.[6]

Other infrastructure challenges exist overseas as well. For example, as hard as it may be to believe, differences in rail gauges and rail delivery reliability between

Western and Eastern Europe still exist. In addition, there are questions about the capability and efficiency of technology and information systems in some countries. A lack of adequate technology may create problems for Western partners when these inadequate or outdated systems are used. When communications systems that link via satellite with road transportation are lacking, companies may lose the information that they need to successfully manage the supply chain.

Differing Shipping Terms, Laws, and Acts

To manage international logistics well, one must be good at jugging many balls at once—transportation services; origins and destinations; equipment; service providers; service contracts; quality control; government and agency regulation compliance; cargo insurance; transit times, product payment; and customs clearance, to name a few. Related to these challenges are the differing shipping terms used internationally and locally. For example, in the U.S., *Incoterms* are used internationally and the Uniform Commercial Code (UCC) is used domestically. It is important to know and understand Incoterms when conducting business overseas. Without question Incoterms add a layer of complexity to a buyer/seller transaction.

Incoterms are broadly defined as internationally accepted commercial terms that define the roles of the buyer and seller in the arrangement of transportation and other responsibilities and clarify when the ownership of goods takes place. These terms, developed by the International Chamber of Commerce, are used in conjunction with a sales agreement or some other method of transacting a sale. Although not obligated, buyers and sellers are encouraged to use this standardized set of terms to facilitate international trade.

Table 2.1 provides an overview of 13 main Incoterms, which are reviewed every 10 years. Incoterms 2000 is the current version. Knowledgeable observers do not anticipate any major revisions during the next review period. Incoterms address various ways to handle risk of loss and transportation responsibility as goods move from a seller to a buyer. The following list highlights the primary characteristics of the terms within each group:

- **E terms**: departure contract in which the buyer bears all transportation costs and risks from the seller's premises
- **F terms**: shipment contract in which the main carriage or shipment cost is paid by the buyer, but the transportation to get to the main carriage is paid by the seller
- **C terms**: shipment contract in which main carriage is paid by the seller to the buyer's named destination
- **D terms**: arrival contract in which the seller bears all costs to the country of destination

The UCC is one of a number of uniform acts that have been developed to harmonize the law of sales and other commercial transactions in 49 U.S. states (Louisiana has historically followed French law rather than the more common British influence). Domestic contracts are generally drafted according to the basic principles of U.S. contract law, primarily those set out in Article 2 of the UCC that governs contracts for sales of goods. Article 2 establishes rules for how contracts are formed; the rights and obligations of the buyer and seller; what constitutes a breach of contract; and a party's remedies for such breach.

In addition, the United Nations Convention on International Sales of Goods (CISG), a treaty that the U.S. and 71 other countries are party to, may govern international contracts. Many U.S. trading partners (including Canada, Mexico, most European countries, China, Korea, Argentina, Chile, Australia, and Singapore, but excluding the U.K. and Japan) are parties to this agreement. A contract for a sale of goods between parties in countries that have signed the treaty will be governed by the CISG.

Broad range of laws when conducting international business. A supply manager will encounter a broad range of laws when conducting business internationally; and these laws and conventions also have some degree of conflict with each other. For example, depending on the country, the CISG can represent a small or great departure from local legislation relating to the sale of goods.[7] Each country has developed (and uses) its own set of commercial laws, creating a tangled web of information for companies to sort out. Certain laws require that passage of title and the risk of loss take place upon conclusion of the agreement between the seller and buyer. In other cases, passage takes place when the bill of lading consigned to the buyer is issued. In certain other countries commercial laws require actual physical delivery to the buyer at the place agreed upon between the buyer and the seller. There are also variations in some of these laws that specify functions in the transaction that will trigger the passage of title and risk.[7] Examples of some of the areas that can lead to confusion include:[7]

- Many countries that have signed the CISG have made declarations and reservations as to the treaty's scope.
- Discrepancies might exist in the seller's offer and the buyer's purchase order. The CISG and the UCC treat these discrepancies differently.
- Unless otherwise specified by a ratifying state, the CISG does not require that a sales contract be in writing. The CISG recognizes oral contracts for any amount. Under the UCC, oral contracts selling goods for a price of $500 or more are generally not enforceable.
- Various statutes apply to bills of lading and passage of title for export shipments under the U.S. legal system.
- When a trade term is used without reference to a specific set of trade term definitions and issue dates, a conflict might arise as to the responsibilities of the parties.

Table 2.1 Incoterms 2000: Overview of Terminology

Incoterm	Description
Ex Works (EXW)	The buyer bears all costs and risks involved in taking the goods from the seller's premises to the desired destination. The seller's obligation is to make the goods available at his premises (works, factory, warehouse, etc.). This term represents a minimum obligation for the seller. This term can be used across all modes of transport.
Free Alongside Ship (FAS)	The seller has fulfilled his obligation when goods have been placed alongside the vessel at the port of shipment. The buyer is responsible for all costs and risks of loss or damage to the goods from that moment. The buyer is also required to clear the goods for export. This term should only be used for sea or inland waterway transport.
Free on Board (FOB)	Once the goods have passed over the ship's rail at the port of export, the buyer is responsible for all costs and risks of loss or damage to the goods from that point. The seller is required to clear the goods for export. This term should only be used for sea or inland waterway transport.
Free Carrier at (FCA)	The seller's obligation is to hand over the goods, cleared for export, into the charge of the carrier named by the buyer at the named place or point. If no precise point is indicated by the buyer, the seller may choose within the place or range stipulated where the carrier shall take the goods into its charge. When the seller's assistance is required in making the contract with the carrier, the seller may act at the buyer's risk and expense. This term can be used across all modes of transport.
Cost and Freight (CFR)	The seller must pay the costs and freight required in bringing the goods to the named port of destination. The risk of loss or damage is transferred from seller to buyer when the goods pass over the ship's rail in the port of shipment. The seller is required to clear the goods for export. This term should only be used for sea or inland waterway transport.
Cost, Insurance, and Freight (CIF)	The seller has the same obligations as under CFR; however, he is also required to provide insurance against the buyer's risk of loss or damage to the goods during transit. The seller is required to clear the goods for export. This term should only be used for sea or inland waterway transport.
Carriage Paid to (CPT)	The seller pays the freight for the carriage of goods to the named destination. The risk of loss or damage to the goods occurring after the delivery has been made to the carrier is transferred from the seller to the buyer. This term requires the seller to clear the goods for export. This term can be used across all modes of transport.
Carriage and Insurance Paid to (CIP)	The seller has the same obligations as under CPT, but also has the responsibility of obtaining insurance against the buyer's risk of loss or damage of goods during the carriage. The seller is required to clear the goods for export, but the seller is only required to obtain insurance on minimum coverage. This term requires the seller to clear the goods for export. This term can be used across all modes of transport.

Table 2.1 (continued) Incoterms 2000: Overview of Terminology

Incoterm	Description
Delivered at Frontier (DAF)	The seller has fulfilled his obligation when the goods have been made available, are cleared for export, and are at the named point and place at the frontier, but before the customs border of the adjoining country. The term "frontier" may be used for any frontier including that of the country of export. Therefore, it is important that the frontier in question be defined precisely by always naming the point and place in the term. The term is generally used when goods are to be carried by rail or road, but may be used for any mode of transport.
Delivered Ex Ship (DES)	The seller has fulfilled his obligation to deliver when the goods are available to the buyer on board the ship, but not cleared for import at the main port of destination. The seller is responsible for all costs and risk of loss or damage in bringing the goods to the named port of destination. This term should only be used for sea or inland waterway transport.
Delivered Ex Quay (DEQ)	The seller has fulfilled his obligation to deliver when the goods are available to the buyer on the quay (wharf) at the named port of destination and cleared for importation. The seller is responsible for all risks and costs including duties and taxes in making available the goods at the port of destination. This term should only be used for sea or inland waterway transport.
Delivered Duty Unpaid (DDU)	The seller is required to deliver the goods to the named place in the country of importation. The seller is responsible for costs and risks involved in bringing the goods to the import destination (excluding duties and taxes) and arranging customs formalities. This term may be used regardless of the mode of transport.
Delivered Duty Paid (DDP)	Similar to DDU; however, in DDP the seller is responsible for delivering the goods in the named place in the country of importation and all costs and risks in bringing the goods to import destination including duties, taxes, and customs formalities. This term may be used regardless of the mode of transport.

All of these conflicting statutes, laws, and terms can lead to confusion if the governing laws for the countries where the goods are being sourced are not fully understood. Best practice companies ensure that a full understanding of these laws exists, often by retaining legal counsel that is intimately familiar with local laws and regulations. In our experience it is simply not feasible for supply managers to be familiar with the extensive rules that change from country to country. Obviously, this complexity will only increase the total cost of sourcing internationally.

An overall best practice is to ensure that all goods leaving a company have warehouse-to-warehouse insurance. With warehouse-to-warehouse insurance, goods are insured against risk of loss no matter where they are in the supply chain. Under this arrangement, the insurance certificate is payable to the "Assured." It may be passed from seller to buyer. When the seller that obtained the insurance endorses the certificate, the coverage passes to the buyer.[7]

Reverse Logistics Requirements

In order to cut costs and improve customer relationships, managing returns—or reverse logistics—is a critical area of focus for a company. Product returns impose heavy financial costs on a business, and often returns-management procedures detract from a customer's experience. Returns reduce net revenues by increasing the costs of inventory, packaging, and customer-service-processing. If a product is defective, and the returns process is inefficient, the impact could be negative on a retailer's reputation, perhaps causing future sales to decline.

When sourcing globally, reverse logistics takes on an even more significant role in the supply chain because of the greater distances and time involved. A key issue in cross-border logistics is the management of reverse logistics from two overall points of view. First, the distances involved present challenges. Careful coordination and control is required, with the necessary information systems being in place to support reverse logistics. Second, different countries have different rules and regulations regarding the impact of logistics (and reverse logistics) operations on the environment. In Western Europe, for example, there is a high degree of emphasis on protection of the environment with strict regulations in place. This in turn has specific implications for the disposal of items and packaging in the reverse logistics flow and the effect of these items on the environment. (This point is further addressed in a following section, *Environmental Issues and Concerns.*)

Increased Use of Agents and Third Parties

As firms increase their global reach, they often find that they need to review their internal capabilities in managing the global supply chain. In many cases firms decide to outsource this function in whole or in part to agents or 3PL firms. Primary services offered by agents and 3PL firms are outbound transportation, warehousing, inbound transportation, freight-bill auditing and payment, customs brokerage, freight forwarding, and customs clearance.

Companies often do not have in-house lawyers, accountants, or IT personnel that are familiar with overseas issues. This is a key reason for turning to the use of agents and third parties with global capabilities, including an understanding of the requirements for doing business in foreign countries from a supply chain perspective.

Companies look to agents and third parties to provide financial and operational performance improvements. Outsourcing often requires decentralizing the operational aspects of supply chain management to ensure they occur in the most advantageous locations and are performed by best-in-class suppliers. Strategic outsourcing requires a collaborative approach to removing cost and time from the supply chain, often through a different set of processes enabled by technology. In addition, most executives understand the need for better decision-making and strategy execution supported by sharing of valuable information. Therefore, it is incumbent upon 3PL companies to position themselves with resources and processes to exceed their customers' expectations.

Agents and 3PL companies. In today's world of global sourcing, agents and other third party logistics firms are required to have sophisticated logistics teams that understand everything from air to ocean to rail to port-related activities; customs clearance activities; regulatory issues; and compliance issues, as well as the idiosyncrasies at the individual country level. Some major 3PL firms offer a range of services that can be combined to provide end-to-end supply chain management capabilities. These services combine stand-alone services to provide clients with door-to-door delivery of shipments from points outside a country to the final recipient within a country. Providers offering this service typically also provide in-transit sorting and consolidating services and provide the ability to track goods while in transit. Also included in the package of services might be cross-border services such as providing assistance with customs clearance. These services save time and money by combining smaller loads into larger loads to optimize transportation costs, helping to speed up customs clearance through understanding the necessary procedures and documentation requirements and reducing the number of times goods need to be transferred between different carriers.

Some powerful trends are at work that should ensure the growing reliance on worldwide 3PL providers continues. Perhaps the greatest driver behind transportation and logistics outsourcing comes from a relentless pressure to reduce costs, making the efficient use of resources a mandate. Next, many companies are becoming increasingly specialized in what they do. In other words, they can't be everything to everybody, nor can they be everywhere at all times. Additionally, companies will increasingly focus on what they do best while outsourcing non-core business areas. More and more companies are deciding that transportation and logistics, although integral parts of an effective supply chain, are not part of their core business. A focus on core capabilities and competencies combined with cost reduction pressures may be the two strongest drivers behind the worldwide outsourcing of transportation and logistics services.

Selecting an agent or 3PL company. When selecting an agent or third parties, best practice companies work hard to understand:

- The global supply chain functions that are best outsourced to agents or 3PL companies
- The third-party companies that are most capable of delivering global supply chain services
- The pros and cons of outsourcing specific supply chain functions to a service provider, including a full cost-benefit analysis
- The development of selection criteria for working with a partner firm in this regard
- A comprehensive selection and implementation plan

Companies should conduct a careful analysis of these issues to select the functions to be outsourced and to set up the selection process for choosing their agent or 3PL provider. Poor selection decisions can have long, lasting, and painful consequences. And unless you enjoy long, lasting, and painful consequences, we suggest you view the selection of worldwide service providers as one of your most important corporate decisions.

Environmental Issues and Concerns

In today's environmentally conscious world, the affect of supply chains on the environment is a major concern. Practices such as Just-in-Time manufacturing; low-cost offshore manufacturing; pollution around ports from ocean-going ships; and the reduction-of-cycle time using premium freight options can have a negative environmental impact. In this section we briefly discuss the key environmental issues from a supply chain and logistics management perspective and provide some examples of how companies are dealing with these issues.

Reducing the carbon footprint. A key environmental concern for Europe as well as the U.S. is the need to reduce their carbon footprint. Specific laws exist in the U.S. and Europe with regard to vehicle emissions that affect the carbon footprint. However, recent studies suggest that the transportation-related carbon footprint worldwide is growing. Increasingly, companies are reducing their footprint by optimizing travel routes and using hybrid-powered vehicles. Besides creating fewer emissions, optimized routes reduce costs by eliminating waste. The effect of packaging materials on the environment is also a concern. In the U.S., packaging materials are being examined to make them recyclable and more environmentally friendly. Companies such as Proctor and Gamble and General Mills have moved aggressively to reduce the size of their packages for popular products such as Tide detergent and Hamburger Helper. Logistics providers are also under pressure to conform to new environmental expectations. For example, DHL is using route-optimization tools to map out best-delivery routes that reduce delivery mileage and fuel consumption. DHL and its parent company,

Deutsche Post World Net, are also exploring alternatives such as bio fuels and natural gas that can save money.[8] As another example, over the last several years UPS has invested $600 million in a route-optimization system that maps daily delivery schedules. Each day drivers check a hand-held device that contains an optimized delivery schedule that minimizes the distance each driver travels that day. This system is so smart it even minimizes the number of left turns made during the day, a feature that improves fuel mileage and reduces idle time. Without question the route optimizer has reduced waste and increased driver productivity. In a recent month, UPS drivers logged 3 million fewer miles compared with the year before. Naturally another primary concern is the use of energy in the ongoing "greening of the supply chain." For example, the Timberland Company in the U.S. is attempting to make its distribution centers as green as possible. To this end Timberland uses 100% renewable energy—mostly hydroelectric—at one of its plants in Holland and uses solar technology to generate 60% percent of the energy at a facility in California.[9]

Differing environmental directives. A complicating factor of how best to serve the environment is that different countries have different rules, regulations, and requirements regarding the environment. Rules and regulations concerning the environment are particularly stringent in the European Union (EU) countries. Two major environmental directives exist in the EU. First is the directive on the restriction of the use of certain hazardous substances in electrical and electronic equipment, commonly referred to as the Restriction of Hazardous Substances Directive (RoHS). This directive restricts the use of six hazardous materials in the manufacture of various types of electronic and electrical equipment. It is closely linked with the Waste Electrical and Electronic Equipment Directive (WEEE), which sets collection, recycling, and recovery targets for electrical goods and is part of a legislative initiative to solve the problem of toxic waste. Second is a relatively new set of environmental laws in the EU, called REACH, which regulate chemicals and their safe use. REACH deals with the registration, evaluation, authorization, and restriction of chemical substances. The aim of REACH is to improve the protection of human health and the environment through better and earlier identification of the intrinsic properties of chemical substances. The EU also mandates that producers of certain energy-using products document the environmental impact of their products through the complete life cycle of the product from sourcing through manufacturing to recycling. This information will be used for inspection purposes by European regulators.[10] Although these strict rules and regulations apply in the EU, such rules and regulations do not necessarily apply in the same way in other parts of the world. For example, China has a comprehensive set of environmental laws that are not always followed. The penalties for noncompliance are often low, an outcome that encourages some companies to pay the fine rather than comply with the law.[11] As companies in the

U.S. send goods to China that comply with laws that protect the environment, the reverse is not necessarily true. Companies that outsource to foreign countries must comply with environmental laws and collect data that documents this compliance. They must also be prepared to produce these documents for regulators on demand. Companies that use 3PL providers must also rely on these providers to comply with these laws and to collect this data. This comprises an area of concern when shipping products from countries such as China.

Supply Chain Security and Post 9-11 Requirements

The world is becoming a less secure place with increasing terrorism, piracy on the high seas, and increasing industrial crime. A major concern for global supply chain managers involves supply chain security.

Supply chain security refers to the efforts to enhance the security of the transport and logistics systems that move cargo throughout the world. It combines traditional practices of supply chain management with security practices that are influenced by threats such as terrorism, piracy, and theft. Typical supply chain security activities include the provision of security credentialing to participants in supply chain security programs; ensuring the validity and screening of cargo; providing advance notification to countries of goods being shipped; the application of locks and tamper-proof seals to ensure the security while in transit; and cargo inspection on entry into other countries.

Additional security measures have been instituted worldwide since the attacks of terrorism in 2001. Companies must now comply with regulations that pertain to increased cargo security measures and regulatory compliance issues. Noncompliance can result in penalties and even the seizure or destruction of shipments. A number of supply chain security initiatives in the U.S. and around the world today are shown in Table 2.2.

Companies should develop an understanding of the various government security programs that exist. Having an understanding of these government security programs enables a participating company to measure its risk profile and security measures against a set of established and recognized standards. For instance, under the U.S. C-TPAT program and the Canadian FAST program, participants are rated according to a tier system. Tier 1 comprises certification into the program. Tier 3, the highest level, recognizes a company's security measures as going beyond minimum requirements to the level of best-practice accomplishment.[12]

Yet compliance with all of these government programs will not necessarily ensure that a company is in the best position to mitigate security risks. These programs provide a useful benchmark to identify potential weaknesses, but companies still need to take the measures necessary to ensure excellent security is taking place across the supply chain.

Table 2.2 Key Supply Chain Security Initiatives

Security Initiative	Description
The Customs Trade Partnership Against Terrorism (C-TPAT) Initiative	A voluntary compliance program aimed at helping companies to improve the security of their corporate supply chains
The Canadian Free and Secure Trade (FAST) Initiative	Expedites border clearance and reduces delays for preapproved, low-risk truck drivers, carriers, and importers; a joint Canada/U.S. initiative involving the Canada Border Services Agency (CBSA) and the U.S. Customs and Border Protection (CBP) Agency
The Authorized Economic Operator (AEO) Initiative	Part of the World Customs Organization SAFE framework of standards aimed at securing safe trade
The Container Security Initiative	A program led by U.S. Customs and Border Protection in the Department of Homeland Security; focuses on screening containers at foreign ports
The International Ship and Port Facility Security Code (ISPS Code) Initiative	Initiatives by countries around the world to implement and enforce the International Ship and Port Facility Security Code (ISPS Code); an agreement of 148 countries that are members of the International Maritime Organization (IMO)
The International Organization for Standardization (ISO) Initiative	The International Organization for Standardization (ISO), which has released a series of Standards for the establishment and management of supply chain security (ISO 28000:2007)
Internal security initiatives	Initiatives implemented by companies in the private sector; implemented to track and monitor the integrity of cargo containers moving around the world using technologies such as radio frequency identification (RFID) and global positioning system (GPS)

CONCLUDING THOUGHTS

After reviewing the broad range of issues involved with international purchasing and logistics, one might wonder how global trade can even occur. As supply organizations embark on the international purchasing efforts, they inevitably find themselves confronted by a need to understand many logistical issues. These logistical issues arise from extended supply chains, the additional complexity associated with managing them, and rules and regulations that often differ widely across countries. The bottom line is that supply managers must have a solid knowledge of the global logistics component of the supply chain; use supply chain best practices when managing the flow of goods, information, and funds; be willing to work with best-in-class supply chain intermediaries; and take advantage of synergies that can be created with those intermediaries. Failing to do so will ensure the total cost of international purchasing far exceeds the price of international purchasing.

REFERENCES

1. *The Economist Magazine. Industry Briefing* electronic newsletter, December 31, 2008.

2. J.J. Coyle, E.J. Bardi, and C.J. Langley, Jr. *The Management of Business Logistics, 6th ed.* 1992. St. Paul, MN: West Publishing Company; 15.

3. International Monetary Fund website. *World Economic Outlook Database.* Retrieved from http://www.imf.org/external/data.htm#data.

4. Global Supply Chain: New Supply Chain Digest Report Identifies the 10 Keys to Global Excellence. *The Supply Chain Digest's News & Views* 2007 Apr 12. Retrieved from http://www.scdigest.com/assets/newsViews/.

5. R.B. Aronsen. Offshoring Pleasures and Pitfalls. *Manufacturing Engineering* 2008 Jan 1; 140(1): 81.

6. Press Release. *WHO Warns of Mounting Death Toll on Asian Roads.* World Health Organization. Retrieved from http://www.wpro.who.int/media_centre/press_releases/pr_20040405.htm.

7. D. Ewert. Passage of Risk and Passage of Title. *Shipping News* electronic newsletter, September 15, 2001. Retrieved from http://www.shipsolutions.com/newsletter/new0109.html.

8. R.J. Bowman. The Greening of the Supply Chain. *Global Logistics & Supply Chain Strategies* 2006 Nov; 10(11): 32.

9. R.J. Bowman. The Greening of the Supply Chain. *Global Logistics & Supply Chain Strategies* 2006 Nov; 10(11): 30.

10. R.J. Bowman. The Greening of the Supply Chain. *Global Logistics & Supply Chain Strategies* 2006 Nov; 10(11): 34.

11. C.R. McElwee, II. Who's Cleaning Up This Mess. *China Business Review Online* 2008 Jan-Feb. Retrieved from http://www.chinabusinessreview.com/public/0801/mcelwee.html.

12. S. Richer. There's More to Compliance Cooperation than Just C-TPAT. *World Trade Magazine* 2008 Mar. Retrieved from http://www.worldtrademag.com/.

3

SOURCING IN EMERGING AND LOW-COST COUNTRIES

The geographic search by U.S. and Western European companies for lower-cost goods and services is constantly ongoing. And that search increasingly takes us to emerging and low-cost countries. Therefore, a book that includes international purchasing and global supply management as major topics would be incomplete if it did not have a chapter on emerging and low-cost country sourcing.

Chapter 3 takes a closer look at a specific but growing subset of international purchasing—sourcing in emerging and low-cost countries. First, an overview of emerging and low-cost country sourcing is provided, including potential problem areas. Second, the all-important topic of sourcing in China is addressed. Then emphasis is given to international purchasing offices (IPOs) as a way to establish a presence in emerging and low-cost countries, including a detailed company case example. Except for the discussion of IPOs, Chapter 3 does not deal extensively with ways to overcome the risks of sourcing in emerging and low-cost countries.

OVERVIEW

Part of the challenge when discussing emerging and low-cost countries is that no definitive definitions exist that define these terms. Although some observers simply use the term *low-cost country sourcing* (LCCS) when referring to any purchasing outside the first world domain, it is important to distinguish between emerging and low-cost sourcing. From our perspective, emerging countries compete primarily in the areas of lower labor costs and prices, but do not necessarily present the same level of risk that is present with traditional third world or low-cost countries.

It is mistake to label any low-cost country as an emerging country. For instance, Bangladesh and Honduras are low-cost countries for certain items (e.g., textiles), but are not thought of as emerging countries. A country can be a lower-cost provider for a narrow range of commodities or products, but not necessarily an emerging sourcing country, which is often looked to for a wider range of goods or services. An emerging country resides in an "in-between" status between a third world, developing, or low-cost country and first world countries that are characterized by mature institutions, political stability, legal protection, sophisticated production capabilities, and prosperity. An emerging country has the potential to move, or has already moved, beyond developing country status.

Think about the continent of Africa. The problems that plague that continent, including rampant corruption, AIDS, war, inadequate health and education services, and poor infrastructure are so severe they almost guarantee that African countries will retain their third world status for the foreseeable future. Are you looking for a good supplier in Algeria, Cameroon, or Somalia? We didn't think so. The reality is that Africa has few emerging countries for sourcing or selling. Unless forced to do so (which is true for certain raw materials), most of the African continent is off the radar screen of most supply managers. A characteristic of an emerging country is that supply managers usually willingly include that country in their domain of potential supply options.

Survey after survey tell us that U.S. and European supply managers look to emerging and low-cost countries to take advantage of lower-cost goods and services. Some observers argue that these lower costs are party the result of lax environmental compliance, government subsidies, and unfair labor practices—an argument that does have merit. A surge in gold mining using mercury in remote Asian countries, a substance known to wreak havoc on human health and the environment, anecdotally supports this point.

In the primary set of emerging sourcing countries, we include China, India, certain Eastern European countries (reluctantly including Russia), certain Latin American and South American countries (primarily Mexico and Brazil), and certain Southeast Asian countries. Within Southeast Asia, the country that is receiving attention as a sourcing location is Vietnam. Already the electronics industry is shifting some production and assembly from China to Vietnam, where, at least for now, wage rates are about a third lower.[1] Other observers might have a different list of emerging countries compared with the one provided here.

Locations for lower labor costs are transitory as some low-cost countries evolve into emerging countries and some emerging countries evolve into emergent countries. At one time, the southern U.S. was considered a low-cost location for textiles and other manufacturing previously done in the northern U.S. The South was soon replaced by Mexico as a location of choice, which was then largely replaced by China. Now, other countries are taking much of the textile business from China. Not too long ago, Japan was considered to be an emerging country before, like the U.S., it evolved into a high-cost country that competes on intellectual value-added and technological innovation. To bet on a longer-term purchasing strategy that is based solely on labor costs pegged to a certain country might be short sighted.

The challenge when sourcing from suppliers in emerging and low-cost countries is that it can both decrease *and* increase a company's risk exposure. Many examples demonstrate that sourcing from China has allowed a company to maintain or even increase the competitiveness of its end products. And many examples also reflect the risk from sourcing in less-developed economies.

Sourcing in emerging countries demands that risk management plans become a major part of the buying process. One only has to read the news to see reports of counterfeit products from China that have worked their way into supply chains, a situation that has placed human lives at risk and has even jeopardized national security.[2] And let's not forget about tainted toys, paint, pharmaceuticals, and dairy products that tarnish a brand in the blink of an eye. Long lead times and distances that make planning difficult also do little to reduce supply chain risk.

Potential Problem Areas

Although some of the challenges encountered when sourcing internationally can be similar to domestic challenges, the ability to prevent a problem or manage one after it happens is usually more difficult when dealing with suppliers located in faraway places. It is not well publicized, but Western food and pharmaceutical companies rely extensively on ingredients from low-cost and emerging countries. And if managers at these companies are not losing sleep over the integrity of their supply chain, they should be. A recent Chinese scandal involving the selling of tainted milk resulted in death sentences for two individuals and prison sentences for 12 others, including some life sentences.[3] Some food companies have gone so far as to advertise that their products contain no ingredients from China. The bottom line is that most Western companies have no plans to eliminate sourcing in emerging and low-cost countries. So, let's take our heads out of the sand and manage the issues that exist.

The potential concerns when sourcing around the world are fairly extensive. The list includes:

- Inconsistent supplier quality
- New tariffs and taxes

- Currency fluctuations
- Unreliable infrastructure leading to variable lead times
- Longer lead times that make planning difficult
- Inadequate intellectual property protection
- Lack of supplier adherence to contract terms and conditions
- A total cost that exceeds unit price
- Government interference
- Lack of supplier flexibility and responsiveness
- Language and cultural barriers
- Challenges associated with transferring work to distant suppliers

No wonder risk management must be part of the international purchasing discussion.

Research reveals that the top problem areas when sourcing in emerging and low-cost countries are (in order of severity):

- Lack of lead time stability
- Lengthened logistical movement
- Inconsistent supplier quality
- Lack of supplier flexibility and responsiveness
- Protection of intellectual property

The possible effects of these issues are not trivial. A study by Accenture revealed that between 2001 and 2003, annual inventory turns in the retail industry declined from 14 to 11 and in the consumer goods industry declined from 17 to 13.[4] It is no coincidence that this time period corresponded to an increase in purchases from lower-cost countries, particularly China.

A study by Industry Canada revealed that only 42% of Canadian companies reduced their total landed cost via low-cost country sourcing. (Chapter 4 examines the topic of total landed cost in depth.) Industry Canada also found that over 80% of Canadian shippers experienced longer lead times and that only 10% of shipments from low-cost counties were on time. These figures compare with on-time deliveries of 90 to 100% from domestic suppliers.[5] We cannot ignore the effects of changing supply patterns on some important supply chain metrics.

Inconsistent supplier quality. For many companies, supplier evaluation and selection is among their most important organizational processes. Perform this process well and life will be a whole lot simpler. Perform this process poorly and be prepared to witness some nasty outcomes, many of which relate to supplier quality and delivery. The importance of supplier selection becomes even more important as companies begin to rely on global suppliers (addressed in Chapters 9 through 13). Yet when a company lacks in-country resources or representatives, the selection process for international suppliers is often not as rigorous as it is for domestic suppliers. This becomes a serious issue when limited resources are available to support supplier visits in emerging and low-cost countries. Perhaps supply managers think the cost of international supplier visits is too costly in terms of time and dollars. But the double-digit price reductions promised by the foreign supplier are so enticing. We can almost taste the savings! So the appeal of rapid cost savings can lead to a risky temptation—the selection of suppliers based largely on product samples or cursory supplier visits performed by third parties.

Consider the following example that affects home builders, an industry that already had its fair share of problems. Some home builders in Florida are finding that the Chinese drywall they selected based primarily on samples emits an unpleasant, sulfur-based odor that corrodes air conditioner coils, computer wiring, and metal picture frames. And new home buyers are concerned about respiratory problems.[6] The builders are likely thinking that the low drywall price they received is not looking like such a good deal.

What do we have against relying on product samples that are used during supplier selection, especially samples provided by suppliers in emerging and low-cost countries? Actually, quite a bit—and so should you. Samples focus attention on the output of a process rather than the process that produces the output, a clear violation of a very important quality management principle. Samples also do not provide any objective insight into a supplier's process capability, another violation of an important quality management principle. And let's not forget that samples provide no insight into the supplier's working conditions, capacity, financial stability, delivery performance, management capability, or any other non-product factor that affects performance. Samples also provide no evidence of how well a supplier manages its suppliers and supply chain. Samples usually do not come with a guarantee that they were produced under normal operating conditions. Did the supplier even produce the sample? Suppliers can handpick samples that represent only their best output. Who would send a bad sample? We think you get the idea. Some upfront work during the selection process might prevent some quality embarrassments later. The world is full of suppliers that are willing to promise lower prices. Getting consistent performance from these suppliers might be a totally different story. Do not let the attraction of quick cost savings warp your good judgment.

Let's face reality. Sourcing in China and other emerging countries, even with all the additional challenges it presents, will be around for the foreseeable future. Table 3.1 provides some advice when purchasing in emerging and low-cost countries.[7] Even though we suspect that many readers are aware of these issues either through experience or as seasoned graduates of the school of hard knocks, Table 3.1 still provides a good review.

Table 3.1. Tips for Sourcing in Emerging and Low-Cost Countries

Advice	Comments
Improve supplier evaluation and management.	Plan on visiting suppliers on a regular basis; avoid a reliance on product samples when selecting suppliers; establish IPOs.
Establish a clear strategy.	Understand how emerging and low-cost country sourcing fits into your broader supply strategy; work with engineering and logistics personnel when sourcing.
Build relationships that are longer term.	Relationships matter in a country where the rule of law is still incomplete; guanxi (*gwan-shee*) or "social capital" is crucial to successful business dealings; symbolic importance is attached to long-term relationships.
Consider going direct.	Instead of shifting sourcing and supplier performance responsibility to third parties such as traders who help locate suppliers, companies should consider placing their own people on the ground to ensure performance.
Protect IP.	IP theft is still a concern; work closely with trusted in-country representatives.
Pay careful attention to contracting.	Be precise in written and spoken language; address quality requirements and other expectations clearly; agree on where and how disputes will be resolved.
Become familiar with local customs officials.	Good relations with local officials can allow shipments to be inspected and cleared at the factory, avoiding delays at a port or airport.
Know who you are negotiating with.	State-owned enterprises take longer to reach a deal; private companies move more quickly due to the profit motive.
Move beyond price to total cost.	Unit price *never* equals total cost; the gap can be surprising; develop total landed cost models.
Selectively use third-party help when needed.	Many companies, particularly smaller ones that lack in-country resources, could benefit from having a trusted party represent their interests with suppliers.

THE CHINA SYNDROME

When thinking of emerging sourcing countries, the one that quickly comes to mind is China. One only has to see the growing trade deficit that China has with Western countries to appreciate the mad stampede of buyers and manufacturers into that country. The pace of economic growth within China over the last 10 years is nothing short of astounding. To put this growth in perspective, the Chinese had virtually no business contact with the Western world prior to 1980. In a relatively short period of time, China has passed the U.S. to become the world's second largest exporter (Germany is first). Certain measures of economic activity now place China as the third largest economy in the world behind the U.S. and Japan. Some prognosticators have boldly predicted that China will be the world's manufacturer of choice for the next 50 years.

Most surveys reveal that Western companies are increasingly concerned about sourcing in China, but these same surveys also indicate that most supply organizations will not take any radical action in the short term. Given this reality, we should not expect a mass exodus away from sourcing in China. Instead we will likely see a slowing in the rate of growth in Chinese exports and a tweaking of supply patterns as macroeconomic forces affect supply planning. Continued sourcing from China will figure prominently in the supply plans of most companies for the foreseeable future. In fact, the Chinese government is actively taking measures to promote export growth.

The Challenges with China Sourcing

A set of possible concerns or problem areas when sourcing in emerging and low-cost countries was identified in a previous section. From our research, China is the highest-rated problem country in 7 of the 12 areas evaluated by supply managers. It earns the second spot for four other areas. A recent study by AMR Research involving 130 international companies identified China as the "winner" in 9 of 15 risk categories, including intellectual property infringement, supplier and internal product quality failure, and security breaches.[8] Are you detecting a theme here?

Overall, earning the first or second spot in almost every problem area (and earning top honors is a dubious distinction here) is not simply a coincidence. The risks are real and being unaware of these risks is a recipe for trouble. As a side note, India earns a top or second-place ranking in 9 of 12 problem areas.

Protecting Intellectual Property

Compared with domestic sourcing, we know that international purchasing presents a new set of risks. One area of particular concern when sourcing in China is the protection of intellectual property (IP). According to the World Intellectual Property Organization (WIPO), IP refers to creations of the mind, including inventions, literary and artistic works, symbols, names, images, and designs used in commerce. IP falls into two main areas—industrial property and copyright. Industrial property includes inventions (patents), trademarks, industrial designs, and geographic indications of source. Copyright protects creative works and gives the copyright holder exclusive right to control reproduction or adaptation of such works for a certain period of time. (Information about WIPO can be found at http://www.wipo.int.)

Although movies, music, books, records, clothing, and other consumer goods are regularly pirated and counterfeited, producers of industrial products must also be prepared to protect what is rightfully theirs. IP theft costs U.S.

companies from $80 billion to $250 billion annually, a figure that rises dramatically when looking at IP theft from a worldwide perspective. As one might expect, precise figures are not readily available. Pirates and counterfeiters are not very open about the scope of their activities.

IP protection is taken seriously, perhaps even for granted, in developed countries. The U.S. views IP protection to be so important that the Constitution addresses patents, copyrights, and trade secrets directly in Article I, Section 8, Clause 8. The founding fathers instilled the importance of IP protection directly into U.S. culture and law.

Various studies have concluded that although IP violations occur in many countries, the Chinese have a particular expertise in this area. As Western companies continue to buy from China, the fact remains that many Chinese believe they have a right to the IP of others. Let's not forget that China is still a communist country. The concept of private property and a legal system to recognize that property are not nearly as developed in China as in Europe and North America. Unfortunately, legal protection of IP is a relatively unknown concept in too many low-cost and emerging countries.

Lost revenue is not the only outcome from violations. Brand erosion, counterfeit parts that can cause injury or death, and higher legal costs to fight the counterfeiters are also possible outcomes. An expert on the subject has commented that supply managers must face some harsh realities when they expand their buying operations internationally. The search for new markets and lower costs, particularly in China and western Asia, forces supply managers to put far more effort into protecting one of their most precious assets—their firm's IP. What are some ways to help manage or even prevent this risk when IP theft may be a problem?

Divide purchase requirements. Disaggregate and disperse purchase requirements among several providers rather than providing a single supplier with access to an entire design. Final assembly must still occur at a trusted location.

Establish proprietary assets in a foreign country. Establish operations in a foreign country or form a joint venture with a foreign partner. This is probably not a realistic option for smaller companies or when buying raw materials or components. Rather, it is more likely when outsourcing finished products. Keep in mind that most companies are reluctant to take on new capital assets.

Seek legal support and remedies. Legal experts are available who can help identify preventive measures as well as legal remedies if IP violations occur. These experts can also help supply managers develop contract language and nondisclosure agreements that address IP protection, including where to establish jurisdiction in the event of an IP dispute. Legal groups can also help with the filing and protection of patents, trademarks, and copyrights before doing business outside a home country.

Work with trusted in-country representatives. A major risk when purchasing internationally is not having a local representative to protect the buyer's interests. This representative, who is usually local to the region where sourcing will occur, can work in conjunction with a company's purchasing office or be an independent representative. Many small and medium-sized companies have found that using a trusted local representative to identify and perhaps even evaluate qualified suppliers is essential for protecting IP.

Use International Purchasing Offices (IPOs). IPOs, usually staffed by foreign nationals, provide an in-country presence. These offices evaluate potential suppliers with an assessment of the supplier's willingness to respect IP. The IPO can also maintain a list of suppliers to avoid by region or country. (This topic is so important that a later section of this chapter discusses IPOs in detail.)

Protect trademarks. Experts provide some solid advice for companies that want to protect their trademarks within China.[9] First, transliterate your language into Chinese characters to avoid embarrassing mistakes or usage by other parties. Transliterating simply means to represent or spell in the character of another alphabet. Although transliterating into Chinese is not easy, and embarrassing mistakes do occur, the process is critical to avoid infringement. It is essential to engage the services of competent specialists to transliterate a trademark. Second, move quickly to the Chinese trademark office. In the U.S, the first entity to use a trademark commercially owns the trademark. In China, the first to file the trademark owns the trademark. Speed is of the essence—otherwise you could wake up to find that someone else in China has ownership of your trademark.

Avoid countries or areas within countries that are IP offenders. This option is not as easy as it sounds. IP violators tend to not advertise. And unfortunately, no published list separates the good guys from the bad guys. Although we have a good idea about the worst offenders internationally, we often disregard this information and source in that country anyway. How many companies have walked away from sourcing in China? If nothing else, knowing where the potential trouble spots are located should result in using greater caution. The good news is that the Chinese government is beginning to recognize its obligation to better protect IP. China is a member of the World Trade Organization and is therefore required to adhere to some basic rules. Chinese government officials finally appear to be more serious about addressing this issue.

Is the Allure of China Fading?

Certain changes are underway that are causing an increasing number of companies to rethink their sourcing plans. A study by the American Chamber of Commerce in Shanghai found more than half of all foreign manufacturers in China believe the mainland is losing its competitive edge to countries such as

Vietnam and India.[10] Some good arguments can be made that the allure of China sourcing is losing some of its luster. More and more publications are addressing the dynamics of bringing work back to North America or Europe, a trend that is called a variety of names, including near sourcing, home sourcing, and near shoring.[11]

Fluctuating exchange rates. The Chinese currency is technically called the *renminbi*, which translated literally means the "people's currency." The principle currency of the *renminbi* is the *yuan*, a name with which most of us are probably more familiar. For many years the Chinese pegged its currency at a fixed rate of 8.2677 yuan to $1 U.S., removing currency fluctuation as a risk. Under international pressure, the Chinese government has allowed its currency to fluctuate a bit more freely, a move that resulted in strengthening of the yuan relative to the dollar. Suddenly, and this relative comparison could change quickly back to China's favor, Chinese products that looked so inexpensive are not as inexpensive with the new exchange rate.[12] One survey revealed that when the yuan strengthened 20% against the dollar, 40% of supply managers said that the exchange rate now had an effect on where they would source their requirements.[13] This is a topic where readers must have a high comfort level. Fluctuating exchange rates can change the dynamics of international purchasing in the blink of an eye. You do not have to be an economist to appreciate the basics of exchange rates.

Pressure to use remote suppliers. The Chinese miracle has not been evenly distributed across the country. The eastern coastal regions of China are the primary benefactors of economic growth while the more remote inland regions still often resemble third world countries. To help correct this situation, the Central Chinese government is pressuring foreign companies to source further inland. Although labor costs might be lower as companies move inland, the inland regions can also present some real disadvantages. Workers and managers are generally not as experienced as the coastal regions. Equally, if not more important, the Chinese infrastructure deteriorates rapidly further inland from the coast, making already long lead times and distances even more of a concern.

Rising costs. It may come as a shock, but the typical Chinese worker does not plan to work for next to nothing forever. Simple economics tells us that rapid growth creates a demand for workers, which places inflationary pressures on wage rates. Until recently, this has been the case as Chinese labor rates increased 10 to 15% annually. Furthermore, a new law requires that Chinese companies provide employee benefits such as pensions, guaranteed collective bargaining rights, and hiring for the long term.[10] The Chinese government also reduced or canceled tax rebates on more than 2000 items used to make exported goods (although some of these rebates have been brought back to encourage export growth). An American Chamber of Commerce official noted that ending the tax rebate raised the cost to manufacture many goods by 14 to 17%.[10] Rising global protectionism also has the potential to increase costs through higher taxes and tariffs on imported goods. During times of economic stress, it is not unusual for countries to talk about trade protection rather than free trade.[14] Trade restrictions, often in the form of higher tariffs and other import restrictions inevitably have the effect of raising costs. In the Western world, no country is more in the crosshairs of protectionists than China. The economic meltdown of 2008 decimated demand across many industries, which took some pressure off wages, commodity demand, and transportation prices; but over the long term, cost structure and the labor wage trend in China should be upward, particularly as world economies recover. (For data regarding the trends in import prices in the U.S. see www.bls.gov.)

Health, safety, and environmental changes. Certain international companies are making a very public display of demanding that Chinese suppliers conform to Western standards regarding working conditions, hours worked, and environmental compliance. Although this stance plays well in the arena of public opinion, the irony is that at some point these suppliers might no longer be cost competitive. The reality is that most purchasers do not consider human or environmental issues when selecting suppliers. A survey by KPMG International revealed that only 43% of buyers consider human rights issues in procurement decisions, while a mere 30% regard a supplier's environmental record as important or very important.[15] You decide if this is good or bad. The probability that costs will increase due to stronger health, safety, and environmental standards is strong. Suppliers in Honghe, China, long known for making a large portion of the world's sweaters, say that the Chinese government's tougher protection policies for workers and the environment has made competing internationally more difficult.[16] The Honghe region has witnessed the closing of hundreds of its factories.

Changing total landed costs. A study by the Council of Supply Chain Management Professionals found that 100% of companies it surveyed sourced from China. Less than 50% of the companies sourced from the next highest-rated countries. Perhaps more importantly, over 80% of these same companies said they were reexamining their offshore sourcing decisions. And what is the reason? Product prices may still be low compared with home market sourcing, but particularly in China the total cost picture is changing rapidly.[17] Over half of the companies surveyed say that rising costs and excessive lead times are causing them to rethink their sourcing networks. (Chapter 4 addresses total cost in detail.)

Quality lapses. It is well known that Chinese manufacturers are responsible for some high-profile quality lapses. Over the last 10 years, the number of consumer imported products into the U.S. has doubled. And over 40% of these products now originate in China. Perhaps more importantly, the U.S. Consumer Products Safety Commission reported that over 60% of all recalled products in a recent year were made in China.[18] Unless these numbers radically change,

Table 3.2. Selected Major Recalls of Chinese Products

March 16	A series of recalls of more than 100 brands of dog and cat food begins across North America because of melamine contamination
May 14	RC2 Corporation recalls 1.5 million toy trains and components because of lead paint contamination
June 1	The FDA issues an alert for Chinese-made toothpaste because of the presence of diethylene glycol, an inadequate substitute for glycerin
June 27	The National Highway Traffic Safety Administration orders a New Jersey firm to recall 450,000 truck tires because of missing components that make the tires unsafe
June 28	The FDA blocks imports of certain seafood reportedly containing carcinogenic antimicrobial drugs
August 2	Mattel's Fisher-Price division issues a global recall of 1.5 million plastic toys because of lead paint hazards
August 14	Mattel announces a global recall of 18.6 million toys because of a design flaw and lead paint hazards
September 4	Mattel announces a third global recall of almost 850,000 products manufactured with lead paint
September 26	The U.S. Consumer Products Safety Commission (CPSC) announces seven recalls totaling 600,000 toys because of excessive amounts of lead paint
October 4	The CPSC announces another recall of more than 635,000 products because of excessive lead
October 9	Starbucks issues a recall for 250,000 plastic children's mugs that are easily broken when dropped, presenting the risk of sharp edges and choking hazards
November 7	The CPSC announces the recall of 4.2 million sets of Aqua Dots because their coating contains a chemical that can be toxic if swallowed orally
January 17	Baxter Healthcare begins a massive recall of the drug heparin due to an increase in the number of reports of adverse reactions and possible deaths

Sources: S. Hughes. *Baxter Recalls Heparin*. Retrieved from http://www.medscape.com/viewarticle/569325; US-China Business Council as reported in G.P. Fremlin. Careful Contracts Reduce Risk. *The China Business Review* 2008 Jan/Feb; 35(1): 36.

quality concerns will raise costs and tarnish China's image as a sourcing destination. Table 3.2 summarizes some recent recalls of Chinese products in North America (2007 and 2008). The purpose of this table is not to embarrass the Chinese. Instead, its purpose is to create awareness among readers about the seriousness of the risk. These recalls are not something that will only happen to "someone else." Do not think that because your company did not manufacture a faulty item means forgiveness in terms of liability. Lawyers will go after just about anyone in the supply chain with deep pockets.

What are some conclusions we can make regarding sourcing in China?

1. Macro factors affect the sourcing decisions made by buyers (which supports a point made in Chapter 1). Labor market, government regulation, and currency rates are three of these factors.

2. Few observers believe that China will cease to be an export power anytime soon. Compared to most other emerging and low-cost countries, China has an abundant workforce, an improving infrastructure, a government that actively promotes exports, and an increasing ability to produce industrial goods that are less susceptible to labor cost increases. Over a recent 12-month period, exports from almost every major country into the U.S. declined at double-digit rates in terms of their dollar value. One country, however, saw its exports decline by a relatively modest 5%. That country was China. Some experts believe that even in a slumping economy China could continue to take export market share from other countries.[19]

3. Sourcing in China is entering a more mature stage where thoughtful analysis by supply managers will replace low-price exuberance and frenzy. "Total cost" is no longer just a buzzword.

4. Make sure your "Plan B" is current. The economics that favor China sourcing (and this is true for all emerging and low-cost countries) can change rapidly, making other regions more attractive.

5. The Chinese economy is entering a phase in which relying on cost-cutting and simple production methods to boost exports might be a thing of the past. It is easy to understand why the Chinese government wants to accelerate a move into higher-value goods such as capital equipment and aerospace.

6. On the marketing side, few global Chinese brands exist today. Western firms should expect to see the entrance of new competitors as marketing and brand development increases by Chinese firms.

INTERNATIONAL PURCHASING OFFICES

Most supply managers recognize their limited ability to manage activities that happen thousands of miles away. An important element of international purchasing that does not receive much attention, particularly as it relates to managing risk in emerging markets, is the use of international purchasing offices (IPOs).

At some point, companies realize that constantly traveling from the home market or relying on third parties to represent their interests in a sourcing region just doesn't do the job. Establishing IPOs is a natural progression in the international scheme of things.

Some companies call IPOs foreign or international buying offices, international procurement centers, or international procurement organizations. No industry standard exists regarding what to call these offices. This topic receives extended coverage in this chapter because this approach represents the most sophisticated way to reduce the risk of working with suppliers (and governments) in emerging countries. Relying on IPOs is an international purchasing best practice.

IPOs are usually a formal part of a company's organizational design and will increase in importance as global supply management expands. We say *usually* here because some companies hire IPO service providers as needed rather than maintaining a dedicated office. These companies have taken what is essentially a fixed cost and turned it into a variable cost.

Research reveals that half of larger companies (those with sales greater than $1 billion dollars a year) have at least one formally established IPO somewhere in the world. This figure declines rapidly as company size decreases. In fact, it is hard to imagine that very many smaller companies maintain an IPO. Large companies not only have the purchase volumes to justify international offices, but they also usually have the resources to support them.

A company that understands the value of IPOs is Oshkosh, a maker of specialty vehicles and vehicle bodies. IPOs are an important part of the global growth strategy of Oshkosh. Oshkosh now operates Asian procurement centers located in Shanghai, Hong Kong, and Beijing. The CEO of Oshkosh maintains that these locations allow Oshkosh to support its global manufacturing efforts by leveraging a local supply of parts. He further says, "Broadening our global footprint with local offices increases the scale of our operations, which is key to fueling our future growth."[20]

It would be wrong to conclude that IPOs are located only in emerging countries, although Eastern Europe and China are well represented as locations. An IPO provides a company with a day-to-day presence in any supply market or region where it intends to buy. Most supply managers know that IPOs are an important part of their company's global footprint.

We know one thing with certainty—overwhelming consensus exists regarding the importance of IPOs. Over 85% of companies with IPOs say these offices are extremely important to their international success; 10% say IPOs are moderately important; and only 5% say IPOs are less than moderately important, with no company indicating these offices have limited importance. About half of all companies that maintain at least one foreign buying office say their IPOs are more than meeting or exceeding expectations while a third indicates their IPOs are meeting expectations.

Although the most common number of IPOs that a company maintains is one (a quarter of companies with an IPO maintain a single IPO), no consensus exists regarding the number of IPOs that a company should maintain around the world. Almost half of all companies with an IPO maintain four or more international offices. And a positive relationship does exist between the number of IPOs that a company relies on and the percentage of total purchases that are obtained worldwide. As worldwide purchases increase as a percentage of total purchases, the likelihood of having more than one IPO increases.

Some subtle differences exist regarding where U.S. and European-based companies locate their IPOs. Although Asian countries are the primary locations for IPOs, U.S. companies are more heavily concentrated in China compared with their European counterparts. In fact, U.S. companies are almost twice as likely as European companies to establish an IPO in China. Logically, U.S. companies are also more likely to have IPOs in Canada, Mexico, and other parts of Latin America compared with their European counterparts. European companies are more likely to maintain a wider Asian IPO presence outside of mainland China (e.g., Japan, Taiwan, South Korea, and Vietnam) compared to U.S. companies.

The kinds of services that an IPO provides are important and varied. At least 70% or more of companies with at least one IPO say these offices somewhat or extensively identify suppliers and evaluate their capabilities; negotiate and execute contracts with suppliers; resolve quality and delivery problems directly with suppliers; develop supplier capabilities; measure supplier performance; evaluate product and service designs and samples; facilitate import and export activities; and perform logistical coordination.

The use of IPOs should only increase as supply organizations scour the globe for buying opportunities. However, challenges could also increase as new IPOs are staffed with foreign nationals hired away from other IPOs. Anecdotal evidence is already emerging that some companies are experiencing unhealthy turnover due to the "poaching" of staff by other companies. Turnover will have the inevitable effect of increasing the cost of operating an IPO as well as affecting overall performance. The discussion in the following section provides more detail concerning the important role that IPOs play when pursuing international objectives.

USING IPOs TO SUPPORT GLOBAL OUTSOURCING—A CASE EXAMPLE

This case highlights the supply management objectives and organizational design of a privately owned, consumer products company with 25,000 employees and annual revenues of over $4 billion.[21] (*Note*: The company has requested that its name remain confidential.) The company sells its line of products through franchise and company-owned retail outlets that appear in virtually every mall in North America. The company's primary business involves the retailing of keepsake gifts, personal correspondence products, party items, family entertainment products, and personal development products. Although the correspondence products are produced almost exclusively in the U.S., virtually all the finished goods sold through retail outlets are sourced overseas.

The company faces intense customer and competitive pressure to manage costs, particularly as web-based and PC-generated entertainment products threaten the growth of its core businesses. Computer-based and electronic activities for children are a direct threat to its personal development products for children. As a result, the company is keenly aware of the need to remain competitive in its worldwide markets by focusing on four critical areas—process improvements, business simplification, new product development, and low-cost country sourcing of finished goods. This discussion focuses on the company's approach for sourcing finished goods for resale in its franchise and company-owned stores.

Finished Goods Outsourcing

This company has a long history of buying in Asia, but had lacked the structure to support a full-scale push into China and surrounding areas. Now a major part of the company's total purchases involves finished goods outsourcing through a Hong Kong-based IPO. The Hong Kong IPO is a separate company called Hong Kong Finished Goods and it is responsible for sourcing finished goods, primarily keepsake items, for resale in the company's retail outlets. These keepsakes simply are not available from North American suppliers. Therefore stocking its shelves with competitively priced finished goods is forcing the company to buy from Asian suppliers. (Remember from Chapter 1 that sometimes we engage in international purchasing simply because we have no choice. This is one of those times.)

The total workforce of the company in Asia, including those outside of procurement, is about 250 people with 6 expatriates serving in key managerial roles. (An expatriate is simply someone who leaves his or her country to live, and in this case work, elsewhere.) The majority of the Asian staff works in the Hong

Kong office with smaller field offices in Thailand and Sri Lanka and three smaller offices throughout China.

A key component of the company's IPO is that it resembles a mini-business with many of the same functions and skills that are present in the company's U.S. headquarters. The IPO houses personnel that manage product design, supplier, and logistical areas, including quality management and assurance, engineering, procurement, creative design, transportation and logistics, and supplier code of conduct governance and compliance.

A unique aspect of the IPO is that the entire organization reports directly to the chief procurement officer in the U.S., although only a small percent of the IPO staff is aligned to traditional procurement and supply chain activities. This IPO office has much greater responsibilities than traditional IPOs, particularly in the area of product design. IPO personnel conduct supplier audits, identify new suppliers, approve finished good designs, negotiate supply agreements, and manage supplier quality and transportation directly from the Hong Kong office. Although focusing primarily on finished goods, the IPO also works with Asian suppliers that provide direct materials. Any currency risk management issues are handled by the corporate treasury group.

A continuous objective of procurement leaders is to replace the expatriate presence with highly skilled local leadership. A single expatriate assigned to the Hong Kong office costs the company several hundred thousand dollars annually. Because the cost of supporting expatriates in places such as Hong Kong and Singapore requires serious cash outlays, moving more nationals into key leadership roles will provide overhead cost savings.

Critical success factors. Experience with the Asian offices provides the luxury of looking back and commenting about the factors that make this IPO successful. One success factor centers on the way the company has built its organization in Hong Kong and the neighboring regions. The idea of having each of the core business functions from the corporate office represented within the IPO has allowed this office to add value in quality management, creative design, transportation, supplier code of conduct, and other important functions. A second critical factor involves shifting IPO leadership from expatriates to local representatives. Creating a strong local presence with minimal expatriate support lessens the concern that local representatives are assuming less autonomous roles with a perceived lower status. Furthermore, the cost of employing expatriates supports the business case of developing local capabilities. Relying on expatriates was the right choice during the IPO ramp up, but developing strong local leadership is proving to be a sound steady state strategy.

Lessons learned. A primary lesson learned over 30 years of doing business in Asia is that developing a cross-functional IPO staff, consisting primarily of in-country nationals, ensures that local suppliers and other service providers can interact easily with company personnel. This interaction ranges from quickly addressing tactical issues to participating in finished goods design. A growing risk, however, is that the nationals who staff the Asian IPOs will increasingly be in demand as U.S. and European companies expand their Asian presence. Next, establishing a long-term commitment through a regional footprint has been an important success component in this company's Asian sourcing strategy. The lesson learned? The commitment requires patience and perseverance, traits that are often in short supply. From a human resources perspective, this company is finding that about half of the expatriates that return to the U.S. do not stay with the company. Sourcing leaders believe this is due primarily to the inability of these individuals to adapt to an environment that does not have the same independence and power they had on their overseas assignment. The lesson learned is that the company now gives considerable scrutiny to the individuals who take on expatriate assignments. Corporate leaders also believe they have established an effective way to manage suppliers in Asia by using local nationals to evaluate market changes, understand cultural sensitivities, and appreciate the political subtleties of doing business across the region. With the objective of managing its three-dimensional finished goods business, the company's structure has provided a solid platform that is meeting or exceeding quality, cost, time-to-market, and other critical business metrics. As commodity teams develop international purchasing strategies for the company's direct and indirect items, such as ink, paper, and other categories, the ability to leverage the skills already in Asia will support these evolving strategies.

CONCLUDING THOUGHTS

A common saying, which some might describe as a management theory, is "if you can't beat them, join them." And that is precisely what many Western companies have done as they source in emerging and low-cost countries. We know that an increasing number of purchase categories and products are never coming back to North America or Western Europe, making sourcing in low-cost regions an important part of the supply management model.

Something else we must recognize is that global economic changes and forces exert a strong affect on a company's sourcing decisions. A 2009 study found that almost 90% of manufacturers are contemplating changes to their overseas manufacturing and supply strategies. This includes 30% that are considering a change, 26% that are planning to relocate manufacturing or sourcing (some of it back to the home market), and 33% that are being more selective when making offshoring decisions. Only 11% are content with the status quo.[22] Sourcing in emerging and low-cost country markets is not going away anytime soon, so decisions about what and where to source will always demand our attention.

REFERENCES

1. J. Carbone. Next Stop for Electronics Sourcing and Manufacturing Could Be Vietnam. *Purchasing* 2008 May 8. Retrieved from www.purchasing.com.

2. D. Butow. Dangerous Fakes: How Counterfeit, Defective Computer Components from China Are Getting into U.S. Warplanes and Ships. *Business Week* 2008 Oct 13 (4103); 34–44.

3. B. Loyd. Death Sentences in China Tainted-Milk Scandal. January 22, 2009. www.abcnews.com.

4. L. Sullivan. Global Sourcing Crates Supply Chain Challenges. *Information Week* 2005 Mar 21 (1031): 18.

5. G. Chow. Getting Back to Basics. *Canadian Transportation Logistics* 2008 Oct 2008; 111(10): 40.

6. M. Corkery. Chinese Drywall Cited in Building Woes. *The Wall Street Journal* 2009 Jan 12; A3.

7. N. Shister. A Pro's Tips to Newcomers about Trading in China. *World Trade* 2006 Jan; 19(1): 24–28; G.P. Fremlin. Careful Contracts Reduce Risk. *The China Business Review* 2008 Jan/Feb; 35(1): 24–39; K. Kedl. Risk Strategies for the Chinese Market. *Risk Management* 2008 Jun; 55(6): 54–55; and W. Atkinson. 10 Tips to Better China Sourcing. *Purchasing* 2008 Jun 12; 137(6): 16.

8. Anon. China Contributes the Most Risk to International Companies. *Inside Supply Management* 2009 Feb; 20(2): 8.

9. Anon. Protecting Trademarks in China. *Industry Week* 2008 Dec; 257(12): 63.

10. D. Roberts. China's Factory Blues. *Business Week* 2008 Apr 7: 80.

11. J. Ferrieira and L. Prokopets. Does Offshoring Still Make Sense? *Supply Chain Management Review* 2009 Jan/Feb; 13(1): 20–27.

12. See www.x-rates.com for perhaps the most comprehensive website for exchange rate information.

13. J. Katz. Welcome Back U.S. Manufacturing. *Industry Week* 2008 Aug: 37.

14. B. Davis. Surge in Trade Protection Threatens to Deepen Global Crisis. *The Wall Street Journal* 2009 Jan 12; A2.

15. Anon. Buyer's Discourse. *Industry Week* 2008 Dec; 257(12): 34.

16. J. Areddy. China's Export Machine Threatened by Rising Costs. *The Wall Street Journal* 2008 Jun 20; A1.

17. Anon. Companies Are Rethinking Offshore Sourcing. *CSCMP Supply Chain Quarterly* 2008 Quarter 2: 16-17.

18. M. Trottman. When Recall Isn't Total. *The Wall Street Journal* 2008 Jul 15; A12.

19. M. Mandel. China Hangs Tough as Trade Craters. *Business Week* 2009 Jan 26/Feb 2 (4117): 28.

20. Anon. Oshkosh Opens Procurement Office in Shanghai. *Industry Week* 2008 Jul: 30.

21. Case study authored by R.J. Trent. Adapted from *Effective Global Sourcing and Results for Superiors Results.* Tempe, AZ: CAPS Research, 2006: 63–65.

22. J. Ferrieira and L. Prokopets. Does Offshoring Still Make Sense? *Supply Chain Management Review* 2009 Jan/Feb; 13(1): 26.

4

TOTAL COST
OF OWNERSHIP

Imagine walking into a room populated randomly with 100 supply managers. Next, imagine asking those present to raise their hand if they would like to be able to make important decisions based on total cost rather than simply unit price. A betting person knows that the likelihood of almost every hand shooting up in the air is high. (Why would anyone be against making more informed decisions?) Then, ask how many of those supply managers work for companies that have well-developed total cost systems to help make these well-informed decisions. Don't be surprised to find most of those hands suddenly dropping.

Although the concept of total cost applies whether we are engaging in domestic or international buying, the added complexity that surrounds international purchases also means a greater opportunity to experience a wider set of total cost elements. The bottom line regarding total cost of ownership systems is that everyone wants them, but few have them. The information is "out there," but with so many cost variables to consider, the job of consolidating this information into a useful package can be intimidating.[1] More than a dozen total cost categories with over 125 separate cost elements embedded throughout these categories have been identified.[2]

Total cost of ownership is a topic companies simply cannot ignore as they search for new sources of supply. The first section of this chapter defines the concept of total cost, including the reasons to measure total cost. Next, three common types of total cost models are discussed. Then the cost elements that typically comprise a total cost model are presented followed by a case example that shows the development of a total landed cost model. The chapter concludes with one company's experience when it pursued low-cost country sourcing and total cost thinking.

WHAT IS TOTAL COST?

Total cost includes the expected and unexpected elements that increase the unit cost of a good, service, or piece of equipment. Total cost systems, and there are a variety of them, attempt to capture these cost elements. The logic behind the development of total cost systems is clear. Stated simply, unit cost or price *never* equals total cost. If we believe this proposition (and we should), then our concern becomes one of trying to understand the size of the gap between a unit price and its corresponding total cost. We also want to know in some detail what makes up that gap.

Those who are involved in international purchasing are increasingly buying into the notion that variables such as long lead times and distances carry additional costs and risks that are not as relevant to domestic purchases. And supply managers are increasingly buying into the notion that we need to quantify these cost elements, as abstract as some may be, whenever possible. One expert has noted that the "soft costs" that are rarely included in off-shore cost models are starting to become painfully clear.[3]

Measuring Total Cost

It should be obvious why almost every purchasing measurement system includes price-related measures rather than total-cost measures. Price is by far the easiest of any metric to identify across a supply chain. Without a total cost system, however, it is difficult to make sourcing decisions that do not contain a fair amount of subjectivity. It becomes almost next to impossible to select a higher-price sourcing option (but a lower total-cost option) without a total-cost system supporting that decision. Having a "gut feeling" that a higher-price supplier will actually be the lower total-cost supplier doesn't cut it. The "gut feeling" becomes much more certain with total cost data.

The reasons for measuring total cost are compelling. A study by Industry Canada found that over 80% of companies that employed total landed cost analysis did in fact reduce their total landed cost.[4] If anyone can logically argue against the following reasons for measuring total cost, we would like to hear their arguments. Total cost models help companies:

- Identify the impact of different cost elements, including quality non-conformance.
- Track in real terms cost improvements over time.

- Gain management's attention regarding the areas where cost reduction efforts will have their greatest payback.
- Target specific areas for improvement or elimination.
- Make fact-based rather than subjective supply chain decisions.
- Gain a better understanding of the supply chain.

Although this list probably could be longer, we think you get the idea. Prior to the economic meltdown of 2008, importers were experiencing some serious product and logistics cost increases. A survey by Archstone Consulting and the *Supply Chain Management Review* reported that 35% of manufacturers experienced a 25 to 50% increase in material and component costs from foreign suppliers over a 3-year period. Over 50% of survey respondents reported up to a 25% increase in product costs. Similar increases were reported for logistics and transportation costs.[5] So, why measure total cost? The answer: in uncertain times the need to understand every element of cost has never been greater.

The Hidden Costs

The obvious costs of purchasing internationally, which can alter any savings realized from the practice, are only part of the cost equation. Most sourcing experts acknowledge that sourcing offshore contains a variety of hidden costs that can undermine the effectiveness of any global strategy. So, what are the hidden costs from international sourcing?[6]

- Internal expenses: the higher skills, communication, and time required to evaluate and work with foreign suppliers are not free.
- Supplier health: gaining visibility into the financial stability of foreign suppliers is not always easy.
- Post-contract lull: failing to monitor supplier and contract performance after signing an agreement can result in "cost creep" or even performance failure.
- Duty and tariff changes: employing resources to determine correct duties and monitor changes adds to total cost.
- Contract noncompliance: internal noncompliance with a foreign contract reduces the total anticipated savings.
- True inventory costs: although everyone agrees that longer pipelines increase inventory carrying charges, few companies fully account for these charges in their cost models.
- Logistics volatility: managing rapid changes in shipping costs adds an element of complexity.
- Technology: extended supply chains require greater tracking capabilities.

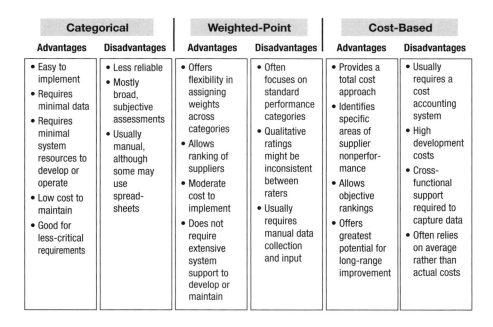

Categorical		Weighted-Point		Cost-Based	
Advantages	**Disadvantages**	**Advantages**	**Disadvantages**	**Advantages**	**Disadvantages**
• Easy to implement • Requires minimal data • Requires minimal system resources to develop or operate • Low cost to maintain • Good for less-critical requirements	• Less reliable • Mostly broad, subjective assessments • Usually manual, although some may use spread-sheets	• Offers flexibility in assigning weights across categories • Allows ranking of suppliers • Moderate cost to implement • Does not require extensive system support to develop or maintain	• Often focuses on standard performance categories • Qualitative ratings might be inconsistent between raters • Usually requires manual data collection and input	• Provides a total cost approach • Identifies specific areas of supplier nonperformance • Allows objective rankings • Offers greatest potential for long-range improvement	• Usually requires a cost accounting system • High development costs • Cross-functional support required to capture data • Often relies on average rather than actual costs

Figure 4.1. Types of Supplier Measurement Systems.

• Quality breakdowns: managing quality problems offshore can be more costly and complex to resolve, including the impact on corporate brand equity.

Traditional cost models reveal that the net cost savings from international buying average around 25%. The Procurement Strategy Council has extended this model by considering the impact of hidden costs not factored into the traditional model. And, guess what? Under this revised model, the actual savings realized from foreign sourcing are only 4 to 6%. If the Procurement Council's model is correct, it shows why total cost calculations must become an integral part of every international sourcing analysis.

TYPES OF TOTAL COST MODELS

All total cost models are part of a family of measurement systems called cost-based systems. A primary objective of these systems is to replace subjective measurement or assessment with data that are more objective. Figure 4.1 summarizes the advantages and disadvantages of the three kinds of supplier and supply chain measurement systems:

Categorical. Categorical systems involve subjective check-offs for various items. A user assigns ratings such as excellent, good, fair, and poor to selected performance categories. In terms of sophistication, categorical measurement is the lowest level of measurement.

Weighted-point. Weighted-point systems, which are widely used in supplier performance scorecards, rely on scales with defined values. This approach weighs and quantifies scores across different performance categories. As it stands now, the most-common system used when making sourcing decisions is a weighted-point approach. Neither categorical nor weighted-point systems consider total cost, although a total cost metric instead of a price measure could be included in a weighted-point system.

Cost-based. Like any measurement system, cost-based systems offer advantages and disadvantages. In fact, these systems can be extremely challenging to develop and use. If these systems were easy to develop, then everyone would have total cost models in place. And that is just not the case. No standard typology of total cost systems exists. As it relates to supply management, we should see total cost models applied within three major areas, regardless of whether this involves domestic or international suppliers: total landed cost models, supplier performance cost models, and life cycle cost models. Although at first glance these may appear to be three unique or independent types of models, these models can have overlapping cost categories. For example, a life-cycle cost model for capital equipment should include the purchase price along with any charges incurred to transport and install the equipment. Be assured that transportation costs usually appear in total landed cost models. The remainder of this section discusses these three models in more detail. (The *Total Cost Elements* section identifies the kinds of cost elements or categories that may populate these models.)

Total Landed Cost Models

A total landed cost model is ideally suited for use when evaluating suppliers prior to making purchase decisions, although that is not the only time or place when total landed costs are determined. Landed cost is the sum of all costs associated with obtaining a product, including acquisition planning; unit price; inbound cost of freight, duty, and taxes; inspection; and material handling for storage and retrieval.[7] Of course, each of these cost categories will contain numerous subcategories.

Whenever we see the word "landed" we can assume we are likely dealing with total cost estimates or calculations that involve international shipments. We can also use total landed costs models when evaluating domestic shipments. In that case, some of the cost elements (such as tariffs) simply have no costs assigned to them. The bottom line is every company that is serious about controlling costs should develop total landed cost models. Best practice companies require their commodity teams or buyers to attach spreadsheets that show the total landed cost whenever they propose a supply strategy or make a selection decision. Few supply managers should question the importance of these models when making foreign sourcing decisions.

If your company can only develop one type of total cost model in the international arena, this should be the one. (Chapter 3 identified various costs that are present when sourcing internationally but are not present when sourcing domestically.) Let's say your company is evaluating a supplier in China, one in Mexico, and one in California. Simply looking at price (and many buyers still look largely at price) might reveal that the Chinese supplier is an obvious choice. But how confident are you that a detailed total landed cost analysis will reveal the same thing? What about all those hidden costs, such as inventory carrying costs and increased logistical handling, that erode the unit price savings? Unless a total landed cost model is developed, you will never know for sure if the correct decision was reached.

Total landed cost models should also be used when doing business with international suppliers on an ongoing basis. After all, the factors that affected the sourcing decision in the first place are dynamic and subject to change. Keeping these models current is also a continuous challenge.

When developing total landed cost models, it is best to start with the unit price and build up the total cost as a good moves from origin to destination. Ideally every cost element is presented in the same unit of measure. If the product is priced by the pound, then every corresponding cost element in the model should appear as a cost per pound. Costs for discrete piece parts may be calculated at the per unit level.

A potential issue with total landed cost models involves whether to include only costs that the buyer incurs or whether to include all of the costs incurred from the point of origin to the point of destination. One school of thought argues that it is best to include only those costs that are incurred directly by the buyer. If a supplier maintains the title and risk of loss for a shipment until it reaches the buyer's dock door, why include the inventory carrying charge for the inventory? Isn't that the supplier's concern? Another argument will say it makes sense to have visibility to all supply chain costs. After all, it's hard to improve what we don't measure. And it's probably safe to conclude that the costs assumed by the supplier are driving up the supplier's unit price.

We have checked and can find nothing that says a buying company cannot have parallel total landed cost models. One model can include the direct costs that the buyer is going to experience firsthand. The second model, which will have a higher total landed cost than the first one, can include all the costs that are spread across the supply chain. Supply chain purists should appreciate this dual model approach.

Total landed cost models are so important that a later section will illustrate in detail how they are constructed. Even the smallest of companies should develop total landed cost models. Spreadsheet software is ideal for developing these models. And almost everyone on earth has spreadsheet software. If your company does not make its international purchasing decisions based on total landed cost, then it is time to assemble a team and charge it with developing a total landed cost model.

Supplier Performance Models

Various models attempt to capture the true cost of doing business with a supplier on a continuous basis. Perhaps the best known of these models is something called the supplier performance index (SPI). Just as total landed cost models often consider total cost during the evaluation phase of supplier selection, the SPI measures costs incurred during a supplier's ongoing performance. SPI calculations are helpful when tracking supplier improvement over time, quantifying the severity of performance problems, deciding which suppliers should exit the supply base, and when establishing minimum acceptable levels of supplier performance. The SPI approach applies to domestic and international suppliers.

The SPI is a total cost model that presents its output in the form of an index or ratio. It assumes that any quality (or other) infraction committed by a supplier during the course of business increases the total cost (and hence the total cost performance ratio) of doing business with that supplier. This approach is more applicable after supplier selection because it is populated with cost occurrences that *have happened* rather than *are expected to* happen. If a company can track each nonconformance and assign a cost to it, the calculation of a standardized SPI becomes relatively easy. The SPI calculation for a specific period is a straightforward formula:

$$\text{SPI} = (\text{cost of material} + \text{nonconformance costs})/(\text{cost of material})$$

Assume a supplier delivers $280,000 worth of parts to a company in the second quarter of a year. The supplier also commits three infractions that quarter: a late delivery, missing documentation, and some defective units. The buying company assigns in its cost accounting system $13,500 in total nonconformance charges for these infractions. The usual warnings apply regarding whether the data are reliable. So, the supplier's SPI for the second quarter is 1.05 [or ($280,000 + $13,500)/$280,000)].

How do we interpret this figure? The SPI of 1.05 means the total cost of doing business with this supplier is 5% higher than the unit price. If the unit price of a supplier's good is \$127.24, then the estimated total cost of that item is really \$133.60 (\$127.24 × 1.05). Because the SPI is a standardized metric (and this is one of its virtues), it allows comparisons between suppliers. A supplier with a higher SPI has a higher total cost than one with a lower SPI. It is important to compare suppliers within the same commodity to ensure "apples to apples" comparisons. Along with total landed cost models, SPI calculations are essential for managing the supply chain from a cost perspective. An efficient and accurate way to identify infractions and their charges is an absolute necessity when using an SPI model.

SPI shortfalls. The SPI has two issues that could make using it problematic unless the user takes these issues into account:

- The SPI does not directly present the unit price of a good. Two suppliers could have the same SPI, but one could provide an item that is 15% less than a competing supplier. Because the SPI is an index that starts with a baseline ratio of 1.0, price tends to get lost in the shuffle. Price will affect the total value of the shipments during a particular period. Keep this in mind when comparing suppliers.
- The base SPI calculation also has a built-in bias against suppliers that provide deliveries with a lower total value. Assume three suppliers within a commodity group commit the same infraction that resulted in a \$1000 nonconformance charge. The first supplier provided \$12,500 worth of goods during a quarter; the second supplier provided \$8700 worth of goods; and a third supplier provided \$35,000 worth of goods. The SPI for the first supplier is 1.08 (\$13,500/\$12,500); the SPI for the second supplier is 1.11 (\$9700/\$8700); and the SPI for the third supplier is 1.03 (\$36,000/\$35,000). This hardly seems fair—each supplier committed the same crime, but will not do the same time. The smaller supplier appears much worse from a total cost perspective while the larger supplier looks like a star. It makes sense to calculate an adjustment factor that removes this bias if suppliers within a commodity provide widely differing volumes. A "Q" adjustment factor allows valid SPI comparisons by removing the inherent bias against suppliers with a lower total value of deliveries. If we want to make our total cost models as accurate as possible, then we have to talk about the Q adjustment factor. Table 4.1 shows how to calculate the SPI as well as an adjusted SPI. In this example, assume that each supplier committed the same infraction with a nonconformance charge of \$1500. Mathematically, we can see how this affects the SPI calculation given the different volumes provided by the three suppliers. SPI users can compensate for this bias by calculating an adjustment factor for each supplier, which is arrived at as follows:

Q = (average cost of a lot or delivery by a supplier)/
(average cost of a lot or delivery from all suppliers
within a commodity)

The adjustment factor is applied against the nonconformance charges within the SPI calculation, which the bottom of Table 4.1 shows.

Two final points about the SPI are important. First, SPI comparisons and average lot calculations should be between suppliers within the same commodity group. It doesn't make sense to group or compare suppliers that are very different in terms of what they provide. Second, the SPI does not necessarily require a major IT effort. Like total landed cost models, the development of SPI spreadsheets by commodity or supplier relationship managers is not an unreasonable burden.

Life Cycle Cost Models

Life cycle cost models may be what comes most readily to mind when thinking about total cost analysis. The life cycle cost model is most often used when evaluating capital decisions such as equipment and facilities that cover an extended time period. For example, buyers at a global energy company cannot propose the purchase of any pumps or compressors unless they attach a life cycle cost model that shows the decision will result in the lowest total cost of ownership. In another example, the controversial competition between Boeing and Northrop Grumman for providing refueling tankers for the U.S. Air Force illustrates the difficulty in calculating life cycle costs for complex projects.

Life cycle models are very similar to the net present value models used in finance. When we start talking about present values, however, we are entering a more complex analysis arena. Most life cycle cost models are used (or should be used) to evaluate capital decisions rather than the purchase of everyday components and services. The other cost models described in this chapter are more applicable for repetitively purchased goods or services.

Life cycle costs apply whether equipment is sourced domestically or internationally. Companies should compare the assumptions made during the development of life cycle estimates with actual data as they become available. This will help identify the validity of the life cycle model while providing insights regarding how to improve the process.

Table 4.1 Supplier Performance Index with Volume Adjustment

	Supplier A	Supplier B	Supplier C
First quarter deliveries	15	15	15
Total value of deliveries	$7,500	$15,000	$30,000
Average delivery	($7,500/15) = $500	($15,000/15) = $1,000	($30,000/15) = $2,000
Nonconformance charges	$1,500	$1,500	$1,500
First quarter SPI	($7,500 + $1,500) /$7,500 = 1.20	($15,000 + $1,500) /$15,000 = 1.1	($30,000 + $1,500) /$30,000 = 1.05
Average shipment from all suppliers	$2,700	$2,700	$2,700
Q adjustment factor	$500/$2,700 = 0.185	$1,000/$2,700 = 0.37	$2,000/$2,700 = 0.74
Adjusted SPI	1.04	1.04	1.04

Adjusted SPI for Supplier A = $7,500 + ($1,500 × 0.185)/$7,500 = 1.04.

Adjusted SPI for Supplier B = $15,000 + ($1,500 × 0.37)/$15,000 = 1.04.

Adjusted SPI for Supplier C = $30,000 + ($1,500 × 0.74)/$30,000 = 1.04.

TOTAL COST ELEMENTS

Regardless of where a company applies total cost models, these models all attempt to capture data beyond unit price. A popular misconception is that total cost models inherently provide better information than not having a total cost model. Although we like to think this statement is correct, the reality is that total cost models, like forecasting models, almost always have some degree of unreliability. The question becomes how much unreliability is embedded in the model? This section explains how the categories of information that populate total cost models contribute to inaccuracy.

The Four A's of Total Cost Data

The data that populate a total cost model can usually be segmented into four major categories that start with the letter "A." How the data are allocated across these categories affects the reliability of the total cost model.

Actual. The first category, and the one that presents the highest degree of reliability, includes actual data. Unit price, insurance on an overseas shipment, and tariffs are examples of actual cost data when dealing with international suppliers. Few, if any, total cost models have the luxury of including only actual data. The ones that do include only actual data are probably excluding some cost elements or data.

Approximations/averages. The second category includes approximations or averages. The predominant characteristic in this category is the data are at least based on figures derived from internal sources. The challenge with many cost elements is that the cost of identifying the true cost of something could outweigh the value of the actual data. Let's say that a supplier is half a day late with a delivery. Should we conduct a detailed study to identify the true cost every time a late delivery occurs? Who has the time, resources, or expertise to undertake a study every time a nonconformance occurs? Overcoming this issue often results in the identification of various costs categories or accounts with standard or average charges applied whenever there is a need to allocate a charge. The following example illustrates the use of averages. In a recent year, 67 late supplier deliveries cost a buying company an estimated $400,000 in total nonconformance costs. The average standard charge in the total cost system for a late delivery, therefore, is $5,970 ($400,000/67) per occurrence. Other cost categories could apply standard or average charges per hour. Reworking a supplier shipment might require 12 hours of labor. The model can include standard labor rates per hour. The usual warnings about using averages apply. A wide dispersion of true costs around this average creates a concern that the average charges may under or overstate the actual cost.

Assumptions. The least-reliable total cost data are based on assumptions. Assumptions come from external sources that form the basis for applying total costs. Let's say a study by researchers at a university concluded that it costs $169 every time a buyer issues a material release. Therefore, every time a buyer issues a material order to a supplier, a $169 charge is applied to the total cost model for that item. But does the $169 charge have anything to do with what really occurs at your organization? What if your company relies extensively on electronic data interchange (EDI) to reduce ordering costs while others in the study do not? Be careful not to develop total cost models that are loaded with external assumptions. Doing so can make the model highly suspect.

Absent. A fourth data category is possible. This category includes data that are absent from a total cost model. The challenge with any cost model is that at times the cost to collect data outweighs the value of the data. At other times the sheer number of possible cost elements that could be part of the model becomes overwhelming. Although we would never say this about product or service quality, close enough is probably good enough as it relates to total cost models.

Regardless of the type of cost model used the need to understand the data that are populating the model cannot be understated. Relying on a model that includes data based largely on assumptions is a recipe for trouble. Supply managers might make decisions based on data that fall largely at the bottom of the reliability scale. Like forecasting models, total cost models usually arrive at some number to report in the way of total cost. The question becomes how confident

Table 4.2 Percent of Companies that Include a Specific Cost Element in Their Total Cost Models

Cost Element	Percent of Firms
Material/component price	88
Logistics and transportation	72
Exchange rate differentials	59
Supplier payment terms	50
Country specific costs (VAT, customs, etc.)	41
Cost of quality	41
Inventory charges	41
Product qualifications	34
Overhead and administrative costs	34
Increased procurement staff costs	31
Material handling and warehousing	28
Tooling cost	25
Packaging cost	22
Customer service cost	19

VAT, value added tax.

Source: Adapted from J. Ferreira and L. Prokopets. Does Offshoring Still Make Sense? *Supply Chain Management Review* 2009 Jan/Feb; 24.

are you in the accuracy of the output? Although beyond the scope of this book, sophisticated statistical techniques are available that help identify confidence intervals associated with total cost estimates.

Specific Total Cost Elements

Research for this book reveals multiple sources that, in one way or another, attempt to identify the cost categories and elements that make up total cost measurement systems. And guess what? Although there is some overlap, not one of these sources agrees about what these models should contain. This issue becomes more complex once we accept that different types of cost models exist. It is easy to see that models that attempt to measure cost elements from point of origin to final point of consumption at the customer (end-to-end models) can be quite broad.

One way to approach this issue is to present the cost elements that are most likely to be included in total cost models. Table 4.2 presents findings from a study of manufacturers regarding the cost elements they include in their total cost models. Examining this table should lead to two conclusions:

- A variety of elements are included in total cost models. Literally dozens of cost elements could populate a total cost model, particularly those that relate to international transactions.
- Except for price and transportation costs, no clear consensus exists regarding the elements to include.

As applied to total landed cost models, cost elements are often divided into categories that reflect a logical progression of material through the supply chain. The following list illustrates these categories along with examples of costs that fall within each category. Most landed cost models will use a supplier's quoted price as the primary cost for the "within country of manufacture" unless the buyer is engaged in some serious cost analysis with the supplier:

- Within country of manufacture: materials, storage, labor, quality, overhead, obsolescence, packaging, risk or disruption, exchange rates, inventory carrying charges
- In transit to country of sale: transportation charges, fuel surcharges, insurance, port charges, handling, security, banking fees, broker fees, potential detention charges, duties, handling agency charges, inventory carrying charges
- Within the country of sale: local transportation and handling, storage fees, taxes, safety stock, inventory carrying charges, yield, productivity implications, maintenance, quality, overhead allocation, payment terms

Developers of life cycle cost models often allocate their cost elements across four broad categories that reflect usage over time:[8]

- Unit price: the price paid including purchase terms
- Acquisition costs: includes all costs associated with delivering equipment, such as buying, ordering, and freight charges to the customer
- Usage costs: includes all the costs to operate the equipment, including installation, energy consumption, maintenance, reliability, spare parts, and yield and efficiency during production
- End-of-life costs: includes all costs incurred when removing equipment from service less any proceeds received for resale, scrap, or salvage

The flow through a life cycle is essentially one of buying, shipping, installing, using, maintaining, and disposing.

CALCULATING TOTAL LANDED COST AT PETS SUPPLY, INC.

The following example, based on an actual international purchasing case, illustrates the key elements that comprise the total landed cost of an internationally sourced good and how these costs can be compiled and calculated to identify a total landed cost. It's time to get down and dirty with the numbers.

Chris Smith is a supply manager with Pets Supply, Inc., a company with operations in California. (*Note*: The name of the company has been changed.) The business is family-owned and processes and distributes cat and dog food throughout the U.S. As one might imagine, the company uses a wide variety of ingredients to manufacture its products. These ingredients include meat, fish, grain, vitamins, and vegetables. A key ingredient used during the manufacture of cat food is fishmeal, which is the clean, dried, ground tissue of whole fish or fish cuttings with or without the extraction of part of the oil.

Because of the rising costs to source ingredients in the U.S., a decision has been made by supply executives to review the costs associated with outsourcing the fishmeal, including the use of foreign suppliers. Pets Supply has performed supplier research and has identified several potential suppliers. This example focuses on a Vietnamese supplier that supply managers believe has the potential to help the company meet its longer-term cost requirements. Chris Smith has been tasked with estimating the total supply chain costs associated with using the Vietnamese supplier.

Identifying Total Landed Cost Elements

The Vietnamese supplier processes fish, which it obtains from its fishing fleet, to produce fishmeal. Fishmeal is made by cooking, pressing, and drying the fish. Once the fishmeal is dried, it is ground, screened to the correct particle size, and packed into vacuum-sealed bags that contain 50 pounds of product. Each of these bags is in turn packed into corrugated boxes (one bag to a box) and sealed. The fishmeal is currently priced by the supplier at $0.29 per pound delivered at the ocean-going vessel.

For overseas shipments the supplier stacks 40 boxes to a pallet. Pallets are then loaded into a shipping container that holds 20 pallets. The containers are sent to a port for loading onto an ocean vessel. At this point, the transportation costs become the responsibility of Pets Supply. The purchase agreement, however, calls for title transfer once the container reaches the U.S. port. The ocean carrier will charge Pets Supply $2500 to ship each container to a California port. Once the containers reach the U.S., they will be moved to a local warehouse at a cost of $350 per container. Applicable U.S. customs charges and import duties are 15% of the original purchase price. Demand planners believe the company will require the equivalent of one container per month. Fortunately, the demand for cat food is fairly level throughout the year. Cats, while known for being finicky, are predictable in their eating habits.

Pets Supply plans to store each container in a public warehouse for a month until the fishmeal is required for processing. This one month of storage helps cover any demand or supply chain uncertainty the company might face. Monthly storage costs are expected to be $6.50 per pallet, with an additional warehouse handling fee of $6.25 per pallet whenever a pallet leaves the warehouse. Fresh foods inventory carrying costs are 24% annually, which the company must apply to the fishmeal that is held in storage.

When a container of fishmeal is required at the Pets Supply processing facility, a local freight company will deliver the container at a cost of $275 per container. Additionally, Chris estimates the cost of incoming receiving and quality control procedures to be $4 per pallet. He further estimates that the company will incur a 3% loss of the total purchased fishmeal. This loss results from the nature of the product, the supply chain distance involved (such as in transit damages), and the longer-term effects of storage.

Chris also determined, in conjunction with the industrial engineers in the processing facility, that the historic yield of fishmeal when blended into various products is 98%, which means that the company wastes an additional 2% of the product by volume. This loss is not recoverable and is in addition to the 3% loss mentioned earlier. Some companies might exclude this yield loss from the total landed cost calculation because it occurs during processing. Other companies might also include the effect of payment terms or rebates provided by the supplier. Finding two total cost models that include exactly the same cost elements is difficult because no standard exists defining what these models should contain. Finally, in addition to the costs noted above, corporate accountants at Pets Supply require that a 17% assessment on the unit price of the fishmeal be included to cover general and administrative overhead costs at the company.

With any total costs model, the challenge involves getting complete and reliable data. Chris must identify and collect the data he requires before he can develop a cost model that progressively builds up the total cost per pound. Companies that undertake this build up often find that their estimated total cost far exceeds the more obvious unit price. So who can possibly know with precision the true cost of international purchasing without undertaking this kind of exercise?

Table 4.3 provides some important information, such as annual usage (i.e., demand), that is required to calculate the per pound cost for each cost element. Table 4.4 presents the analysis that arrived at the total cost per pound of fishmeal. Table 4.4 also includes explanations for the determination of each cost. An ingredient that has a $0.29 unit price per pound is estimated to have a $0.49 total

Table 4.3 Total Fishmeal Requirements

	Equals
1. Fishmeal per bag (one bag inserted into one box)	50 lb per box
2. 40 boxes per pallet	2,000 lb per pallet
3. 20 pallets per ocean shipping container	40,000 lb per container
4. One container required per month	480,000 lb of fishmeal required annually (40,000 lb × 12)

landed cost per pound, an increase of almost 70% over the unit price! What we don't know at this point is the estimated total cost per pound of doing business with Pet Supply's current supplier or the other suppliers that the company is considering. That information is critical for making relative comparisons.

Inventory Carrying Charges

Although most of the costs presented in Table 4.4 are clear given the explanations provided, the table does contain one element that requires elaboration. That element is the inventory carrying charge. Although usually not easy to calculate, inventory carrying charges can occur at any part of a supply chain where inventory is present. Until the final customer purchases an item, someone has to retain title to goods and therefore accrue carrying charges. Within the international arena, this issue is important because the material pipelines are much longer in terms of time and distance. Most companies disregard these charges because they don't seem real or are too hard to quantify.

Although there is disagreement on the specifics, inventory carrying costs generally include three major components:

- *Cost of capital.* Inventory consumes capital that could have been put to other productive uses. Some companies may also view this component as an opportunity cost.
- *Cost of storage.* Inventory storage can include insurance, heat, lighting, rent, and cycle counting.
- *Combined costs of obsolescence, deterioration, and loss.* Factors such as expired shelf life, scrap, and theft can all be part of this category.

If all goes well, the finance department is able to quantify these components and arrive at a carrying charge that is expressed as a percent of the inventory's unit cost. For example, a piece of inventory with a unit price, whether it is a raw material, work-in-process, or finished good worth $10, with an assigned carrying charge of 25%, results in an annual carrying charge of $2.50 per unit. Inventory held less than a year is prorated accordingly. Companies that are interested in

Table 4.4 Total Landed Cost Calculation for Pets Supply, Inc.

Cost Element	Explanation of Cost Calculations	Cost per Pound	Cumulative Percent
Fishmeal unit price	Supplier quoted unit price per pound	$0.29	59.2
Ocean shipping	$2,500 per container/40,000 lb per container	$0.062	12.6
Tariffs and duties	15% × unit price ($0.29)	$0.043	8.8
Transfer charge from U.S. port to warehouse	$350 per container/40,000 lb per container	$0.009	1.8
Warehouse storage charge	$6.50 per pallet/2,000 lb per pallet	$0.003	0.6
Warehouse handling fee	$6.25 per pallet/2,000 lb per pallet	$0.003	0.6
Inventory carrying charge	40,000 lb held in inventory each month × unit price ($0.29) = $11,600 inventory value; $11,600 × 24% inventory carrying charge = $2,785 annual carrying charge; $2,784/480,000 lb annual demand = $0.006 carrying charge per lb	$0.006	1.22
Local freight from warehouse to plant	$275 per container/40,000 lb per container	$0.007	1.43
Receiving and quality control	$4 per pallet/2,000 lb per pallet	$0.002	0.41
Product loss before production	3% loss × unit price ($0.29) (This reduces the annual available fishmeal for use during production to 465,600 lb.)	$0.009	1.8
Production yield loss	2% × 465,600 lb = 9,312 lb lost during production; 9,312 lb × $0.29 unit price = $2,700.48 yield loss; $2,700.48/465,000 lb = $0.006 per lb	$0.006	1.22
Administrative overhead	17% × unit price ($0.29)	$0.05	10.2
Estimated Total Cost		**$0.49**	**100.0**

managing carrying charges as a cost element pay particular attention to a set of measures that report inventory turns.

In the Pets Supply example, the company incurs carrying charges prior to production when the fishmeal is held in storage for a month. This example does not include carrying charges when the fishmeal is in-transit from Vietnam because title (i.e., ownership) does not transfer to Pets Supply until the goods arrive at the U.S. port. We could engage in a lively debate about whether in-transit carrying charges should be part of the total landed cost model when the buyer does not own the inventory. The model developed here only includes charges that are directly incurred by the buyer.

So how exactly is the carrying charge determined? In our example, the buyer imports a container of fishmeal each month and then expects to hold that container for 1 month in a warehouse. This is the equivalent of holding one container in storage for a year. So, one container of fishmeal is valued at $11,600 (40,000 pounds multiplied by $0.29 unit price per pound). Next, the 24% carrying charge is applied against $11,600 to arrive at an annual carrying charge of $2,784. Because this is an annual charge, it is divided by the annual demand to arrive at a relatively insignificant charge of $0.006 per pound.

This analysis shows how total supply chain costs can be allocated to provide a more complete picture of total supply chain costs. After completing this analysis, it becomes possible to compare supplier costs across common cost categories; identify cost elements that are unusual or require attention; compare the total cost for obtaining similar products from different suppliers and regions; and make better decisions. Total landed cost calculations are an indispensable part of managing supply chain risk.

The next section looks at offshore sourcing costs and risks at a company that we all recognize.

LOW-COST COUNTRY SOURCING AT UPS

The UPS Procurement Group in Atlanta, Georgia, is responsible for purchasing goods and services for UPS. Among the group's key responsibilities is ensuring continuity of supply and reducing cost. Recently, UPS management made a decision to consider offshore sourcing for certain commodities to realize cost savings. A team of sourcing professionals was formed and tasked with reviewing the requirements for such an undertaking.

UPS is a global company. Therefore, a key consideration for the team, and also one of the key reasons for UPS undertaking this initiative, is the potential for leveraging UPS spending across the world. An integral part of this exercise is to determine what items are conducive to offshore production (or are currently being sourced offshore) and where it makes the most sense to source them from a total cost perspective. UPS provides products from the U.S. to its customers in foreign countries, so the company is also interested in learning if there are viable sources in those countries that could provide these products at lower cost. In addition, although the UPS Asia operation has been relatively small in size, it is growing both as a source of supply and demand. UPS wants the Asian operation to develop a local supplier base to ensure continuity of supply as well as to reduce cost.

Options Considered by UPS

In order to achieve the objective of cost reduction, UPS considered several low-cost countries outside the U.S. that could produce items at a much lower cost and with comparable quality as domestic suppliers. Although in the final analysis, suppliers in Mexico, China, and Malaysia were selected as potential sources of supply, this case study deals mainly with UPS sourcing in China.

Several problems and issues can arise when sourcing from a foreign country, including using an unknown and untested supplier base; finding significant variations in material availability and quality; confronting social responsibility issues; encountering language barriers and cultural differences; and facing trade restrictions. With operations in over 200 countries, UPS had experience with all of these issues, but UPS wanted additional information on the supplier base in China. When planning for this initiative, UPS considered whether they should hire staff or partner with a company that has knowledge of local suppliers. In order to accelerate the process, UPS management felt that the best choice would be to work with a third party that has knowledge of the global supply market.

After identifying several qualified third parties, UPS decided to partner with an experienced global consulting firm that had a presence in China. Working with its consulting firm, one of the first tasks for UPS was to determine which products would be best suited to offshore sourcing and how much of the total volume of these products would be obtained offshore.

How UPS Identified Qualified Suppliers

UPS spends billions of dollars annually to procure thousands of products. As a first step, UPS wanted to identify those products that could benefit from offshoring. In order to accomplish this, UPS procurement identified items that would *not* be ideally suited to offshore manufacturing. This included items with volumes that were too small to justify the time and effort; items that had a relatively long design or testing cycles; and items that required customization and short order lead times. After a 2-month process, the team identified several categories of items that should benefit from being sourced offshore.

This case study primarily focuses on two of the selected product categories: those made from paper/corrugated and polypropylene materials. Needless to say, UPS requires vast amounts of these goods. It might appear that these categories would not be suited to offshore manufacturing. The relatively low unit cost and high logistics costs associated with transporting products of this nature might seem to outweigh any savings. However, the sheer volume of these products that UPS and its customers consume globally, and the potential associated cost savings, made them worthwhile candidates for foreign sourcing. When UPS initially looked at the costs to purchase these items offshore, the product costs were on average 40% less per unit. UPS believed it could realize an estimated total savings of around 15% after factoring in its total costs. With the volume that UPS requires, this translated into potential savings of millions of dollars per year.

UPS initially identified around 100 potential suppliers in various regions, with the majority located in China. Members of the team went through an initial evaluation process of these suppliers and reduced the field to 35 potential suppliers that appeared to have the necessary capabilities. After further analysis, the number of potential suppliers was reduced to 20. Four members of the UPS procurement team, along with support from the consulting firm, carried out factory visits and conducted on-site interviews with these suppliers. After grading and ranking these suppliers, 12 finalist suppliers were identified with 1 located in Mexico, 1 in Malaysia, and the remainder in China.

Managing the Risks of Low-Cost Country Sourcing

Prior to commencing the study, UPS procurement managers were aware of potential pitfalls when undertaking low-cost-country sourcing. If not managed properly, each of those pitfalls could erode the total cost savings the company expected to achieve. Therefore, UPS spent considerable time planning for this initiative, including dedicating a team of sourcing professionals to the project. UPS planned for and mitigated potential issues in the following ways:

Communication and language. UPS was aware of the potential for problems and misunderstandings due to language problems and miscommunication when working with suppliers in foreign countries. UPS also felt that if the company tried to manage the work from afar, it would be less effective. The company established a local procurement team in Asia to provide an on-the-ground presence. To educate this team, UPS used its U.S.-based commodity managers who had many years of experience in sourcing the selected items. UPS also invested a considerable amount of time and effort on the ground with foreign suppliers before and during the sourcing initiative, as well as continuing its local reviews on a continual basis once outsourcing began.

Cost changes. UPS found that the initial cost elements that were used in the total cost model changed over time, mainly due to unpredictable economic conditions: the cost of gasoline increased; local wages increased because of a government regulated overtime policy change; and local inflation rates as well as currency exchange rates changed. UPS learned some valuable lessons from this experience. Supply managers kept track of these cost changes and acted accordingly, inputting these changes into the total cost model as they took place. Thus,

UPS was poised to react in a timely fashion with up-to-date information on projected savings. If rising costs could not be contained, UPS would consider shifting volume to lower-cost countries until market conditions improved.

Price changes. Certain suppliers, in their eagerness to obtain UPS business, provided low-cost bids and then sought to raise their prices once production began. In other cases, suppliers had not accounted for all the costs in their cost models and subsequently tried to raise prices. Anticipating some of these tactics, UPS met extensively with suppliers prior to signing contracts to agree on all costs. These meetings revealed that some suppliers were receiving Chinese government subsidies and were not including certain costs, such as the cost of management or capital equipment, in their pricing. UPS realized that these suppliers might try at a later date to include these costs and raise their prices. To build fair and lasting relationships with suppliers, UPS worked closely to help them understand their true costs. UPS provided detailed information on product requirements, including detailed performance specifications and product samples.

Defects and returns. Defects and returns can present an issue when procuring goods from overseas because greater time, distance, and cost are involved. UPS reached an agreement with suppliers on a procedure for dealing with defects and returns, contractually establishing who has responsibility and how this process would work in practice. Allowances were also made in the total cost model for defects and returns. It was agreed that for defects below a certain value, UPS would destroy these items and submit a claim to the supplier. Above a certain value, UPS could return defective items at a supplier's expense. Also, given the additional time and distance in the supply chain, UPS reserved the right to send defective items back within 12 months of their purchase date.

Use of logistics intermediaries. Companies that engage in global sourcing often need to rely on logistics intermediaries with global reach to provide transportation, distribution, and freight-forwarding services. Fortunately, UPS has this capability in house, through its UPS/SCS subsidiary, to provide transportation, warehousing, freight forwarding, customs brokerage, and other services for itself and UPS customers. The company was able to leverage this expertise and resources.

Maintaining consistent quality. UPS adopted several strategies to maintain quality and availability when sourcing from low-cost countries. UPS employed foreign nationals on the ground in China to conduct ongoing site visits. A local presence is essential when buying direct from manufacturers, so UPS foreign nationals work with suppliers to ensure quality and product availability. Furthermore, UPS procurement personnel, based in the U.S., also spend time working from their locations to accomplish these objectives. UPS also relies on independent laboratory product testing and independent quality audits to ensure supplier quality. The company also requires normal quality controls for products leaving a supplier's facility as well as when they are received in the U.S. UPS regularly reviews these quality control procedures.

Raw material supply. UPS needed to ensure its suppliers could obtain the necessary raw materials for the items sourced in China on a timely, consistent, and cost-effective basis. In addition, it was important to know where these raw materials originated to ensure that the raw material suppliers were not adversely impacting the environment. In order to minimize this problem, UPS worked early on with its local procurement professionals to evaluate each supplier's source of raw materials as well as each supplier's history of conformance with accepted environmental protection practices.

Environmental and weather-related risks. UPS understood the environmental and weather-related risks involved in transporting goods from overseas. In the summer months, containers can be exposed to high, humid temperatures and can be in transit for up to 6 weeks. At times water can seep into containers, causing damage and increasing costs. UPS determined by item whether it was cost effective to provide additional packaging and outer wrapping for cartons. Furthermore, UPS reduced the impact of this issue through use of a reliable third-party logistics firm (UPS/SCS) that had the equipment and controls in place to protect goods while they were in-transit.

Supply continuity risk. UPS supply managers recognized quite well that sourcing from a low-cost country carries inherent risks that may jeopardize continuity of supply. UPS made a decision that approximately half of its required volume was to be sourced in China with the balance sourced in the U.S. This decision reduced the total amount of savings but helped maintain supply continuity and flexibility.

Lessons Learned

Supply managers who are involved in low-cost country sourcing are able to identify various lessons learned from their experience. During the process of deciding what to outsource, UPS gained an important insight: the savings made in offshore manufacturing could be reduced or negated by the costs associated with distributing the products once they arrived at U.S. shores. A company cannot simply add a general cost factor to a product's cost and decide whether it is cost effective to purchase it offshore. A variety of factors must be considered: how much must be produced and shipped to achieve lower prices; usage frequency; the warehouse space and time needed to store a product; and ultimately the cost associated with additional handling and shipping an item to its final destination. It is important to monitor these costs continuously as economic and other conditions change. Total cost and risk management are not simply buzzwords.

An additional lesson learned is that these initiatives are not short term. Time and effort are required before suppliers are at the point where they consistently perform. Therefore, companies should not underestimate the required effort, resources, and associated costs when working with suppliers located in low-cost countries. Forming strong relationships is still a vital component of the supply management process.

Provided the appropriate actions are taken to manage risks, the UPS Procurement Group thinks that low-cost country sourcing offers attractive savings opportunities. With over 2 years of experience, the results of UPS offshore initiatives are solid. UPS continues to realize significant cost savings. (*Note*: The authors would like to thank Andy Criscuolo, Commodity Family Manager, Corporate Procurement, UPS, and James P. Thompson, Vice President, Corporate Procurement, UPS, for their generous support in developing this section.)

CONCLUDING THOUGHTS

Managing international purchasing costs from a total cost perspective is perhaps one of the best ways to manage supply chain risk. Imagine the benefit of making decisions that are backed by objective data rather than incomplete or subjective analysis. If your company has not developed total landed cost, supplier performance, and life cycle cost models, then we have just identified one of your strategic supply management objectives for the next year. The development of reliable total cost models is without question a best practice that far too many companies have yet to endorse or perform well. Given the growth in international purchasing and the uncertainty that surrounds supply chains today, these models should no longer be thought of in theoretical terms.

REFERENCES

1. L. White. Determining Total Cost of Ownership. *Food Service Equipment and Suppliers* 2006 Feb; 59(2): 28–32.

2. B.G. Ferrin and R.E. Plank. Total Cost of Ownership Models: An Exploratory Study. *The Journal of Supply Chain Management* 2002 Summer; 38(3): 25.

3. J. Ferreira and L. Prokopets. Does Offshoring Still Make Sense? *Supply Chain Management Review* 2009 Jan/Feb; 13(1): 23.

4. G. Chow. Getting Back to Basics. *Canadian Transportation Logistics* 2008 Oct; 111(10): 40.

5. J. Ferreira and L. Prokopets. Does Offshoring Still Make Sense? *Supply Chain Management Review* 2009 Jan/Feb; 13(1): 22.

6. D. Hannon. 9 Hidden Costs of Global Sourcing. *Purchasing* 2009 Mar; www.purchasing.com.

7. K. Cowman. Material Costs. *Materials Management and Distribution* 2004 Sep; 49(7): 73.

8. R.M. Moncka, R.J. Trent, and R.H. Handfield. *Purchasing and Supply Chain Management* 2005.Mason, OH: Thomson-Southwestern; 364–365.

5

ADDITIONAL INTERNATIONAL TOPICS

This chapter discusses two topics that deserve more than passing reference. The first part of the chapter addresses culture and cultural differences and provides examples of differences that exist across the broad concept known as "culture." The second part of the chapter deals with sourcing services internationally and discusses choosing the right service provider and ensuring that an international services strategy does not expose your company to new risk. The chapter concludes with a look at India, the current leading destination for many types of outsourced services.

UNDERSTANDING CULTURAL DIFFERENCES

In a review of a book about India, *Business Week* wrote that one of the most valuable assets any global business person can possess today is cultural understanding: a deep understanding of how other countries really operate.[1] Yet this understanding is something that most of us lack. An elaboration of the cultural mistakes people make could fill volumes of books! Many of these mistakes might even come across as humorous. For example, have you heard about the employee at a call center in India who ended his conversations with U.S. callers by saying, "I love you?" When his manager asked why he said this, he responded by saying that he wanted to show his customers that he cared. Although *I love you* is a noble sentiment, most North Americans do not respond well to receiving unsolicited statements of love from a stranger over the telephone! Or what about the representative from Boston who publicly gave a Chinese official a green hat during a reception for his trade delegation? Who would think that in China a green hat symbolizes that one's wife is being unfaithful? Apparently the "luck of the Irish" was not working that day. And probably the conversation around the Chinese official's dinner table that night was quite interesting!

Several years ago, a colleague was invited to lecture to a group of applied mathematics students in China. As he was writing calculations on the board, he sensed that the students were not following along, even after they nodded *yes* when he asked if they understood what he was doing. So he next asked, "Would you tell me if you did not understand me?" The students shook their heads *no*. This reaction is completely different from what we expect from Western students—and it's a classic example of a cultural difference.

Culture is the sum of the understandings that govern human interaction within a society. These understandings result in two broad areas of differences: the first is values, or the way people *think,* and the second is behavior, or the way people *act*.[3] It's no surprise that cultural differences exist between countries and societies. What might also be surprising is the extent to which these differences can create potential problems for supply managers who want to do business in foreign countries. The bottom line is that the global scope of supply management is increasing. An appreciation that the differences between cultures are very real must also increase.

The following sections outline differences in business culture from country to country and, although not intended to be exhaustive, they point out areas where some notable cultural differences exist. Throughout these sections, a piece of advice applies: before engaging in international business, it is worthwhile to review a comprehensive reference about the country you are about to visit or to consult with someone who has experience with that culture. We also include some words of warning here: culture is an area where we relentlessly engage in stereotyping. Often we make statements as if they apply to everyone in every part of a country. The reality, however, is not always that clear because most countries are comprised of a variety of subcultures. Geographic borders and cultural borders are often two different things. Table 5.1 summarizes some key points that relate to various dimensions of cultural differences.

Eastern vs. Western Culture

Because an increasing amount of international business is taking place with Asian countries, a useful starting point is to consider some of the differences between Eastern and Western cultural values. Interestingly, the skills that are most highly prized among Western businessmen (technical and business skills) might not be the primary attributes required for success in the East (patience, flexibility, and adaptability).[4]

Table 5.1 Advice When Working Across Cultures

Category	Some Good Advice
Greeting rituals	• Arrive in a country ahead of time to observe greeting rituals in practice. • Speak with individuals in your company who have experience with greeting rituals and/or with foreign nationals who understand proper greetings.
Gift giving	• If gift giving is accepted practice, do not give lavish gifts; a gift might be misinterpreted as a bribe. • Ask your hosts about the gift-giving practice that is considered acceptable in the country where you will be conducting business. • Speak with individuals in your company who have experience with gift giving and/or with foreign nationals to understand the practices in the country where you will be conducting business.
Gestures and eye contact	• Arrive in a country ahead of time to observe these rituals in practice. • Speak with individuals in your company who have experience with using gestures and eye contact and/or with foreign nationals who work for your company to understand their use; practice beforehand.
Time perception	• Plan to have extra time in the country where you will be doing business if you find from your research that meetings are conducted at a different pace. • Be on time for appointments even though your counterpart might not be to avoid any sign of disrespect. • Expect time perceptions to be different. Do not allow perceptions to affect your interaction with foreign business individuals.
Meeting customs and conduct	• Understand the proper way to enter a room and the typical seating arrangements where you will be conducting business. • Attempt to mimic behaviors by observing meeting customs and conduct. • Speak with individuals in your company who have experience with the use of meeting customs and conduct and/or foreign nationals who work for your company to understand proper protocol.
Use of names, titles, and business card presentation	• Convert one side of your foreign business cards into the language of your counterpart. • After receiving a business card, take time to study the card and ask questions regarding the individual's position and responsibilities. • Use a business card holder or case to hold your business cards. Keep the business cards you receive.
Negotiation styles	• Adapt your negotiation style to that used in the country where you are conducting business. • Practice negotiation with foreign nationals who are experienced in the negotiation style of the target country. • Understand who the true decision maker is in a negotiation. • Plan extra time for negotiation.

Table 5.1 (continued) Advice When Working Across Cultures

Category	Some Good Advice
Language and communication	• Adjust your communication style and pace to that used by individuals in the country where you are conducting business. • Write out long numbers. • Avoid slang, acronyms, and jargon. • Understand that if you work through an interpreter, confusion might arise. It is important to understand what level of expertise the interpreter has in understanding cultural and communication nuances. • Ask interpreters to restate the questions or statements you make back to you to ensure clarity of understanding. • Double translate contracts to avoid misunderstandings.

Westerners, particularly Americans, tend to establish business relationships fairly quickly, but these relationships might not be deep or necessarily long lasting. And if all a Westerner wants to do is purchase something through a straightforward transaction, the need to think about a longer-term relationship is not that great. In Asia, time is usually required to establish and build business relationships that are based on trust. Once a relationship is established, however, it tends to endure. Although the tendency for Americans is "to get down to work," business people from the East tend to take their time getting to know their counterparts. Furthermore, the first group of people that one meets when doing business in the East might not be the ultimate decision makers. In fact, decision making might take place by consensus within a group.

A common practice with Western companies involves sending staff members (expatriates) overseas on temporary assignments. The inherent challenge with this practice (besides the high cost of maintaining expatriates) is that time is required to develop relationships in the East. Not long after a relationship is fully developed, however, the Westerner is likely to be transferred back home.

Greeting Rituals

Greeting rituals differ from country to country. Good business practice demands that supply managers understand the various forms of greetings used in foreign countries and comply accordingly.

In the West, shaking hands when being introduced to a foreigner for the first time is customary. Subsequent meetings are also characterized by handshakes. This can become extreme if one person, usually from the West, moves beyond the handshake and engages in the dreaded hug or even a kiss on the cheek. It should come as no surprise to find that not all cultures respond favorably to this level of physical contact, particularly with relative strangers.

In Japan, a bow is a common means of greeting a person, and the depth of the bow is a way of respecting the relative status of an individual. Japanese business people will shake hands with Westerners to make them feel more comfortable, but shaking hands is not their first instinct when meeting or greeting a counterpart. In the Middle East, only touch another person with the right hand because the left hand is considered unclean. Filipinos greet each other with an "eyebrow flash," which is a quick lifting of the eyebrows.[5]

Gift Giving

In many cultures, presenting a gift is common when meeting someone for the first time. In the West, however, gift giving is generally frowned upon and receiving a gift might even be viewed as accepting a bribe. In fact, many companies forbid their employees from accepting gifts of any form.

If giving gifts is a common practice, however, be aware of the appropriateness of the gift selected. For example, in the Middle East giving gifts is acceptable, in fact even appreciated, at a first business meeting. Unacceptable, however, is giving gifts that are made of pigskin or contain alcohol. Also unacceptable is giving a gift of personal clothing. Furthermore, do not present a gift to a Muslim with the left hand or give a gift to a Muslim's wife. Both are practices that are considered highly inappropriate. In China, the presentation of a sharp object as a gift, such as a knife or scissors, represents the severing of a friendship or relationship. Around the world, symbolism can take on entirely different meanings.

In certain cultures, such as the Middle East, the person receiving a gift might wait and open it in private. Yet Westerners might construe this practice to be rude or an expression of disinterest in the gift. In certain parts of the world, such as Japan, how a gift is wrapped, including the color of the wrapping materials, carries certain significance. Clearly, in gift giving, the practice, manner, and type of gift given differ from country to country. Standard advice applies here: supply managers are well advised to understand the differences before presenting a gift within a foreign country. (*Note*: A useful website that provides more information on this subject is http://www.cyborlink.com/besite/international_gift_giving.htm.)

Gestures and Eye Contact

Never assume that the gestures used will convey the same meaning around the world. At times gestures can mean the exact opposite of what is intended. In the U.K. indicating "V" for victory with your hand and fingers is shown with the palm facing out toward your audience. Shifting the "V" with the back of the hand toward the audience is a rude gesture. Using the fingers to beckon someone or pointing at an individual is considered insulting to most Middle and Far Easterners. In the U.S., a person who is reluctant to maintain eye contact is called "shifty-eyed" and arouses suspicion. In other countries, such as Japan, South Korea, Taiwan, and other Asian countries, an attempt to maintain eye contact might be perceived as being aggressive, so maintaining eye contact is not acceptable. Conversely, in Saudi Arabia, eye contact and gestures of openness are important and can actually facilitate communications.[7] (*Note*: A website containing useful information about body gestures is http://www.ehow.com/how_2129585_learn-body-language-foreign-culture.html.)

Perception of Time

Time perception differs greatly from country to country. To say these differing perceptions can be a source of frustration is an understatement. In Germany being punctual for business meetings is important. The Spanish, however, are not quite as concerned about punctuality. Italians expect their counterparts to be on time for a meeting, but they might make a point by turning up late to show who is in charge.[8] In India, an instructor teaching a professional development course noted that almost every student arrived 15 or 20 minutes late. Thinking that the cause of lateness might be due to traffic conditions, the instructor shifted the start and end times of the course to begin and conclude later. To his surprise, the participants still arrived 15 to 20 minutes late. Although arriving late for scheduled business appointments is accepted practice in many countries, doing so is highly irritating to most Westerners.

How meetings are conducted and how decisions are arrived at also differ from culture to culture. In the U.S., common practice is to start business meetings on time, have clearly defined goals and objectives for the meeting, and end on time. Arriving at an agreement in a reasonable amount of time during a meeting is also an expectation. Yet in other cultures, such as in Brazil, becoming familiar with the person with whom you are doing business, including getting to know that person on a personal level, is more important. So concluding a business deal just might take a bit longer south of the equator.

Many cultures, including those in the Middle East, consider finishing the interaction with the person they are currently dealing with before moving to the next meeting important.[7] As a result, the next meeting might start later, a situation in which the person who is late does not see as rudeness. Oftentimes the late individual actually sees himself as having been considerate of the participants in the previous meeting. (*Note*: A useful website that addresses this topic can be found at http://www.latpro.com/cms/en/recruiter/time_management_in_other_cultures.)

Meeting Customs and Conduct

It should also come as no surprise to find that business meetings are structured differently from country to country. In many instances, these differences become apparent during the first meeting between business associates. The way meetings are handled helps set the tone for success or failure. Therefore, supply managers must be aware of regional and national differences when conducting business in foreign countries.

In Asia at an initial business meeting, describing your position within your company's organizational structure is common. Seating arrangements are also highly structured, often indicating seniority. In Asia, the most senior person usually sits at the middle of the table with his or her back to a window. If there are no windows the senior person faces the door with the next most senior people seated to his left- and right-hand side.

In the U.S., the most senior person commonly sits at the head of the table. In Sweden, however, the setup of the meeting room goes to great lengths to avoid acknowledging the existence of a hierarchy, something that is reflected in the seating arrangements. Managers sit among their subordinates instead of sitting at the end of a meeting table. In the U.K., almost invariably, managers sit at the end of the meeting table.[9]

The Chinese conduct meetings in a more formal manner. Usually the Chinese contingent participating in a meeting is already present before the other meeting participants are escorted into the room. Participants are also expected to enter the room in hierarchical order. Unlike in many parts of the U.S., the beginning of a meeting in China features informal talk, with business being addressed once the participants feel more at ease with one another.[10]

Use of Names, Titles, and Business Cards

The use of names and titles is important in many cultures. As mentioned earlier, sometimes hierarchy determines the seating arrangements at business meetings and who enters the room first and who speaks and in what order. In China when addressing a businessperson, use that person's family name. In a business context, it is acceptable behavior to call Chinese persons by their last names together with his or her title.[11] Yet in the West, a common practice is to revert to first names once formal introductions are completed.

Across most cultures, using a business card is an internationally recognized method of providing information about contact details and rank within the corporate hierarchy. In Asia the general practice is for an individual's last name to appear first on the business card followed by the first name, a practice that is the reverse of that normally seen in Europe and North America. In Asia, an accepted practice is to give and receive business cards with both hands, another practice that is uncommon with Europeans or North Americans. After receiving a business card, an Asian often studies the card carefully before placing it in a cardholder. In the U.S., a business card is often placed in a pocket or wallet, something that is considered to be disrespectful in Japan.

Negotiating Styles

Between cultures, some important differences exist in negotiating styles. North American negotiators either negotiate singularly or, if they rely on a team approach, have a clear leader that the other team members follow. Cultures such as the U.S, Canada, and the U.K. generally focus on individual performance, initiative, and accomplishments. Many cultures outside of North America place a primary emphasis on the group rather than the individual, which extends directly into the negotiation session. Group-oriented cultures in Latin America include, but are certainly not limited to, Mexico, Argentina, Brazil, Venezuela, and Columbia. Most Asian countries are also group oriented, particularly Japan, Malaysia, and China. Most cultures in Southern Africa emphasize the group. (As already mentioned, in Spain, business is conducted in a more relaxed way when compared to other Western European nations.) Because of the emphasis on group decision making, negotiations tend to take longer in these countries.[12] Table 5.2 compares key indicators of success for negotiations ranked in order of importance for four national backgrounds.

Language and Communication

In most Western European nations and in India, English is the most commonly accepted and used business language. English is also widely spoken in business circles in Pacific Rim countries and in Latin America. In several Middle Eastern countries, English is used when conducting business with Westerners. Some exceptions, however, do exist. The French prefer to conduct business in French. In certain parts of Germany, the native language is preferred. In countries where English is not as common, particularly in Russia, Eastern European countries, China, and Japan, an interpreter is required.[12]

The manner in which conversations take place can also differ in terms of directness, speed, and clarity. U.S. conversation features a very direct style that some cultures might perceive as being rude, which tends to hinder good communication. By attempting to be clear and concise, Americans also tend to increase the directness of their style of communication. Often Americans try to bring someone with a less direct style back on point. Frequently Americans clarify the discussion to stay focused. Many cultures, however, do not like this style of communication.

Table 5.2 Characteristics of Negotiators as Reported by Managers in Each National Setting

Ranking in Order of Importance	American	Japanese	Chinese (Taiwan)	Brazilian
1	Preparation and planning skills	Dedication to job	Persistence and determination	Preparation and planning skills
2	Thinking under pressure	Perception and exploitation of power	Winning respect and confidence	Thinking under pressure
3	Judgment and intelligence	Win respect and confidence	Preparation and planning skill	Judgment and intelligence
4	Verbal expressiveness	Integrity	Product knowledge	Verbal expressiveness
5	Product knowledge	Demonstrate listening skill	Integrity	Product knowledge
6	Perception and exploitation of power	Broad perspective	Judgment and intelligence	Perception and exploitation of power
7	Integrity	Verbal expressiveness		Competitiveness

Source: Adapted from N. Adler. *International Dimensions of Organizational Behavior, Third Edition* 1997. Cincinnati, OH: South-Western College Publishing; 217.

Westerners, particularly Americans, often miss the communication subtleties that exist in some cultures. U.S. culture places a higher value on direct verbal messages than do cultures in Asia and parts of Latin American. Americans tend to say what they mean and mean what they say. Yet when conducting business, the Japanese and Chinese might not directly say *no* or express overt disagreement. Therefore, understanding how different cultures express disagreement so one can identify it and react accordingly is important. For example, in many cases, disagreement is implied, perhaps taking the form of a question being asked or through an expression, such as "this is a difficult question to answer," or by periods of silence. Americans, in particular, are extremely uncomfortable with periods of silence. (*Note*: As mentioned previously, body language and gestures are an integral part of human communication, but the same body language and gestures may mean different things in different cultures. A useful reference on this topic is http://www.ehow.com/how_2129585_learn-body-language-foreign-culture.html.)

General Cultural Differences and Mannerisms

General cultural differences are in a category that is very broad. Topics in this category include personal space, privacy, environment and control, and the inclusion of women.

Personal space. Personal space, like every other topic presented here, can vary widely depending on the culture. In the U.S. and U.K. (which are similar across many cultural dimensions), personal space is greater compared to some Latin American countries and India. In those places individuals tend to stand closer to one another when conversing. It is important to be aware of these preferred distances and to provide a reasonable distance between individuals.

Privacy. Different cultures also have different perspectives on privacy. In some cultures, asking if a person is married or asking personal questions about his or her family is considered rude. In other cultures, asking these sorts of questions is common practice. In almost every culture, however, asking how much money someone earns is unacceptable. Acceptable timing of business calls after hours also differs from country to country, especially when business calls are received at home.

Control of environment. Research has shown that certain cultures feel more in control of their environment while other cultures do not. Individuals who think that they control their environment believe they can influence their environment or even their destiny through hard work and overcoming obstacles. Individuals who think they have less control tend to believe that external forces such as fate and nature control their environment and that there is little that an individual can do in this regard. These individuals might view business in terms of accommodating to and adjusting for unpredictable and uncontrollable events rather than exerting managerial control to make events more predictable.[13]

Women. In Western companies, the likelihood of women acting in positions of authority as compared to Middle Eastern or Asian countries is much greater. The acceptance and treatment of women within and outside of business, however, still varies across the world, which creates difficult issues to address when planning a foreign buying trip or putting together a negotiating team.

Most individuals are forgiving, to a point, when errors are made that violate their cultural sensibilities and norms (accepted patterns of behavior). Committing too many of these errors increases the perception that an individual is out of touch with his or her operating environment. In North American slang, we might say that this individual is "operating out of his league." Wandering around in a cultural haze increases the likelihood of violating a taboo (something that is banned on the grounds of morality, taste, or strong cultural belief). Supply managers who are involved with international purchasing are doing their companies a disservice if they remain unaware of cultural practices outside of their home region.

Culture plays an important role in international purchasing. A lack of understanding of how other cultures conduct business can influence the success of an international experience. A key to understanding and working with other cultures is conducting research and preparation prior to engaging with these cultures. Another key to success is appreciating that other cultures might see the world differently from your perspective, which affects the way they conduct business. For supply managers, to be on the safe side, adjusting their style in accordance with a prevailing culture rather than expecting their foreign counterparts to adjust to them makes sense. Now let's move to the second major topic in this chapter.

OUTSOURCING SERVICES INTERNATIONALLY

A major trend affecting international outsourcing is that outsourcing does not apply only to tangible items. Over the last 15 years, we have come to realize that any product or service that can be digitized or handled via telecommunications is a candidate for outsourcing. One observer maintains that any job or occupation with high information intensity and low need for physical presence is a candidate for offshoring.[14] Although forecasts of the number of service-related jobs that could be outsourced from the U.S. are at best rough estimates, a study has concluded that 3.3 million service jobs will move offshore by 2015.[15] The worldwide economic crisis and the pressure it creates to manage costs could even accelerate rather than slow this shift.

A major area of outsourcing involves business processing outsourcing (BPO). At times this activity is referred to as outsourcing the "back office functions." Some of the more common services managed by BPO providers include customer call center support; technical support; accounting and tax returns; accounts receivable and payable; telemarketing; medical transcription; digitizing of medical records; legal services such as the review of litigation documents and patent research; insurance processing; software development; financial services and analytics research; and data entry. Each of these broad service categories also contains many subservices. For example, one company that provides medical transcription services divides its services into physician information from office visits; progress notes; operative reports; emergency notes; discharge summaries; X-ray reports; consultation reports; history and physical reports; clinical notes; psychiatric evaluation; laboratory reports; and pathology reports. Medical transcription is apparently a broad area.

Like many topics, what looks easy on paper (saving money by outsourcing services to a foreign company) isn't always easy in reality. More than one hospital has been held hostage by disgruntled foreign medical transcribers who have threatened to post sensitive records on the Internet if they were not paid more money. Being blackmailed by an offshore service provider is generally not something hospitals want to publicize. At other times, business changes and trends occur at a pace that is faster than the professional questions can be answered. Consider preparing tax returns—a service that raises legal and ethical issues when outsourced. Each year several hundred thousand U.S. tax returns are prepared overseas, primarily in India.

Various professions are beginning to grapple with the ethical concerns raised by the outsourcing of sensitive services: is the skill level of the overseas employee the same or better as that required of in-firm personnel; how safe is confidential information; should a client or patient be informed that services are being provided by an offshore provider; does professional liability insurance cover work performed by the employees of the outsourcer?[16]

The trend is clear: BPO is increasing. Included with that increase is the potential for greater supply chain risk.

Choosing the Right Service Provider

The key to a successful outsourcing experience, whether the provider is domestic or foreign, centers on the effectiveness of the supplier selection process. Sometimes it is surprising, perhaps even disturbing, to see how often a process that is so critical to corporate success can be treated as an afterthought. Anyone who believes in the total quality precept of prevention (and in a perfect world everyone would wholeheartedly endorse the idea of preventing problems before they occur) recognizes the importance of selecting the right service providers.

The selection decision takes on added risk when the search is global. Unfortunately, distance is a great barrier. So much cannot be determined by a review of product samples, testimonials from other customers, or a review of a supplier's purchase proposal. Another issue is the low industry barriers to entry for service providers: the pool of possible providers can be populated with some risky choices. How should supply managers handle the selection of service providers when these providers are located thousands of miles away?

Having a trusted party available to visit and evaluate potential suppliers and serve as a source of primary contact is hard to beat. Unfortunately, unless they are the size of a multinational, few companies have this luxury. Yet most observers agree that small and medium-sized companies will increasingly pursue services offshore to capture cost savings and to focus on their core business activities.[17] Companies that have established international purchasing offices (IPOs; see Chapter 3) have an inherent advantage because a primary responsibility of these offices is to evaluate suppliers.

Even if a company does not have an IPO or a trusted party to evaluate potential suppliers, there are steps that any company should take when considering an overseas service provider. If the provider will be handling sensitive or confidential information (and it is safe to assume that at some point most of these providers will handle sensitive information), insist that every employee sign a nondisclosure agreement with penalties clearly identified. The company should also insist on certain computer protections that prohibit employees from downloading, printing, scanning, or copying confidential information. The service provider should also have firewall security that prevents outsiders from hacking into the system.[18] In fact, the company should insist on seeing all procedures and processes the provider has in place for protecting client information. Retaining the services of a local law firm that specializes in outsourced service contracts is also a good idea.

Ask the provider for customer references (which will be checked), state licenses, and evidence of any industry trade association affiliations and accreditations. Also, don't forget about financial risk. Ask to see the provider's financial statements. Clearly identify who the business contact will be besides the salesperson. Finally, ask the service provider to detail the tools and technology as well as how that technology is used to increase efficiencies and decrease human error.[19]

Don't ever forget about quality. A major factor that comes into play when doing business with service providers involves service quality. Clearly this issue takes on added importance when service providers operate on the other side of the world. You must move beyond saying that quality is simply conformance to requirements (the Crosby approach) or fitness for use (the Juran approach). How could anyone really manage service quality using these broad definitions as their guide? Although service quality is a broad construct, it includes multiple dimensions that are as applicable to consumers as they are to industrial buyers. It is relatively easy to take the dimensions of service quality and create an assessment tool that supply managers can apply when evaluating a service provider, assuming that good information and data are available. These are the dimensions that relate to the quality of a service:[20]

- *Access.* Is there a clear point of contact between your company and the service provider? Do your customers and employees have easy access to the provider, including the Internet and telephone? (What good is a call center if a customer must wait 45 minutes on the telephone only to be shuffled between call center employees?)
- *Communication.* How well does the service provider maintain contact during the course of normal operations as well as during times of problems or crisis? How well does the provider communicate with its customers when it detects problems in its part of the world?

- *Competence.* Do service employees have the proper knowledge and skills, including language skills, to fulfill their duties? Do they have access to training and development opportunities?
- *Courtesy.* Are employees polite, respectful, and considerate when dealing with you or your customers? (It is easy to see that this dimension is critical when using overseas service providers for call centers and technical support.)
- *Credibility.* Are the service provider and its employees trustworthy and honest? How credible is the provider in the eyes of your employees and customers? Are employee backgrounds thoroughly checked?
- *Reliability.* Is the service provider's performance reliable? If an IT group is expected to send updated software code by a certain time each day, is the code sent on time? Does the service provider meet or exceed your expectations? Is there a high degree of absenteeism and turnover? Does the provider have adequate capacity to manage the volume of work?
- *Responsiveness.* How well does the service provider respond when contacted by you or your customers with questions or concerns? Is the service provider able to respond using different methods of communication? Does the service provider have employees available during off hours to respond to inquiries or problems? Do you have contacts at the service provider who are responsible for managing the business relationship?
- *Security.* Can the service provider ensure freedom from danger, risk, or doubt? (The importance of this dimension is obvious when sharing sensitive digital information and records.) Are medical records, tax information, and credit card numbers safe with the provider?
- *Tangibles.* Can the service provider provide physical evidence of the facilities? How modern is the call center? What is the state of telecommunications equipment? What are the working conditions at the service provider?
- *Understanding the customer.* How well does the service provider understand your industry and your specific needs?

Some of these dimensions are easier to assess after doing business with a service provider, but this does not mean they should not be part of the discussion during the evaluation and selection process. Never assume that a service provider that promises major savings has the ability to perform as expected. In fact, you might want to hold off reporting the projected incredible savings to senior management until you actually realize those incredible savings. The industrial world has more than a few companies that witnessed the painful effects of an ill-advised or poorly executed outsourcing strategy that involved overseas service providers. Just ask Dell Computer.

We are constantly reminded that magnificent savings are just waiting to be captured with BPO. Listening to outsource proponents might even lead us to believe that savings of up to 90% are easily within our grasp! Unfortunately, this just isn't true. Five studies have reported actual savings of 20 to 40% for IT offshoring compared with using high-cost domestic labor.[21] The companies that outsourced expected to realize savings that were easily double the actual savings (but as Chapter 4 revealed, this thing called total cost almost always comes into play). An outsourcing analysis demands more than a comparison of labor rates. Keep this in mind when evaluating potential service providers.

Destination India

Perhaps more than any country, India has benefitted from the outsourcing of services. (*Note*: The authors would like to thank Saurabh Goyal, ThinkLink Supply Chain Services Private Limited-India, for help in developing this section.) Outsourcing to India has steadily increased since foreign companies recognized its benefits nearly two and a half decades ago. Just about every industry has benefited from this practice. Called India's "golden goose of the moment" by some, the outsourcing industry in India is expected to grow over the next several years to $47 billion annually. Some estimates place India's worldwide BPO market share at 80%. Being on the receiving end of outsourcing accounts for almost 6% of India's gross domestic product (GDP) and employs over 2 million people.

Major industries benefitting from outsourcing to India include IT and software development and pharmaceutical, apparel, electronics, and automotive aftermarket parts production. Although U.S. companies are currently India's largest clients, accounting for nearly 60% of revenue, vast untapped markets exist in the European Union, Japan, North Africa, and the Middle East. This discussion focuses on BPO within the Indian service industry.

Introduction to the Indian BPO industry. The beginning of the Indian BPO industry dates back to the early 1980s. Companies such as British Airways, General Electric, and American Express pioneered outsourcing their business operations to India. Today, the Indian BPO industry generates $11 billion in revenue and employs 700,000 people. Multinational corporations have aggressively established captive BPO providers in India or leveraged the capabilities of existing providers. Some of the better-known players include Accenture, IBM (Daksh), Infosys (Progeon), Genpact, Tata Consultancy Services, Tech Mahindra, Dell, and HCL Technologies. There are a variety of reasons for the growth in India's BPO industry:

- *Cost of operations.* Perhaps the most visible advantage of outsourcing services to India is the reduced cost of operations. This is no surprise because Chapter 1 clearly indicated that the primary motivation behind international purchasing is cost reduction. The annual cost of a BPO employee in India is $7500. This compares to $10,000 in the Philippines, $17,000 in Australia, and $19,000 in the U.S. To combat the rising costs of real estate in India's large metropolitan areas, BPOs have started operating away from the major cities. Some of these new entrants are cities such as Mangalore, Mysore, Mohali, Ahmedabad, Jaipur, and Lucknow.

- *Talent pool.* India's vast talent pool provides intellectual support to the outsourcing industry. With a country that produces several million college graduates a year, a shortage of talent is usually not a problem. Furthermore, English is India's preferred language and is the medium for disseminating knowledge in schools and colleges. India has so many languages and dialects that the most logical communication platform is English. Moreover, India's education system places a strong emphasis on mathematics and science, further enhancing the technical capabilities of graduates.

- *Time zone.* India's time zone, while at first appearing to be a major drawback, can actually help some BPO providers better serve their clients. The time difference between India and the U.S. is 13 hours or so, depending on where the companies in the U.S. and India are located. Work that is outsourced digitally to India can be completed before the start of business the next day in the U.S. While the customer sleeps, the outsource provider works. While the outsource provider sleeps, the customer benefits from the outsource provider's output. The need to compress cycle times in virtually all aspects of business makes a 24-hr business model attractive.

Some BPO success stories. Several examples highlight how widely different organizations benefit from their services outsourcing strategy in India:

- A British Airways subsidiary in India employs 1200 workers to handle back office operations for its parent and other airlines. These operations include maintaining frequent flyer programs, managing ticket processing, and handling revenue accounting. The subsidiary is saving the company as much as $25 million a year in direct costs and has increased it services to include ticketing work for nine other airlines.

- GE Capital, a subsidiary of General Electric, outsources to two centers in India. These centers, in addition to running call centers, perform a variety of back office processing tasks for other GE companies worldwide. GE has almost quadrupled the size of its Indian operations.

- A clinic in the U.S. having difficulty documenting medical reports and records, and using local medical transcribers in the U.S. at a charge of $0.40 U.S. per line, outsources the work to India where transcription charges are less than $0.09 U.S. per line. Some estimates indicate over 40% of medical transcription services in the U.S. are now outsourced, with India capturing about 80% of that market. Countries such as Pakistan, Australia, Sri Lanka, and the Philippines compete for the remaining business. Pressure to control medical costs will only encourage further outsourcing.

Key lessons learned. Even with the best of intentions, the transition from an internal source or domestic supplier to a foreign supplier is not always quick and easy. Within business process outsourcing, experienced participants in India are able to look back and share what they have learned. And these lessons are often learned the hard way:

- *Cultural differences.* Cultural differences can cause problems, especially in the beginning of a relationship. Across India, for example, it is accepted practice to arrive late for scheduled business appointments, which can lead to frustration and delays when Western companies outsource to India. We know from earlier in this chapter that a failure to understand and deal with cultural differences when outsourcing can add to service costs. A key lesson for anyone who plans on outsourcing services to India is to develop a thorough understanding of the country's culture and assess the impact these differences will have on business start up and practices.

- *Road conditions.* Road congestion in India's major cities is legendary. Besides the presence of vehicles, animals often roam the streets. This congestion increases the probability that workers will arrive late, if at all, to work. A lesson learned is to consider locations or service providers that are located away from the most congested areas. Another lesson is to work with a separate logistics transportation organization that specializes in getting Indian service workers to work on time. A whole new service industry that specializes in transporting workers has evolved in major cities.

- *Time differences.* Time zone differences with India, while at times being advantageous, can also lead to frustration and delay during the start-up phase of a project. The same can also be said of time differences with China. A key lesson learned is to build enough time into project plans to compensate for this issue. The need to work throughout the night can affect the ability to attract qualified Indian employees to work in call centers.

- *Pronunciation of words.* The pronunciation of English words by Indian service workers is different primarily because of the Indian accent. Most of us have interacted with call centers at one time or another when the experience was a bit frustrating, to put it mildly. Although not an easy issue to solve, a key lesson learned by companies is to provide continuous training to improve communication when dealing with English-speaking customers or participants. The employee selection process should also consider this issue directly.
- *Transition costs.* As with any foreign outsourcing, transition costs can be very high. Companies that outsource services to India have learned that they must take transition costs into account by developing total cost models, something that no one should find to be surprising. As Chapter 4 pointed out, these models must become a routine part of the foreign buying decision.

The road ahead. With untapped markets and an ever-growing need to reduce operating costs without compromising quality, the future of the BPO industry in India should remain strong, but with some realignment. Because 60% of BPO outsourcing in India comes from the U.S., and over 40% of that total comes from the troubled banking, financial services, and insurance sectors, the need for Indian BPO providers to rethink their marketing strategies from a risk management perspective becomes obvious.[22]

India has created a center of excellence that should continue to provide the country with a competitive advantage. This does not mean India's success is assured. Some companies have announced they are bringing call center work back to the U.S. Delta Air Lines stopped using India-based call centers to handle sales and reservations. As the chief executive for a company that advises on outsourcing argues, "It is fundamentally cheaper to do it in India, but there's also the question of whether it's better to do it cheaper or better to do it better in terms of the relationship with your customers." Delta's CEO noted that "the customer acceptance of call centers in foreign countries is low." He further stated that Delta's customers are not shy about letting the company know about their discontent. Delta will keep some call center work in Jamaica and South Africa, areas which have not generated such strong complaints.[23]

India is not the only country that expects a lucrative future in business process outsourcing. Although typically China is connected with manufacturing, the Chinese are also eyeing the BPO market closely. Because of China's strong infrastructure, generous tax breaks, and strong government support, plus a desire by multinationals to spread risk away from India, it becomes clear why sourcing services in China is becoming an attractive option for some large corporations. Even some Indian outsourcing companies are establishing a presence in China. Other nations with BPO aspirations include the Philippines, Brazil, Vietnam, Cambodia, South Africa, and some Eastern European countries (to name just a few). In fact, some key Western European countries are bypassing India altogether and focusing on a nearshoring strategy. These companies are working with service providers in the Baltics, Czech Republic, Hungary, and Poland.[24]

Global competition for BPO contracts will only become more intense. Smart BPO buyers will recognize this and broaden their geographic horizons.

CONCLUDING THOUGHTS

Cultural understanding is an area with many subtleties and nuances. Making mistakes when participating in foreign buying trips and negotiations is, unfortunately, not all that hard to do. On her first trip to Russia, U.S. Secretary of State Hillary Clinton presented her Russian counterpart with a "reset" button that resembles the button the U.S. might push to launch a nuclear attack against her hosts. The button was supposed to represent the restarting of U.S./Russia relations. To make matters worse, the printing on the box with the button contained a Russian word that did not mean "reset" as is known in English. Although the spelling was close, the word printed on the box had a more aggressive and negative connotation. Mrs. Clinton laughed publicly about the error, but the probability is high that there was not much laughing later when she met with her staff. In almost every culture, making the big boss look bad in public is a cultural *faux pas*. Cultural errors can affect even the most experienced organizations.

Regarding the purchase of services internationally, the outsourcing of business processes to low-cost service providers can create cost advantages that enhance competitiveness. Given the ease of digitizing many jobs or tasks, the continued globalization of certain services is an inevitable fact of life. At a macro level, in 2000 the U.S. exported $1.33 of services for every $1 of services it imported. In 2008, this ratio shifted slightly as the U.S. exported $1.35 of services for every $1 of services imported (see http://www.census.gov/foreign-trade/Press-Release/current_press_release/ft900.pdf). Although the mix of services exported and imported fluctuates, predictions of doom and gloom from the outsourcing of services may be overstated at the national level.

REFERENCES

1. S. Hamm. Inside India, Inc. *Business Week* 2009 Apr 20 (4127): 88.

2. T.E. Schelmetic. International Call Center Best Practices: a White Paper. *Customer Inter@action Solutions* 2008 Mar; 26(10): 14.

3. R.M. Moncka, R.J. Trent, and R.H. Handfield. *Purchasing and Supply Chain Management* 2005. Mason, OH: South-Western Publishing; 311–312.

4. M. Johannsen. *The Global Leader: Understanding Chinese Business Culture and Business Practices*. Legacee Organization. Retrieved from http://www.legacee.com/Culture/CultureOverview.html.

5. C. Blaufuß. Presentation: Rituals. *Area Studies SS 2001* 2001 Jun.

6. What's A-O.K. in the U.S.A. Is Lewd and Worthless Beyond. *The New York Times* 1996 Aug. Retrieved from http://query.nytimes.com/gst/fullpage.html?res=9D0DEED61039F93BA2575BC0A960958260&sec=&spon=.

7. G. Bonvillian and W.A. Nowlin. Cultural Awareness: an Essential Element of Doing Business Abroad. *Business Horizons* 1998 Nov/Dec; 34(4): 44–50.

8. When in Rome Don't Be Late for Your Meeting. *The Actuary* 2005 May. Retrieved from http://www.the-actuary.org.uk/693101.

9. M. Saksa. Still Searching for a Common Tune at Board Meetings of Nordic Binational Corporations. *Helsingen Sanomat International Edition Business & Finance* 2006 Jan 10. Retrieved from http://www.hs.fi/english/article/Still+searching+for+a+common+tune+at+board+meetings+of+Nordic+binational+corporations/1135218386990.

10. N. Ripmeester. Successful Business in China, Part II. *China Business Success Stories* 2008 Mar. Retrieved from http://www.chinasuccessstories.com/2008/03/31/chinese-management-culture/.

11. S.D. Seligman. *Chinese Business Etiquette: a Guide to Protocol, Manners, and Culture in the People's Republic of China* 1999. New York, NY: Warner Books (as appears in China Briefing Book, Section VI, Business Etiquette U.S./China Business Council).

12. H. Botha. How to Negotiate with Other Nations and Cultures. *HB* 2000. Retrieved from http://www.henkbotha.com.

13. T. Willen. Working with Foreign Cultures. *Ezine Articles* 2006 Nov 10. Retrieved from http://ezinearticles.com/?Working-with-Foreign-Cultures&id=355464.

14. D. Wagner. Success Factors in Outsourcing Service Jobs. *MIT Sloan Management Review* 2006 Fall; 48(1): 7.

15. B. Briggs. Offshore Outsourcing Poses Risks. *Health Data Management* 2005 Feb; 13(2): 68.

16. E.D. Cook, S.E. Hazelwood, and A.C. Hazelwood. Outsourcing Tax Returns Raises Legal and Ethical Concerns. *Practical Tax Strategies* 2005 Aug; 75(2): 68.

17. J. Downey. The Future of Offshore Outsourcing. *Financial Management* 2005 Jul/Aug; 20.

18. E.D. Cook, S.E. Hazelwood, and A.C. Hazelwood. Outsourcing Tax Returns Raises Legal and Ethical Concerns. *Practical Tax Strategies* 2005 Aug; 75(2): 69.

19. C. Rodriguez. Chose the Right Partner. *Accounting Technology* 2007 May; 15.

20. L.L. Berry, V.A. Zeithaml, and A. Parasuramn. Five Imperatives for Improving Service Quality. *Sloan Management Review* 1990 Summer; 31(4): 29.

21. N. Matloff. Offshoring: What Can Go Wrong? *IT Pro* 2005 Jul/Aug; 39–45.

22. Anon. Outsourcing: Tougher Times. *Business India Intelligence* 2009; 2. Retrieved from Dow Jones Factiva.

23. P. Prada and N. Sheth. Delta Air Ends Use of India Call Centers. *Wall Street Journal* 2009 Apr 18–19; B1.

24. C. Beasty. The Bitter Taste of Offshoring. *Customer Relationship Management* 2006 Jan; 10(1): 12.

PART III.
MANAGING GLOBAL SUPPLY RISK

6

UNDERSTANDING GLOBAL RISK

As Chapter 1 made clear, most supply organizations engage in international purchasing primarily to realize lower prices for goods and services. Lower costs can result from lower labor costs, lower cost of capital equipment, and lower cost of material. Buying from suppliers in developing markets, however, entails risk, and supply managers who do not consider these risks leave themselves open to some nasty surprises. Costs of additional inventory, potentially substandard products, longer lead times, and increased transportation costs, to name a few, can potentially outweigh any price savings achieved.

Supply and supply chain risk refers to the probability of an uncertain or unpredictable event occurring that affects one or more of the parties within a supply chain. These events negatively influence the achievement of business objectives. One objective of supply chain risk management is to evaluate, control, and monitor risk in order to safeguard supply continuity and maximize profitability. Experienced supply managers have learned an important lesson: to be successful at international buying, they must understand risk and develop appropriate risk mitigation strategies. Table 6.1 reveals that around two thirds of executives surveyed believe that supply chain risks are increasing.[1] So the need to understand supply chain risk has never been greater.

This chapter deals with the concept of supply chain risk as it relates to international purchasing and, to a related degree, supply chain management. We outline the trends and developments that are taking place in the global economy that affect supply networks and, and in some cases, intensify risk. We also review the major categories of global risk. (Chapter 7 also reviews these categories.) The chapter concludes with a case study that illustrates some of these risks.

Table 6.1 Changes in Supply Chain Risk over the Last 5 Years

Level of Change in Risk	Percent of Respondents
Increased significantly	23
Increased slightly	42
No change	26
Decreased slightly	7
Decreased significantly	2

Source: Adapted from McKinsey & Company. Understanding Supply Chain Risk: A McKinsey Global Survey. *The McKinsey Quarterly* 2006 Oct. Retrieved from http://www.mckinseyquarterly.com/Understanding_supply_chain_risk_A_McKinsey_Global_Survey_1847.

MARKETPLACE TRENDS AND DEVELOPMENTS AFFECTING RISK

To help ensure supply continuity, supply managers need to understand the risks and uncertainties that can occur at any point in the supply chain, particularly with upstream suppliers. As a result of trends and developments, organizations are continually faced with new uncertainties. The effects of these trends coupled with an emphasis on greater international purchasing can, at times, increase rather than decrease global risk exposure. Each trend and development presented here has implications for risk management. The following sections discuss these trends and developments.

Increased Globalization

Global business should continue its growth after the world begins an economic recovery, with many supply organizations continuing to rely on foreign suppliers to provide sources of raw materials and products as well as markets for finished goods. And, as noted earlier, trade barriers continue to fall and global competition continues to increase. Companies are also seeking to forge partnerships with other supply chain members to expand their capabilities and global reach. Technology will continue to play a vital role in providing linkages worldwide and in enabling distribution on a global basis.[2]

The increase in global activity has had a marked impact on purchasing and logistics. Supply organizations need to strategically source materials and components from around the world; strategically position distribution centers when sourcing and distributing products; and learn from those that are achieving excellence in global supply and logistics management.[3]

Whether we like it or not, globalization of business activity is prevalent. Westerners continually focus on cost because of increased foreign competition and the pressures to improve profitability. This focus often requires moving raw material procurement and manufacturing overseas to countries where costs are lower. Additionally, logistics activities such as transportation, warehousing and, in some cases, supply chain management are being outsourced to reduce capital assets and costs. In many cases, contract manufacturing is being utilized to take advantage of lower manufacturing costs.

Risk implications. Although globalization can contribute to increased profitability, it can also create a new set of risks. Stretching supply chains around the world inevitably leads to greater complexity. It is almost a given that lead times and logistics costs will increase with offshore sourcing. Longer lead times also mean that inventories must increase to ensure product availability. Meanwhile, global competitors will exert a continuous pressure on prices. As supply organizations source globally to save costs, several areas of risk become more prevalent, including competition for scarce resources, currency fluctuations, and an array of risks described later in this chapter. The bottom line is that globalization offers tremendous opportunity for reward. It also creates tremendous opportunity for risk, particularly on the inbound side of the supply chain. Increased globalization has almost exponentially increased the need for global risk management.

Outsourcing Noncore Capabilities

Another trend involves outsourcing those parts of the supply chain in which a company offers nothing distinctive while fiercely protecting those areas that are part of the essential core. Businesses are systematically examining (or should be) their internal processes to determine what will remain internally and what will be outsourced. Most automotive producers, for example, are proficient at manufacturing high-quality vehicles, but are not necessarily as good at making the parts that go into the vehicles. A result of the examination of core vs. noncore capabilities has been a well-defined trend toward outsourcing to suppliers that presumably can add value.

Risk implications. Outsourcing noncore activities creates a dependency on third parties. Increasingly, these third parties are located throughout the world. This dependency brings with it any risks involved with relinquishing control. Oftentimes, for example, outsourcing leads to a transfer of supply chain power from a buyer to a supplier. In addition, companies that outsource to third parties become reliant on them to effectively manage supply chain risk, something the buying company previously managed. It is a fallacy to believe the use of third parties or agents automatically leads to lower costs or better service. The use of third-party providers is an important strategic initiative that requires extensive research to identify suppliers that have the capability to meet and exceed the longer-term needs of an organization. Increased outsourcing has introduced quite a few new risk categories.

Reduced Cycle Times

The ability to reduce cycle times, whether in new product development or customer order fulfillment, is essential for winning business today. Fast, flexible, and responsive is the name of the game. Few will argue that speed kills the competition. Developing supply chains built around quick response systems, enabled by technology that can respond quickly to changing customer demand and tastes, is a trend we are confident will continue. There is no shortage of interest in quick response and pull systems that can respond rapidly after an order is placed.

The use of technologies such as electronic data interchange (EDI) that instantly transmit information between entities in the supply chain can contribute significantly to reduced cycle times (more on these types of technologies later). In order to speed up processes and improve responsiveness, day-to-day decision making is being decentralized, reducing the need to seek approvals from higher management. (Later chapters will discuss the kinds of decisions that will remain part of a centrally led supply organization.)

Risk implications. Risks are involved in achieving compressed lead times because the parties in the supply chain are required to work together closely, something that is often problematic. Information sharing is a critical prerequisite for creating a responsive supply chain. Unfortunately, information sharing can be difficult, even risky, when dealing with suppliers that are unfamiliar to the buying company. Other risks come into play when suppliers are scattered around the world. Do these suppliers have a logistics infrastructure and information system that supports quick response? Is the distance between the buyer and supplier too great to support a cost-effective, responsive supply chain? Many would argue that a supply chain that features an extensive reliance on foreign suppliers might not be as responsive as it should be.

State-of-the-Art Information Technology

Information technology advances are having a significant impact on global supply chains. In fact, we often hear the term "information-enabled supply chains" used to describe modern supply chains. Real-time communications throughout the entire supply chain are a reality—systems are now linked between suppliers, manufacturers, distributors, retail outlets, and ultimately customers, often throughout the world. Information is more readily accessible to any party in the chain, allowing inventories to be minimized and enabling the various entities in the supply chain to respond to fluctuations in demand in a timely manner. Increasingly, point-of-sale information is transmitted immediately throughout the supply chain, allowing managers to identify trends; plan capacity requirements; take action when inventories are running low; allocate materials; and notify suppliers.[4] As well, customers want to know the exact geographic location of their shipments. Suppliers and customers are looking to use technology as a basis for providing efficiency and effectiveness.

Risk implications. Information technology is a key enabler of global supply chain management. The expanding scope of supply chains through the opening up of new sources of supply and new markets places an additional burden on information systems within the supply chain. A lack of systems, poor systems, or nonstandardized IT systems can create potential risk when sourcing from certain countries and regions, particularly third world countries. Without adequate technology systems in place, both sourcing and suppliers might not be in a position to successfully prepare for and react to disruptions in the supply chain. They might also not manage the supply chain effectively.

Proliferation of SKUs and Mass Customization

The number and different types of products offered by producers are proliferating. Customers are increasingly requiring products that are less standardized and more tailored to their unique requirements. In many market segments, success will belong to those that are able to mass customize their product or service offering. Mass customization involves producing products in small batches tailored to individual customers at an economical rate. Products and services are also becoming more complex as they come with a greater variety of options.

It is reasonable to conclude that customers will continue to demand more mass-customized products and services. One of the implications for distribution is that although aggregated or overall demand might remain relatively stable, the number of different SKUs will increase, resulting in a fragmented array of customer options. The implication here is that forecasts of product mix, demand at different distribution points and locations, and volumes required will become increasingly difficult to predict, develop, and manage.

Companies are also expected to provide value-added services, such as kitting, through distribution to meet the demand for specialized products. Kitting involves packaging a variety of items together to create a new item, such as a kit or subassembly. The use of postponement techniques as a means of providing mass customization, while keeping inventory at acceptable levels, will become increasingly important. With postponement, the final process steps that differentiate a product are delayed until a final customer provides insight into the product's final configuration.

Risk implications. Practices such as kitting, mass customization, and postponement require a flexible and responsive supply chain. Coordinating SKUs in global distribution centers, as well as the handling, packaging, and transportation issues that arise from shipping multiple specialized SKUs, is also a global challenge. This coordination and control becomes increasingly difficult to manage when dealing with a worldwide supply base that is selected primarily on price.

The Environment and Recovery, Recycling, and Reuse of Products

An important worldwide trend is the recovery, recycling, or reuse of products after they reach the end of their useful life. Supply chains are being extended beyond the end customer to include a return logistics process that often includes disposal or disposition of products. Companies are seeking to close the loop and eventually transform used products into new products or materials that can be returned to the earth without harming the environment, a process that is called sustainability. In the future, more products will be produced entirely or almost entirely of recyclable materials, which will require organizations to make supply decisions within the context of environmental considerations.

Supply managers will increasingly play a central role in implementing environmentally safe practices. The selection of suppliers will be based more on the suppliers' environmental practices: how they reduce surplus packaging; their actions to reduce fuel and other raw material usage; and whether they are using environmentally friendly practices to lower their costs of materials. Environmentally aware enterprises are also looking for ways to reduce scrap and waste.

Risk implications. The trend to recover, recycle, and reuse products presents risks because many suppliers outside the developed world are not known for their environmental prowess. Different countries have different rules and regulations regarding the impact of logistics, including reverse logistics, on the environment. In Western Europe there is an emphasis on environmental protection with a host of regulations in place. This emphasis on environmental protection has specific implications for the disposal of items (including their packaging) in the reverse-logistics flow and the effect of these items on the environment. Not understanding or disregarding these regulations can result in moral and legal ramifications, bad publicity, and disruptions to supply.

Changing Nature of the Marketplace

The consumer market is changing as consumers become much more aware of what constitutes value. Consumers are becoming more knowledgeable and, through use of the Internet, they can easily compare and contrast prices and delivery schedules as well as track shipments. In today's world, consumers want fast service and delivery as well as convenience and flexibility. Consumers are also less likely to be loyal to brand names if they perceive that a matching brand can be obtained at a lower cost with the same or faster delivery.[5] In short, consumers want more, more, and then more.

Demanding consumers have affected the way the retail supply chain operates. Many larger retailers, including the "big box" stores, are requiring tailored services from suppliers, including more frequent deliveries in smaller quantities. They might even insist on goods being sorted on a pallet in the same sequence they will be placed onto the shelves at the customer's location. Suppliers must provide these types of services economically or risk being eliminated from the supply base.

Risk implications. Like the other trends and developments presented here, the changing nature of the marketplace demands flexible and responsive suppliers, two traits where extended supply networks do not rate highly. A number of years ago, Allen-Edmonds shoes worked diligently to lean-out its supply chain. The company understood that maintaining shoe production within the U.S. required some serious changes to the way it conducted its business. As part of its improvements efforts, Allen-Edmonds asked its European suppliers to ship leather hides to the U.S. more often than the traditional schedule of once a month. This change would have the obvious effect of reducing by at least half Allen-Edmond's average leather inventory. Unfortunately, the European producers did not like this idea very much, demonstrating a notable lack of flexibility and responsiveness. Do not conclude from this anecdotal example that all foreign suppliers are not flexible, but an inability to work closely when one party is located thousand of miles from the other is a concern we have witnessed far too often.

Pressure to Reduce Cost

Identifying an industry that has not experienced an increase in global competition over the last 15 years is difficult, leading to ever-increasing pressure to improve, particularly in the area of cost reduction. Even if the number of major competitors in an industry has become smaller, such as in the aerospace industry, sophisticated customers still present their own set of demands. Because relentless pressure to improve is a never-ending journey, supply managers will constantly be searching for the next great source of performance improvement. Even if we live to be 150 years old, it is unlikely that there will not be a time when cost-re-duction pressures are not present. And we know these pressures are the primary driver behind international purchasing.

Risk implications. A trend that features a constant search for lower-cost suppliers presents challenges. Not only do these low-cost locations shift over time, but companies also compete at least partly on the capability of their supply chains. The search for lower-cost suppliers can lead to behaviors that increase rather than lessen a company's risk exposure. Extended global supply networks, switching suppliers in the pursuit of ever-lower sources of supply, and an inability to develop relationships with a portion of the supply base can elevate risk. It is entirely possible that the resulting supply network, while appearing to offer price reductions that are just too good to pass up, also become part of a supply chain that is less flexible with longer order cycle times. When sourcing globally, supply managers often rely on a new or untested supply network that invites certain risks to become a cause for concern. Risk and trade-off management must now take center stage.

CATEGORIES OF GLOBAL RISK

As already noted, the primary reason for international purchasing is to gain access to lower-cost goods and service. As supply organizations relentlessly pursue lower costs, they are finding that international purchasing and low-cost country sourcing come with their own share of risks. Supply organizations that have been sourcing globally for some time have found that some risks are common to all companies. Other risks, however, might be unique to individual supply organizations. The following sections present areas where increased global supply risk originates. (Chapter 7 offers ways to prevent and mitigate these risks.)

Unstable Geopolitical Climates

Events in the Middle East, Western Africa, Venezuela, and other worldwide hot spots illustrate the uncertainty of doing business within certain geographies. Even the French have shown a propensity for taking company officials hostage to protest job cuts. Although many regions offer a cheap source of labor, the risk of political uncertainty and the resulting risk of supply disruptions often outweigh any advantages gained from working within these regions. Unfortunately, at times supply managers have no choice but to source from regions that are not entirely stable. At the very least, risk management measures must be in place that consider any risk due to political instability. If possible, the best risk prevention plan may be to avoid unstable regions.

Insecure Supply Chains

Risk exposure due to sudden supply disruptions is a major threat when operating globally. Terrorism, piracy, and theft are only three of several factors that can cause a supply chain to become less secure. Recent events serve to illustrate the significant impact that these events and others can have on supply chains. Examples include ships being hijacked off Somalia (including an event in which a cargo ship carrying containers with an American crew was hijacked); organized theft of cargo by gangs (including in the U.S.) that are exporting these goods to the growing number of countries where Western goods are in demand; and the threat of bombs being planted in cargo by terrorists. An extreme example of theft in the international supply chain concerns a South African trucking company that transports much-needed goods into Zimbabwe. According to the owner, the company always uses two drivers per truck. The reason for using two drivers has nothing to do with allowing drivers rest breaks. It has everything to do with one driver staying with the vehicle at all times, even when the vehicle is empty. Leaving a vehicle unattended is an invitation to steal truck parts, including the truck's tires, which are in short supply in Zimbabwe.

Acts of God, which include earthquakes, hurricanes, and floods, also make supply chains less secure. Although the potential for these conditions also exists locally, expanding a supply network globally certainly increases the risk. Again, supply managers need to be constantly aware of world events that fall under this category, including knowing in which countries theft and terrorism is rife, and either steer clear of these countries or have the necessary risk mitigation plans in place.

Currency Fluctuations

A major concern when purchasing internationally involves the risk associated with currency fluctuations. A variety of measures are used to address this risk, ranging from benign neglect to sophisticated risk management techniques. Larger companies often employ full-time specialists to review currency fluctuations and will adjust purchasing and logistics practices based on any fluctuations. Over a period of several months, for example, a major U.S. third-party logistics company alternated between Canadian and U.S. rail services to transport goods from the West Coast to Eastern seaboard destinations based solely on which currency provided the best value. (Chapter 7 contains more information on this important topic.)

Local and Regional Economic Changes

As international buyers shift orders to a foreign region, the local or regional economy can change. These changes could lead to higher costs and prices and the risk that conducting business in that region might no longer be economically viable. In addition, local economies might experience radical economic changes for other reasons. For example, in 1997, over a relatively short period, almost every Asian economy and currency experienced a sharp decline. In 2006, a similar decline took place in many Asian economies due to a number of banking and economic events.[6] Many supply managers have become reluctant to do business in certain parts of the world, including some parts of Latin America and Africa, because of the instability of the local and regional economies. (Chapter 3 pointed out some of the factors that are making China a less desirable sourcing location in this regard.)

Logistics Infrastructure

Some countries, including several in Eastern Europe and Asia, have an underdeveloped or poor logistics infrastructure in place. China, for example, has a relatively poor logistics infrastructure compared with Western countries, with fewer railroads, paved roads, and airports. Although this situation is improving, it is not improving fast enough to keep up with the expansion of traffic.[7]

In the authors' experience, the roads in several African countries north of South Africa are often poorly maintained. An example of this involved a convoy of vehicles traveling through Ethiopia that came to a grinding halt several miles short of a town. After sitting behind a long line of stopped cars for several hours, the convoy leader finally went to see what was happening. He walked up the line of cars and discovered a huge hole in the road. In the middle of the hole was a vehicle that had broken down. The hole had been there for several weeks, but vehicles had simply been driving into the hole on one end and then out the other end with the "help" of local townspeople—for a price. Several of the local townspeople had also developed a lucrative trade repairing the vehicles that broke down trying to navigate the hole in the road.

Logistical shortfalls often lead to higher costs and unreliable deliveries. In addition, as already noted, in certain countries the inadequacy of technologies which enable global logistics operations and the interfaces of these technologies with Western partners might create problems. (Chapter 2 covered this risk in greater detail.)

Cultural, Language, and Legal Differences

Cultural differences can impact relationships and constitute risk. Understanding cultural differences can help to improve global sourcing effectiveness. Conversely, not understanding and dealing with cultural differences can lead to some unwelcome surprises. We know that the manner in which negotiations are carried out in Asia, for example, is very different from Western countries, particularly the U.S.

Language differences can also interfere with effective communication. Language differences might lead to misinterpretations, adding an element of risk when sourcing from foreign countries. (Chapter 5 discussed cultural and language differences.)

Legal systems differ from country to country. Advanced countries tend to have legal systems that provide a measure of buyer protection under law. This provision is not necessarily the case in developing countries. Additionally, many countries have minimal protection for intellectual property. (Chapters 2 and 7 include information on legal issues.)

Documentation Requirements and Customs Clearance

Companies that source internationally have the sometimes daunting responsibility of ensuring that their goods clear customs. This process, which is often complex and time consuming, can include:

- Currency conversion
- Clean import documentation
- Precise record keeping
- Use of customs house brokers
- Valuation of goods by customs
- Federal Drug Administration (FDA) compliance
- Proper classification of goods for customs duty
- Adherence to the Customs Trade Partnership Against Terrorism Act (C-TPAT)

These are just some of the areas that require compliance by an importer. If the importer is bringing in goods such as chemicals, pharmaceuticals, and food products that require the involvement of government agencies beyond customs, then the process becomes even more time consuming.

Most of us would probably agree with the notion that complexity and documentation increase costs, time, and perhaps even waste. The inherent risk in bringing goods in from overseas and having to comply with customs requirements, including provision of the necessary international documentation, is that, if not followed correctly, shipments can be delayed. It is not surprising to find a high reliance on third parties to manage this part of the international purchasing process.

In addition, instances of corruption among customs officials are prevalent, even in some of the more developed countries. The issue here involves something called gray customs clearance. Gray customs clearance is a regular practice among Chinese companies that use intermediaries to transport commodities in bulk in planes and container trucks into Russia. These intermediaries are suspected of paying customs duties on only a small portion of the imported commodities, bribing the customs officers to let the rest of the shipment pass through customs. An example of this practice involves a Chinese company exporting shoes to Russia. The exporter had several millions of dollars worth of shoes confiscated from its warehouse in Russia after its intermediary used gray customs clearance to bring the goods into Russia. Supply managers must not only contend with the complexities of moving goods through customs in various countries, but also with how to contend with suspect practices.

Quality and Traceability

Product defects comprise a significant element of risk when sourcing from certain countries. China currently produces approximately 75% of the world's toys, 20% of the world's steel, and 18% of the world's apparel and textiles.[8] One study found that approximately a fifth of food and consumer products in China were substandard or tainted.[9] Regulators said that the broad survey of foods, agricultural tools, clothing, and women and children's products as well as other types of goods revealed substantial quality and safety failure rates. This outcome underscores the risks faced by China's own consumers even as China's exports come under greater scrutiny elsewhere. (Chapter 3 addressed quality concerns when sourcing in emerging countries.)

Lot traceability is also of prime importance for goods coming in from overseas, especially in the context of batches of products that might have quality problems. Often the assumption is that the overseas supplier has the capability to trace defective lots and remove them from the supply pipeline, an assumption which could be incorrect. Quality problems and the absence of lot traceability capabilities, when present, are an invitation to major supply disruptions and potential lost sales.

An example of poor product quality involves a company that imported several million dollars worth of small plastic curtain sliders into the U.S. from China. The sliders were for use with curtain rods manufactured in the U.S. After the sliders and rods were combined and sent to retail stores, they encountered a problem. Despite having provided clear specifications and measurements to the Chinese manufacturer, the plastic sliders did not fit the curtain rods. The stores promptly sent the sliders back with a demand for a refund. Further examination of the sliders by the importer revealed that the sliders were also not made to the correct thickness specification and had already started cracking. But we can't stop here. The white sliders had already started turning yellow. The importer of the sliders, while appropriately horrified, found he had little legal recourse. In an attempt to recoup at least some of his investment, he asked his sales manager to have the sliders melted for scrap. On closer inspection, the sliders were discovered to have been made of such inferior material that they did not even have a scrap value.

This example illustrates the fact that supply managers need to be diligent in ensuring the quality of goods procured from foreign countries. The use of rigorous supplier development programs to help ensure quality of product is one means of accomplishing this (covered in Chapter 7). In addition, supply managers need to ensure that the necessary contractual measures are in place to allow appropriate recourse in the event of quality issues (covered in Chapter 8).

Supplier Financial Solvency

The recent economic meltdown has created an environment in which most supply organizations are concerned about the financial viability of their supply base. As supply chains become more tightly coupled, the impact of supplier closures will be amplified. Toyota estimated that in 2009, 20% of its suppliers were at serious risk of financial insolvency. Although this risk is every bit as real for domestic as foreign suppliers, a lack of transparent information with foreign suppliers, particularly those operating in emerging countries, should make supply managers anxious. If you are not thinking about the financial health of your international suppliers, you should be.

APPRECIATING GLOBAL RISK AT OHIO ART

Ohio Art, a specialized maker of toys for children, was founded in Bryan, Ohio in the early part of the 20th century (see http://www.ohioart.com). During the late 1950s the company acquired the rights to the Etch-a-Sketch, a toy that evokes happy memories for many of us (see http://dic.academic.ru/dic.nsf/enwiki/584001). Ohio Art quickly added Etch-a-Sketch to its product line in 1960 at a price of $3.99. For those who are not familiar with the product, the user plays with the toy by manipulating two knobs that control the x- and y-axis of a line drawn inside a pane of glass covered with an aluminum powder. When the user wishes to start over, he or she simply turns the toy upside down and shakes it to erase the lines. Although the mechanism is fairly complex, the Etch-a-Sketch itself is easy to use. Etch-a-Sketch quickly became an almost iconic toy, not only among children, but also with a niche of artists specializing in Etch-a-Sketch drawings.

During the 1980s and 1990s, stores such as Wal-Mart, Toys "R" Us, and Target became the primary retailers of toys. Compared to specialty toy stores, the objective of these large retailers is to be low-cost sellers. As a result, Ohio Art came under intense pressure from these low-cost sellers to reduce prices if the company expected to sell their products through these retailers. The expectation was that the Etch-a-Sketch would sell for under $10, less than half of its inflation-adjusted price when it was introduced. Faced with the burden of U.S. labor and health care costs, Ohio Art decided to shift production of all its toys, including the Etch-a-Sketch, to China. Although financial reports do not break out results for individual toys, these reports clearly showed that Ohio Art was losing money in the 1990s.[10] By moving production to China, the delivered cost of Etch-a-Sketch would be 20% to 30% less than the cost of making it in Bryan, which was accomplished primarily by paying Chinese workers $0.24 per hour instead of the $9 per hour paid in Ohio.[11]

Ohio Art contracted with Kin Ki Industrial in Shenzhen, near Hong Kong, to make the Etch-a-Sketch. Although the company gained a labor cost advantage by moving production to China, the move came with other costs and risks, most of which were hard to quantify.[11] In some respects, Ohio Art had replaced one set of risks (high-cost production within the U.S.) with another set of risks (the uncertainty associated with sourcing in China).

A New Set of Issues

Although Ohio Art succeeded in lowering product costs, it also began to appreciate the effects that long material pipelines had on the company's ability to plan and to be responsive to market changes. Because the majority of toy sales occur during the end-of-year holiday season, sourcing in China now required Ohio Art to forecast sales far in advance and to place their orders months ahead of when toys were needed. This meant the company had virtually no flexibility in changing the volume of production to respond to market changes. For example, if a media personality were seen using or even mentioned an Etch-a-Sketch in the fall months, demand might increase. If the toy were produced in Ohio, then the company could add overtime or additional shifts to increase production. Conversely, if demand declined the company could relatively quickly reduce its output. But with production in China, once an order was produced and placed on a ship, that order was what Ohio Art received. Ohio Art had lost its ability to increase or decrease orders in response to market changes.

Another important consideration was quality. Although Ohio Art was satisfied with the quality of the work coming from China, if quality issues did arise, the company would not discover them until the toys were delivered in Ohio. The risk of poor quality meant that thousands of defective toys with no easy way to replace them could be delivered before the holiday season. When the toys were produced in Bryan, defects were prevented or detected quickly, allowing the company to take corrective action immediately.

Another hard to quantify concern was the increased risk in the logistics system. The toys were made in China, loaded in containers, and shipped to the U.S. via a major west coast port such as Los Angeles or Long Beach. Then the toys were shipped by truck or rail to Ohio. What was the cost of carrying the inventory for the shipment time, which could stretch to months? A less quantifiable risk was that the containers would not arrive on time or that they would be damaged during their journey.

Longer supply chains almost always feature additional handling and points of contact. There are ample examples of containers full of toys, sporting goods, and other items being damaged, lost at sea or stolen at the ports. Other hazards include treacherous sea lanes and, in some parts of the world, pirates. At the port, containers can be held up for a variety of reasons, from congestion at the port to impoundment by the Customs Service.[12]

Ohio Art quickly discovered another serious risk from shifting production overseas: dealing with a supplier that was not completely honest. A *New York Times* exposé of Chinese toy manufacturers featured Ohio Art. The article suggested that Kin Ki Industrial promised Ohio Art that its workers had work contracts, pensions, medical benefits, good food, and comfortable dormitories as well as earning minimum wage or above. According to the *New York Times* article, this was not true. The workers worked 7 days per week, received no overtime, lived in crowded conditions, were poorly fed, and earned less than the Chinese minimum wage. The CEO of Ohio Art denied having knowledge of any of this and promised to visit China. The company now faced a public relations disaster because it had failed to monitor its supplier.[11] How does a company quantify the adverse effects of poor publicity?

The lesson here is that many of the costs and risks of global outsourcing are not easily quantified and do not necessarily appear in a company's cost accounting system. These costs, however, are quite real. Seeing firsthand what can happen when we fail to take these costs and risks into account makes global risk management an important topic.

Note: The authors would like to thank Dr. James A. Pope, Professor of Operations Management, The University of Toledo (Ohio), for his generous help in the development of this section.

CONCLUDING THOUGHTS

Supply organizations that source globally need to understand the business climate in which they operate, including the trends and market developments that make risk an increasingly important topic. Supply organizations also need to have a thorough understanding of the types or categories of risk that they might be exposed to. Once risk is understood, supply managers can develop the necessary risk management and mitigation strategies. Chapter 7 covers tools for identifying potential sources of risk, categorizing these sources, and developing contingency plans.

REFERENCES

1. McKinsey & Company. Understanding Supply Chain Risk: a McKinsey Global Survey. *The McKinsey Quarterly* 2006 Oct. Retrieved from http://www.mckinseyquarterly.com/Operations/Supply_Chain_Logistics/Understanding_supply_chain_risk_A_McKinsey_Global_Survey_1847?gp=1&pagenum=6.

2. J.J. Coyle, E.J. Bardi, and C.J. Langley, Jr. *The Management of Business Logistics, Seventh Edition* 2003. Mason, OH: South-Western Publishing Company; 163.

3. J.J. Coyle, E.J. Bardi, and C.J. Langley, Jr. *The Management of Business Logistics, Sixth Edition* 1992. St. Paul, MN: West Publishing; 487.

4. J.J. Coyle, E.J. Bardi, and C.J. Langley, Jr. *The Management of Business Logistics, Sixth Edition* 1992. St. Paul, MN: West Publishing; 578–579.

5. J.J. Coyle, E. J. Bardi, and C.J. Langley, Jr. *The Management of Business Logistics, Sixth Edition* 1992. St. Paul, MN: West Publishing; 13–14.

6. Major Financial Crisis in History. *China International Electronic Commerce Network* 2009 Feb 6. Retrieved from http://en.ec.com.cn/article/enfeature/200902/718397_1.html.

7. A. Terreri. China: The Dragon Awakes. *Inbound Logistics* 2004 Oct. Retrieved from http://www.inboundlogistics.com/articles/features/1004_feature04.shtml.

8. R. Moradian. The Logistics of Doing Business in China. *Inbound Logistics.com* 2004 Jul; A1.

9. J.D. Dingell. Diminished Capacity: Can the FDA Assure the Safety and Security of the Nation's Food Supply? Part 2. *The House Committee on Energy and Commerce: The Public Record: Subcommittee on Oversight and Investigations Hearing* 2007 Jul 17. Retrieved from http://energycommerce.house.gov/Press_110/110st68.shtml.

10. 10-K Reports for Ohio Art, Inc. Retrieved from www.sec.gov.

11. J. Kahn. Ruse in Toyland: Chinese Workers' Hidden Woe. *New York Times* 2003 Dec 7.

12. J. Pope. Dimensions of Supply Chain Security. *Southern Business Review* 2008 Fall; 21–27.

7

IDENTIFYING, PREVENTING, AND MANAGING GLOBAL SUPPLY RISK

Supply organizations must have processes and procedures in place that will help them identify potential risk elements; prevent these risks from occurring whenever possible; and manage and mitigate risks when they do occur. "To mitigate" means to make something less painful or harsh. Risk management is the process of planning, organizing, leading, and controlling the activities of an organization in order to minimize the effects of risk on an organization's capital and earnings. Enterprise risk management expands the process to include not just risks associated with accidental losses, but also financial, strategic, operational, and other risks.

In a survey conducted by McKinsey & Company, executive managers reported that more than 50% of respondents indicated their company either undertakes no formal risk assessment or conducts only a qualitative assessment.[1] Table 7.1 presents the results of a study indicating that more than 50% of organizations are either not concerned about risk or have no formal process in place to address it. This can be a serious mistake. The study also concluded that there is a significant disconnect today between supply chain risk and the ability to successfully mitigate this risk.[2]

A first step in managing risk is to identify and assess the key "ingredients" that comprise organizational risk. The next step is to develop plans and approaches

Table 7.1 Level of Concern and Actions Taken—Risk-Related Events

Level of Concern	Percent of Companies
Actively managing risk	11
Actively assessing risk	24
Concerned but no formal process in place	47
Not concerned about risk	18

Source: Adapted from C. Verstraete. Share and Share Alike. CSCMP *Supply Chain Quarterly* 2008 Quarter 2; 32.

to prevent risk whenever possible and then to mange or mitigate risk when risk events occur. In this chapter we identify and assess risk and present approaches and best practices for managing and preventing risk from becoming a reality.

IDENTIFYING AND ASSESSING RISK

As mentioned in previous chapters, supply managers realize that although significant savings can be made when sourcing globally, risk exposure also increases. With an increasing need to minimize inventory levels, traditional buffers against disruptions to supply are often reduced or no longer in place. In order to minimize and prevent disruptions to supply, identifying risk and mitigating disruptions by effectively managing and preventing risk are necessary for companies operating at any level.

A recent example involves a U.S. company that manufactures and distributes products in the Midwest with key suppliers scattered throughout the country. Several years ago the company experienced extensive disruption to its supply of a key component. The failure was a direct result of one of its domestic tier two suppliers not being able to supply components because of a natural disaster. This tier two supplier was located in New Orleans and had shut down because of Hurricane Katrina. The end result was a supply disruption for the end user of the parts. Not surprisingly, end users had minimal knowledge of their tier two suppliers; had not identified potential supply chain risks that far up the supply chain; and were without a plan to prevent or to mitigate risk resulting from failures at this supply level.

Before talking about specific ways to manage risk, stepping back and viewing risk management as a continuous process that contains some specific elements is important. The following sections describe those elements.

Identifying and Categorizing Risks

Global supply chains are vulnerable to many forms of risk, from natural disasters to terrorism to currency fluctuations. These disasters can completely disrupt a supply chain and completely close an operation, as in the Hurricane Katrina example described above. The key to mitigating and then managing risks is to understand a company's vulnerabilities. As a first step, identify all potential disruptions to the supply chain and then categorize these in a way that makes sense for the organization. Examples of broad categories of supply chain disruption risk include:[3]

- Operational risk, including equipment failure, abrupt discontinuity of supply, labor strikes, and quality issues
- Natural disasters such as earthquakes, hurricanes, and tornadoes
- Terrorism or political instability
- Commercial or market risk, including shifting demand and supply patterns and unexpected increases in prices

Each of these risk categories should be divided into subcategories and clearly described in terms of the type of risk and the effects of the risk if it occurs. For example, in the risk category of supply disruption, a risk subcategory could be quality-related issues. The type of quality issue might include defective packaging. The risk element is that packaging for a product might not provide adequate protection for the product in transit from India or China. The packaging might separate when subjected to a certain amount of stress under certain conditions. The number of actual and potential occurrences, including their cost impact, should then be estimated in an objective format.

Dividing risk elements in this way helps to ensure that there is a common understanding of all categories of risk. Dividing risk elements also helps when determining the relative risk severity and implications. Some companies assign these according to categories that affect different business units.

Risk Assessment and Prioritization

After identifying the key risks, the next step is to assess and prioritize risks in terms of how the organization will deal with them if they occur. This process includes assessing risks in terms of the probability of their occurrence and the severity of their impact on supply. Risks with the greatest probability and severity will receive the highest priority in terms of management attention. An integral part of this analysis is the determination of the *implications* of risk occurrences. In other words, if this risk does occur, what will the implications be for continuity of supply?

Risk Mitigation

Once risk assessment is complete, the next step is determining the best means of mitigating risk. The initial focus is on risks that are determined to have high severity and high probability. Actions should be determined that will reduce the level of impact and provide a measure of protection if these risk events occur.

The actions described above should be carried out for those suppliers that a supply organization views as critical to success. This process involves reviewing the following factors for key suppliers:

- *Delivery capability:* Includes the ability of the supplier to deliver the right goods, at the right time, at the right place, and with the correct information/invoice
- *Human resources record:* Includes employee relations and records and employee turnover
- *Supply disruptions:* Includes the nature and extent of previous supply disruptions or weaknesses in the supply chain
- *Location:* Includes geography, political situation, and shipping distance
- *Natural disasters:* Includes, hurricanes, floods, tornados, and other natural disasters
- *Financial strength:* Includes cash flow and capital available for investment
- *Quality capability:* Includes quality history, failures, and improvement plans

The above exercise is repeated for every key supplier. Specific strategies and contingency plans are then developed based on the supplier's criticality and the risk factors for that particular supplier. Strategies and contingency plans could include, for example, changing the risk profile of the supplier by developing supplier quality and reliability capabilities; shifting spend to other less risky suppliers; developing alternative suppliers; and carrying additional inventory in the supply chain. Other risk mitigation strategies include commodity and currency hedging, possession of tooling, and a rigorous supplier selection and evaluation process. These and other approaches and practices for managing and preventing risk are covered in the *Approaches and Practices for Preventing and Managing Risk* section.

Monitoring and Managing Risk

After developing contingency plans, monitoring and managing risk for key suppliers is necessary. This task is often assigned to a buyer or commodity team.

Monitoring should occur on a regular basis for some risk categories such as delivery timeliness, product quality, and quantity. In some cases, the nature and extent of monitoring will be driven by events such as the potential for political unrest in the country where a supplier is located. For example, national, regional, and global monitoring of risk is particularly important when companies have suppliers located in other parts of the country, region, or world that can be affected by events such as political instability and natural disasters.

APPROACHES AND PRACTICES FOR PREVENTING AND MANAGING RISK

This section examines various approaches and practices that leading companies use to manage and prevent risk. These approaches include probability and severity mapping; risk contingency planning; managing commodity and currency fluctuations; a rigorous supplier evaluation and selection process; supplier development; and international purchasing offices (IPOs). Additional approaches include taking a total cost perspective; identifying qualified backup sources; possession of tooling; the use of third-party data services and information repositories; and the effective use of contracts. Literally hundreds of ways exist for supply managers to prevent, manage, and mitigate supply risk.

Probability and Severity Mapping

Some risks have a greater impact and lead to a greater disruption of a company's supply chain efforts. As noted earlier, to effectively manage risk, companies should first understand the types of risk that they may be subject to, then assess the relative impact of risk and the relative probability that this risk will occur. Next they should identify those risks with the highest probability of occurrence and the highest severity (and then use this information to develop contingency plans with a focus on those risks that have the highest probability of occurrence and the highest severity of impact if they do occur). A tool for accomplishing this is the risk severity and probability matrix in Figure 7.1.

The first step in constructing this matrix is the formation of cross-functional teams comprised of individuals who have a thorough understanding of operations and the risks to which a company might be subjected. The next step is to brainstorm all the possible risks that could occur. Then categorize the risks according to their relative severity, in terms of negative impact on the business and their probability of occurrence. Where each risk falls within the matrix determines the time and effort that should be spent in developing contingency plans and on managing these risk elements, including prioritizing the risks and determining

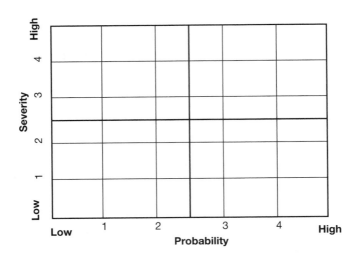

Figure 7.1. Risk Severity and Probability Matrix.

the amount of resources that will be spent on risk management for each element. Those risks that fall within the upper right-hand side of the matrix should receive the most attention in terms of risk mitigation and contingency planning.

The risk matrix in Figure 7.2 is an example of this analysis with risks under the broad categories of operational risk, natural disasters, terrorism, and financial risk. Each of the risks is numbered. The numbers correspond to the list of potential risks derived from the brainstorming session. The list can then be expanded to include risk implications and contingency plans where appropriate.

This exercise is carried out for all risks at a high level. After each high-level risk has been assessed, the team can develop a separate risk matrix, by risk category, as a means of further analysis. All operational risks can then be brainstormed, listed, and positioned appropriately on each matrix.

Risk Contingency Planning

Contingency planning is the development of a management plan that identifies alternative strategies that will help ensure success if specified risk events occur. The key here is to ensure that a contingency plan is in place. Equally important is to ensure that the plan has a good chance for success rather than just being a document that was completed as a result of some corporate requirement. In other words, the plan represents more than somebody's idea of creative writing or "busy work."

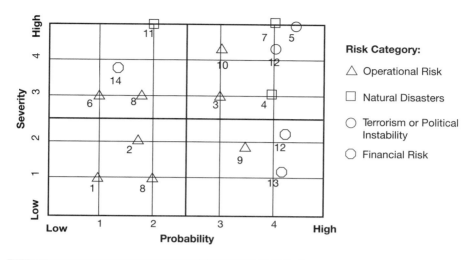

Figure 7.2. Risk Severity and Probability Matrix—Risk Categories.

The following example illustrates the importance of having a formal risk evaluation and mitigation plan in place for key suppliers.[4] (This example is adapted from Reference 4.) A medical equipment manufacturer produces a device used to monitor patient vital signs. The device has specially designed tubing that comes into contact with a patient during the procedure. The supplier of these tubes had experienced production problems and had been unable to provide the tubes. In order to maintain its production schedule, the buyer for the medical device manufacturer was looking at using an alternate source. However, because the tubing physically touches patients, the medical device manufacturer has to meet strict biocompatibility requirements of the U.S. Food and Drug Administration (USDA); so this limited the number of suppliers of this tubing. Meeting the USDA requirements is the responsibility of the manufacturer of the device. In this case, on short notice, the manufacturer had to identify alternate tubing suppliers that were qualified to meet biocompatibility standards, including an ability to demonstrate stringent lot-tracking capabilities.

The subsequent slowdown in product deliveries affected the company's financial performance. Although the medical device manufacturer identified the supplier as being the main problem, the company's own managers were also at fault for not realizing the possibility of the occurrence of this risk and not developing risk mitigation strategies. If the manufacturer had held additional inventory of this low-cost item or qualified a second source of supply, far less disruption would have been experienced.

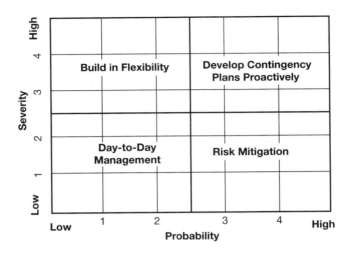

Figure 7.3. Risk Severity and Probability Matrix—Developing Contingency Plans. (Adapted from C. Verstraete. Share and Share Alike. *CSCMP Supply Chain Quarterly* 2008 Quarter 2; 34.

The key steps in risk contingency planning include evaluating the implications of risk, developing contingency plans, and testing contingency plans. Each is outlined below.

Evaluate the implications of risk. This step involves the development of several potential risk implications, which begins, as mentioned earlier, with assembling a group of individuals who have a thorough understanding of the risks that a supply organization might be exposed to and the resulting implications if these risk events do occur. The process then involves brainstorming the implications and moves on to determining the most likely implications, using a rank-ordering technique such as the nominal group technique. Once this exercise has taken place, a risk element previously thought to be of relatively low importance on the probability and severity matrix might be reviewed and "upgraded" in terms of its severity.

Develop contingency plans. In this step, contingency plans are developed based on the relative severity and the probability of occurrence of the risk. Figure 7.3 provides a useful tool for determining the response to risk elements that might occur. Risks that appear in the upper right-hand quadrant (high probability/ high severity) require detailed contingency plans. These plans might include, for example, the development of alternative sources of supply, additional inventory or safety stock in the supply chain, or duplicate technology. In extreme cases, more than one contingency plan might be developed for each risk element. Risks that appear in the upper left-hand quadrant (high severity/low probability) require procedures for risk reaction that build in flexibility and speed. Contingency plans might, for example, include agreements with local sources of supply that are close geographically and can provide a ready or faster source of supply if the risk occurs. Of course, the local source will likely cost more (which in the end analysis is the least of your worries). Risks that appear in the lower right-hand quadrant (low severity/high probability) have a strong chance of occurring. The appropriate action here is to have contingency plans in place to mitigate these risks. In this case, we know that the likelihood of this risk event occurring is relatively high, but the severity is low. An appropriate response might be, for example, to increase local safety stock levels for supply items in this category. Risks that appear in the lower left-hand quadrant (low risk/low probability) do not necessarily need contingency plans because supply managers can usually take care of these issues in the course of normal day-to-day management. The approach here would be monitoring of these risks as part of day-to-day management and taking appropriate action as necessary.

The primary objective of carrying out the above procedure is to develop appropriate contingency plans based on the probability and severity of the risk event—not all risks and not all events are "created equally." In addition it helps to ensure that risks receive differing amounts of ongoing management attention according to relative levels of their severity and probability.

Test contingency plans. Whenever possible, testing the plans is advisable in order to ensure that contingency plans are realistic and will work. For example, if bringing new suppliers on board is part of the contingency plan, doing so might not be feasible in a reasonably short enough space of time for the contingency plan to be effective. However, "practice runs" should occur to test the feasibility of plans whenever possible. How quickly, for example, can a crisis team get together if a crisis occurs? Answering this question might include testing communications procedures and reviewing alternate supplier readiness. (There is a reason why schools and businesses have fire drills.)

Managing Currency Fluctuations

Few observers would argue that globalization has caused nations and regions to become economically interdependent. Because of this situation, a major concern with global supply management is managing the risks associated with currency fluctuations, which leads us to the need to reduce the uncertainty associated with fluctuating currencies. The following situation illustrates the principle of currency fluctuation and risk.

Reed Davis, a buyer at a small Midwestern manufacturer, entered into a contract to purchase plastic extruding equipment from a Canadian supplier. The contract called for Reed's company to pay $75,000 in Canadian currency upon receipt of the equipment. When Reed negotiated the contract, the exchange rate between the U.S. and the Canadian (C) dollar was C $1.37 to U.S. $1.00, making the cost of the equipment equal to U.S. $54,745 (C $75,000/$1.37).

Upon delivery several months later, the Canadian dollar had strengthened to the point that a U.S. dollar was now worth only C $1.20. The U.S. equivalent of C $75,000 now equaled $62,500 (C $75,000/$1.20). Because Reed had not taken any steps to protect his company from currency fluctuations, he could only watch in frustration as the currency change cost his company almost an additional $8000, an increase of 14% over the original price in U.S. dollars.

Purchasing professionals know that currency fluctuations are part of doing business when buying internationally. And many of these same professionals also know that at times they might gain rather than lose from currency changes. For most purchasers, however, the objective should be to protect their firm from risk due to currency fluctuations. Fortunately, a variety of approaches are available to help manage currency changes.

Buy in U.S. dollars. Paying for foreign goods or services with U.S. dollars seems to be the easiest and, at first glance, the most logical way to manage currency fluctuations. Yet an approach that shifts currency risk to the seller might not be as easy as it sounds. Foreign suppliers are aware of currency fluctuations and might be unwilling to accept any risk. Furthermore, when assuming responsibility for currency fluctuations, many foreign suppliers incorporate a risk factor into their price.

Ignore currency fluctuations. Ignoring currency fluctuations might make sense under certain conditions. Some purchases are short term, one time, or involve relatively few dollars. Also, a buyer might be confident that a foreign currency will remain stable against the dollar. The buyer might conclude that ignoring currency fluctuations, at least in the short term, does not present an unacceptable risk.

Buy from countries that peg their currency to the dollar. Some countries maintain or peg their currency at a fixed or relatively stable rate against the U.S. dollar. China is the most notable country that previously pegged its currency at a fixed rate against the dollar. Now, however, China allows its currency to fluctuate against the dollar. The result has been a shift that has made Chinese imports more expensive. As long as a country maintains its currency at a stable rate compared with the dollar, currency risks are minimal.

Share currency fluctuation risk. Sharing currency risk involves the equal division of a change between a buyer and a seller through an agreed-upon price due to currency changes. Although sharing risk does not eliminate risk, it helps minimize the impact of any changes that may occur.

Negotiate currency adjustment contract clauses. In this approach, both parties agree that payment occurs if exchange rates remain within an agreed-upon range. If exchange rates move outside the range, the parties can renegotiate or review the contract. Currency adjustment clauses usually stipulate that exchange rates are reviewed before delivery (delivery-triggered clauses) or at specified time intervals (time-triggered clauses).

Hedge currencies. Hedging involves the simultaneous purchase and sale of currency contracts, often over a time frame that coincides with a foreign purchase. Hedging also occurs for commodity markets. A gain realized on one contract will offset a loss on another contract. The objective of hedging is to avoid risk rather than realizing a financial gain. Hedging simply locks in a position. If the purpose of buying currency contracts is to gain financially, then the purchaser is *speculating* rather than hedging.

Purchasers who enter into longer-term or high-dollar contracts with foreign suppliers should consult with their finance or treasury department. These departments often have extensive international currency experience and can give advice or even take responsibility for hedging, currency forecasting, developing currency contract language and clauses, or making payments to foreign suppliers. (*Note*: For a comparison of currency exchange rates by country, see www.x-rates.com.)

Rigorous Supplier Evaluation and Selection Process

Perhaps the most powerful risk prevention approach today is the development of a rigorous supplier evaluation and selection process. Select a set of world class suppliers and watch how much easier life becomes. Select a set of poor performers and be prepared to dust off the risk contingency plans.

There is no one best way to evaluate and select suppliers. Regardless of the approach used, a primary objective of the evaluation process should be to reduce purchase risk and maximize overall value. The time that goes into selecting suppliers should be a function of the importance of the item purchased. For example, the effort involved in evaluating and selecting suppliers is going to be different for jet engines than for commercial stationary. When sourcing globally, the time and effort will increase proportionately. So when considering foreign suppliers, the selection of the items that are outsourced must be carefully considered from a strategic perspective.

Most supply organizations have at their disposal some well-developed resources available for locating suppliers. These resources include current suppliers that are familiar with suppliers in other industries, sales representatives, information databases, experience, trade journals, trade directories, trade shows, second-party or indirect information, professional associations, internal sources, and internet searches. However, locating and evaluating sources of supply internationally is much more difficult because of travel distance and time, ready availability of information on suppliers, differences in culture and language, and differing expectations in terms of quality and conformance.

Several best practices have been adopted by successful firms when selecting and evaluating suppliers internationally:[5]

- Successful companies consciously search for the best global sources of supply in the world, which specifically includes the consideration of supplier technical, quality, cost, and reliability characteristics in the search.
- Best practice companies perform in-house supplier certification. In order to accomplish in-house supplier certification, they might apply internationally recognized quality standards such as ISO standards. They might also use third parties to assist in the qualification process. In addition, the environment and environmental standards and compliance among potential suppliers are of specific concern in the selection procedure.
- Best practice companies engage in legally binding contracts with their suppliers. Although these contracts stipulate the results and penalties of noncompliance, disputes are often settled out of court.
- Best practice companies often employ foreign nationals that reside in the target country to locate sources of supply and to help in the evaluation process.
- Best practice companies use evaluation criteria for foreign sources of supply that attempt to mirror the criteria used for evaluating local sources of supply. This helps ensure a consistent selection approach across the organization.

The complexity and value of a required purchase will influence how thoroughly a buyer evaluates supply sources. With global sourcing, complexity increases considerably. Methods for supplier evaluation and selection include evaluation from supplier-provided information, supplier visits, and the use of preferred supplier lists. Suppliers are generally rated across multiple categories using selection criteria with assigned weighting according to the relative importance of each of the criteria.

From a global supplier evaluation perspective, a supply manager might consider many criteria during supplier evaluation and selection. The following comprise the key criteria:[6]

- *Location*: Where the supplier is located in relation to the purchasing firm and the relative advantages and disadvantages of that location, including, for example, distance, supply chain infrastructure and cost, and regional political and economic stability

- *Cultural and language differences:* Type of culture in place and language differences and their potential impact on the ability of the parties to communicate clearly
- *Infrastructure and assets:* Age and quality of supplier's buildings and equipment and support infrastructure for maintenance of buildings and equipment
- *Working conditions:* Amount of attention paid to general working conditions, health and safety practices, first aid capabilities, and unacceptable employment practices, including, for example, the use of child labor
- *Management capability:* A broad category that includes management qualifications and experience; practice of long-range planning; commitment to total quality management and continuous improvement; turnover of managers; professional experience and qualifications; vision, strategy, and direction; customer focus; history of labor-management relations; investment to sustain growth; employee training and development programs instituted; and strategic sourcing programs instituted
- *Employee capabilities:* Commitment to quality and continuous improvement, the overall skills and abilities of the workforce, turnover, history of strikes and labor disputes, and general morale
- *Cost structure:* Suppliers total costs, including direct labor costs, indirect labor costs, material costs, manufacturing or process operating costs, and general overhead costs
- *Quality capabilities:* Quality assurance systems and procedures, involvement of workers in quality assurance, quality record, ability to sustain quality consistency for current demand and anticipated increases in demand
- *Process and technological capability:* Current and future capabilities in design, methods, equipment, process, and investment in research and development
- *Environmental regulation compliance:* Demonstrated commitment to protection of the environment and the level and severity of infractions that have occurred, including the company's demonstrated capability in, and history of, toxic waste management, use of environmentally friendly materials, and use of returnable and recyclable packaging and shipping containers
- *Financial stability:* Financial history of the company, levels of capital available for investment in the company, credit history, level of debt,

and current stability (The economic meltdown starting in 2008 has elevated the importance of this category.)

- *Information technology capability:* Types of information technology in place, ability to link and communicate electronically with the technology used at a buying organization or with other supply chain partners, and demonstrated willingness to invest in new and proven technologies
- *Supplier's supply network:* Nature and extent of the network and the potential risk exposure to the target supplier from its own supplier or suppliers as well as second- and third-tier suppliers

Although not exhaustive, this list is close. Each of these criteria should also include a set of detailed questions designed to evaluate capabilities with a rating scale. A thorough supplier evaluation might include the use of foreign nationals as purchasing agents, site visits by commodity teams, and increasingly the use of dedicated international purchasing offices.

Supplier Development

Supplier development is a broad term that comprises those activities undertaken by a purchaser to improve a supplier's performance and capabilities. Companies use a variety of activities to improve supplier performance, including providing help with implementing Six Sigma programs; sharing technology; providing incentives to suppliers for improved performance; providing capital; and involvement of personnel with suppliers through activities such as training and development. For most Western companies, improving supplier performance is an underdeveloped risk management approach.

Although much has been written on the subject of supplier development and relationship management, working with geographically dispersed suppliers presents some unique challenges. Several trends have been identified that will affect global supplier development:[7]

- Global supplier development is essential for unlocking foreign market potential. Many suppliers in developing countries simply are not ready to compete at a worldwide level.
- Companies will tend to retain existing world class suppliers as they grow and expand and, where appropriate, companies will rely on these suppliers to develop foreign manufacturing capabilities. Supplier switching will not be as prevalent as in the past.
- A key trend is to work with existing strategic suppliers to undertake joint ventures with local firms where there is a need for local content.

- Technology, especially information technology, has become increasingly important in enabling global supply chain management and sourcing. Those companies that are expanding their global reach must place additional emphasis on the development of the technology capabilities of suppliers as a means to lessen risk. Competent foreign suppliers are less likely to experience problems or to fail.

In this section, we review some of the key global supplier development practices that supply leaders are using to develop their supply base around the world. A major focus of many supply organizations is to collaborate with suppliers, which often includes joint planning, extensive communication, best practice sharing, and technology sharing. This collaboration can help to strengthen a relationship and inherently reduce risk through shared problem solving and early warning when supply problems occur. Supplier development can include helping geographically dispersed suppliers identify opportunities to grow their own business with the purchaser and with other customers.

An example of supplier development involves Wal-Mart. Wal-Mart was approached by a supplier in Mexico that had a solid core business, yet was not performing on par with the market. Wal-Mart devoted resources to working with the company in joint business planning processes and other key supplier development activities, which helped to increase the supplier's market share and capabilities.[8] Other cases exist, but not as many as one would think, in which major companies have helped overseas suppliers grow their business. Helping to grow a supplier's market share can increase its viability and help ensure its continuity.[9] This in turn helps reduce the level of risk in dealing with geographically dispersed suppliers.

Major companies that rely on global suppliers understand the importance of exchanging information electronically using EDI technology or the Internet. Increasingly, supplier development efforts with international suppliers involve bringing these suppliers up to speed in terms of electronic systems. An important aspect of exchanging information electronically is having the technology in place with geographically dispersed suppliers that will enable visibility throughout the supply chain. This increased visibility allows early action to occur, including the launch of contingency plans should supply problems arise, which in turn helps reduce risk levels.[10]

A further area of supplier development includes a focus on improving the management of supplier relationships through improved coordination and collaboration and through joint performance improvement projects. These projects seek to reduce waste in the supply chain and in the development and implementation of continuous improvement projects. The reduction of waste at distant suppliers helps to make these suppliers more competitive and, therefore, helps to reduce the risk of the supplier going out of business. In addition, the impact of constantly shifting demand and market dynamics in foreign markets and changes in costs and prices as a result, can be countered, at least to some degree, through working with suppliers that are cost competitive.

International Purchasing Offices

International purchasing offices (IPOs; a topic presented in Chapter 3) are mentioned here because of their importance in managing supply risk. Using IPOs to mitigate risk has several benefits. A major benefit of using IPOs is that on-site management in a foreign country can understand and deal with local supplier evaluation and selection, supplier development, and risk management requirements, practices, and issues. The use of foreign nationals in an IPO has the added advantage that local customs, language, and procurement laws are well understood, which allows for more effective procurement and also helps to reduce risk.

Total Cost Perspective

Total cost includes the expected and unexpected elements that increase the unit cost of a good, service, or piece of equipment (see Chapter 3). One way to sum up the state of total cost analysis today is to say that almost everyone wants total cost of ownership systems, but few have them. If you really want to manage the risk that relates to cost elements, then you must have cost visibility.

Understanding total cost of supply from global sources helps reduce risk in several important ways:

- Understanding total cost helps provide a focus for cost-reduction efforts that can become an integral part of supplier development efforts.
- The process of assessing total cost enables supply managers to gain important insights into the component elements of cost and price so that appropriate action can be taken to better manage worldwide costs and risk.
- Understanding the total cost of a product or service, including supply chain costs, helps ensure that negotiations are based on a full understanding of all supply chain cost elements, which can help to ensure competitive pricing is achieved.

Backup Sources

Unexpected supply chain risks can lead to lost sales, lost customers, and lost profits. A proper assessment of supply chain risks might lead to the need for backup sources for certain products or services to help ensure continuity of supply. Supply managers can adopt several kinds of strategies here:

Buffer stocks. Use buffer stocks. If buffer stocks are required, the estimate of buffers should be realistic in terms of quantity of buffer stock and associated inventory holding costs vs. potential risk and associated costs of not having the buffer if a risk event occurs.

Develop risk plans. Develop risk plans that take into account that other companies might be affected by a disruption of supply from the same supplier or market as your own company. A disruption in supply could mean an unexpected burden on the same supply resources that you have in place (especially when several customers use the same backup suppliers as your company). When this situation occurs, one tactic is to source from two suppliers simultaneously for the same commodity. Another tactic is to have emergency sourcing available that can be called on fairly quickly in the case of a supply disruption. In the case of the latter strategy, companies should take into account the cost of using the emergency source (which is often higher than normal supply costs, for example, the cost of using overnight delivery vs. 2- to 3-day delivery); the speed that the emergency supplier can be brought online; the level of additional demand that the emergency supplier can sustain; and the time period the supplier is capable of sustaining this additional demand.[11]

Third-party logistics providers. Use a third-party logistics provider with global reach for critical service parts. Logistics firms, including firms such as UPS Supply Chain Solutions (UPS-SCS) and DHL, offer a global service wherein critical spares are kept in forward stocking locations close to the point of use. Should a breakdown or failure occur, the logistics provider can supply these parts within an agreed upon time period, which can range from within an hour of notification to several hours or days, based on the purchaser's specific needs. The benefits of working with a specialized logistics provider are threefold. The first benefit is a contractually guaranteed replacement interval for spares that provides a measure of risk mitigation to clients that need parts. The second benefit is that these types of service providers often provide the same service for other companies and are able to rationalize common spare parts between customers, which reduces the cost of inventory holding. The third benefit is that technology and other asset costs are shared among multiple clients, thus making this service a more cost-effective option.

Outsource from multiple suppliers. Outsourcing from more than one supplier in a foreign country for the same item or commodity is another risk mitigation strategy that allows the benefits of lower labor costs to accrue while providing some protection against risk.[11] Potential drawbacks to this approach are twofold:

- Time and effort are required to build foreign supplier capability
- Intellectual property rights are not always honored in some countries

Therefore, when using more than one supplier, the risk of having your product compromised might increase. In other words, if a company shares proprietary technology or design information with multiple suppliers, the risk of proprietary information being stolen increases.

Possession of Tooling

Another risk-reduction strategy is to own the tooling used in the foreign country to manufacture the purchaser's products. Owning the tooling provides a degree of flexibility in the event a supplier ceases its operations, but this option should only be pursued when the cost of owning the tooling is justified vs. the risk of not having capacity available when it is needed. The potential life cycle of the product also needs to be considered when weighing the costs and benefits of owning tooling. If the product life cycle is fairly short and the tooling cannot be used for other similar products, the cost of owning the tooling might not be justified.

Third-Party Data Services and Data Repository

A third-party data service provides storage of information on a reliable and secure database that is normally operated and maintained offsite at a secure location. Databases provide a highly efficient means to store and retrieve data.

Organizations often use overseas third-party service providers as an economic alternative to domestic sources or internal technology and data processing functions. Use of these foreign-based entities is not without risk. (For useful guidelines on using foreign-based entities, see http://www.ffiec.gov/ffiecinfobase/booklets/outsourcing/15.html.)

From a risk mitigation perspective, third-party data services serve an important function because they help to mitigate disasters involving information systems. Critical data used onsite within a company is safely stored offsite on secure servers. This type of service also helps ensure the integrity of sensitive data that might otherwise fall into competitors' hands.

A best practice example of using third-party data to manage supplier financial risk occurs at United Technologies Corporation (UTC), a company whose supply organization is widely recognized as being world class.[12] Although UTC works closely with its suppliers, doing so comes with no guarantee that a particular supplier will stay in business.

UTC uses *SBManager*, a risk management tool developed by Open Ratings, a Dun & Bradstreet company, to monitor 25,000 suppliers. *SBManager* is an early warning tool that predicts supplier failures. *SBManager* develops pattern-recognition models that look at the past bankruptcies of suppliers and the events occurring 3 and 6 months prior to these bankruptcies. It also identifies supplier problems, such as failure to pay their own suppliers, legal issues, and problems meeting government and environmental regulations.

Use of Contracts

Having proper contracting procedures is an important approach for mitigating risk. A good contract can help a supply organization mitigate authority limit risks; regulatory noncompliance risks; security risks; terms and conditions risks; environmental, health, and safety risks; intellectual property and patent risks; and reputation risks. In fact, research evidence suggests that when contracts describe clearly what actions a supplier should take and what outcomes should be achieved, the risks of contract failure and the costs of monitoring a contract relationship are lower. With incomplete contracts, the parties might face potential opportunism and costly bargaining later when they attempt to negotiate contract adjustments.

A key risk that contracts help mitigate is poor supplier quality. An effective purchase and supply contract sets the quality standards expected as well as the legal recourses available against suppliers in the event of a breach. Also included are contractual provisions that require the manufacture and delivery of defect-free products. Contract provisions should also be in place that offer legal recourse against a supplier related to product liability insurance, recall insurance, and indemnification. Some best practices that leading companies adopt when contracting internationally include:[13]

- Select suppliers with strong financial health and an excellent quality record. Best-in-class companies seek to avoid the need to enforce contracts by selecting and working with suppliers that consistently provide quality products and services.
- Determine the laws of contract that apply in a particular foreign country and specify under which country's laws a dispute would be adjudicated. The U.S. operates under common law, but many other countries operate under different legal systems. In this case, best practice companies ensure that contracts include an international arbitration clause. In the event of a dispute, a U.S. purchaser might

need to force the foreign supplier to enforce the contract. The supply contract should stipulate that disputes would be resolved through international arbitration governed by U.S. law, preferably in the U.S.

- Determine and specify in the contract responsibility for costs of product liability lawsuits and recalls. Costs that stem from poor-quality products that result in lawsuits and costs of recall should be the responsibility of the foreign supplier. A contract should specify that the supplier has product liability and recall insurance in place that also covers the purchaser.

- Ensure that contract provisions include recourse when a supplier does not carry insurance. In this case, try to impose responsibility for product liability and safety recall costs on the supplier.

- When contracting with a foreign supplier through a middleman or third party, be sure that the necessary actions and contracts are in place to ensure adequate protection in the event of product quality issues or recall. A contract with a sales subsidiary of a foreign company located in the U.S., for example, might not provide recourse against the manufacturer of the product.

- The chance of contract misunderstandings occurring due to language differences is very real. Best practice companies try to prevent this risk by double translating contracts. As an example, assume a company negotiates a contract in English with a Chinese company. The English contract is given to a competent translator to translate into Chinese. The Chinese version is given to another competent translator to translate back into English. Any inconsistencies between the original English contract and the double-translated English contract indicate areas where contract problems may occur.

Aligning Technology Roadmaps with Suppliers

Developing technology roadmaps with a supplier is another way to prevent the future risk that you could wake up one day and find that your company has fallen behind in technology. Roadmapping is a planning tool that shares product development information with suppliers so they have ample time to develop technology that aligns with a buyer's product development plans. It almost goes without saying that roadmapping requires extensive trust and a longer-term commitment between buyers and sellers. Leading companies understand this process well. Figure 7.4 illustrates the concept of aligning technology.

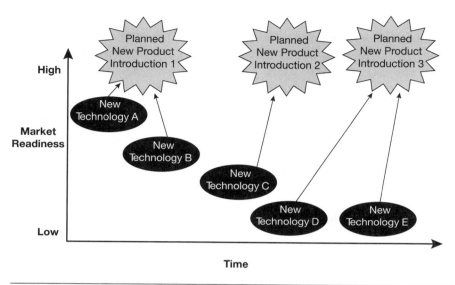

Figure 7.4. Aligning Technology Roadmaps.

THE CHANGING FACE OF RISK MANAGEMENT AT DHL SUPPLY CHAIN

The next sections discuss two examples that help illustrate how risk management professionals at DHL Supply Chain are changing their perspectives about their role in preventing and managing risk. The authors thank Phil Renaud, Vice President Global Safety, Health, Environment, at DHL Supply Chain-DHL for his generous support when developing this section.

The first example involves a global health care products manufacturing and distribution firm, illustrating how the risk management group within DHL Supply Chain developed strategies to mitigate the risks arising from concentrating manufacturing and distribution operations into fewer facilities. Because DHL Supply Chain has also been exposed to the affects of sometimes challenging worldwide weather patterns, the second example illustrates how DHL Supply Chain is evolving its risk prevention and management strategies to meet the world's weather challenges.

Managing Risk for a Health Care Products Company

DHL Supply Chain provides third-party logistics services for a global manufacturer of health care products. As the relationship with the health care product manufacturer has evolved over time, DHL Supply Chain has been asked to provide an increasing range of services to this client. DHL Supply Chain not only provides distribution and transportation solutions, but it has also developed an intimate understanding of the client's business and global risk exposure, including the need to ensure business and supply continuity.

A current project with the health care product manufacturer involves rationalizing globally 130 factories to 30 factories, which will result in fewer, potentially larger, distribution centers to supply these facilities and to store finished goods. Because of the scale and importance of the project, any risk-related disruptions while the project is underway could prove disastrous. Also, with the reduction of the number of production facilities and distribution centers, any disruptions involving this fewer number of facilities could have a negative affect on the overall supply chain.

The DHL Supply Chain risk management team recognized the need for structured risk and business continuity planning early on. Working closely with its client, the team proactively created a risk portfolio comprised of risk identification and risk management strategies that will come into play in the event of a problem so that the customer can continue operating. For example, one major risk involved power continuity for the company's warehousing operations. The DHL team discovered that the power supply for key warehouses in Europe was concentrated with a single provider in one country. Risk analysis identified the effects of a significant power outage, including the maximum amount of time the affected facilities could operate without power. Risk management strategies that evolved out of this exercise included shifting the power supply to several other countries; developing alternative energy sources to lessen the dependence on power providers; and onsite and regional backup generators.

Coping with Hurricane Ike

The second example deals with how a weather event affected supply chains across a large portion of the U.S. The weather event also affected DHL operations in a rather surprising way. When Hurricane Ike made landfall in the Houston area, not only did it have a massive impact in the immediate vicinity, but the storm also disrupted other parts of the country. The aftermath of Hurricane Ike caused states as far away as Ohio to experience the wrath of sustained 75-mile/per/hour winds. Trees snapped in half and power was disrupted from Cincinnati to Columbus. In order to help ensure business continuity, DHL Supply Chain implemented existing risk contingency plans for the Houston area and for surrounding states, including Florida and other coastal states. From a risk management and mitigation perspective, however, no plans had been made for the impact of the storm in other parts of the U.S.

Hurricane Ike knocked out the power supply for a DHL Supply Chain temperature-controlled warehouse in Cincinnati, resulting in rising warehouse temperatures. Although DHL could not prevent the risk of a hurricane, it had to respond quickly with a risk mitigation plan. DHL Supply Chain responded by obtaining a large mobile generator from a company in New York and transporting it to Cincinnati in time to avert a disaster by saving the bulk of the goods in the warehouse from spoilage.

In retrospect, DHL Supply Chain found that its risk contingency planning for Hurricane Ike focused largely on coastal regions. Because the crisis plan targeted only the point of impact and the states in close proximity, regions further inland remained exposed without sufficient contingency planning. As a result, deploying resources to combat the risk event in Ohio when the remnants of Hurricane Ike hit the state was delayed. This situation provided an ideal learning opportunity.

DHL Supply Chain now understands that it needs to take worldwide changing weather patterns into account in risk mitigation planning. As a result, the DHL team has revaluated its contingency plans. Whereas the DHL team previously has only considered backup generators in coastal areas, the company now takes a more holistic view by strategically placing generators in other inland areas. The team has also concluded that to develop the appropriate contingency plans, DHL needs to do a better job predicting the frequency, intensity, and effects of major storms. To enable this, the DHL Supply Chain risk management team now uses *Google Earth Pro*, a software tool that allows the user to see a picture of weather-related events, track these events, and take action as necessary. The changes at DHL Supply Chain have all come about because of the conclusion that weather patterns are changing globally.

Because some think that storms are becoming larger, more widespread, and more sustained, risk management should include not only the direct impact of storms, but also the likely effects as larger storms extend their reach inland. Risk management practitioners must therefore think about expanding their view beyond the obvious areas affected by weather events to include more widespread areas that might be affected.

Insights Gained by the Risk Management Team

The DHL Supply Chain risk management group has gained several insights over the last few years, including from the experiences we have described above. One important insight is that many supply chains are interconnected globally. Therefore, when developing risk management strategies, companies must understand the ripple effect that risk-related events (including weather-related events) could have in a supply chain, plan for these effects wherever possible, and have continuity plans in place when risks occur.

Another important insight is that, in addition to sourcing globally to reduce manufacturing costs, companies are attempting to operate in as lean a manner as possible. Customers are asking providers to ship in smaller lots more frequently, including on a just-in-time basis, which means having fewer inventories in the supply chain to cover undesirable events. Furthermore, the current global economic crisis has contributed to this situation because customers are buying in smaller quantities, and in many cases are shifting their buying patterns to purchase less frequently and to purchase less-expensive goods, which intensifies the situation if a risk-related event occurs. For DHL, maintaining smaller inventories and shifting buying patterns place greater pressure on understanding the potential risks that can occur within the interconnected global supply chains of their customers. DHL is also under pressure to develop strategies to ensure continuity of supply, an area in which they continue to focus attention.

CONCLUDING THOUGHTS

Identifying, preventing, and managing risk is of vital importance to global supply managers. Failing to grasp the idea that risk management is one of a supply organization's most important processes is an invitation to trouble. Global supply chains will almost certainly be interrupted, and supply continuity threatened, at some point from a host of risk categories. Although predicting when various risks will occur is virtually impossible, it is almost certain they will occur.

The issue with risk is not *if* something undesirable will happen, but rather when will it happen and how severe the consequences will be. Global supply managers must therefore plan for risk events and have the necessary contingency plans in place when risk shifts from being a vague probability to a harsh reality. We must understand the type, nature, probability, and severity of the risks we are exposed to and determine the implications for supply continuity.

REFERENCES

1. McKinsey & Company. Understanding Supply Chain Risk: a McKinsey Global Survey. *The McKinsey Quarterly* 2006 Oct. Retrieved from http://www.mckinseyquarterly.com/Operations/Supply_Chain_Logistics/Understanding_supply_chain_risk_A_McKinsey_Global_Survey_1847?gp=1&pagenum=6.

2. W. Browning and A. Bartolini. Supply Risk Increases while the Market Stands Still. *The Aberdeen Group* 2006 Mar. Retrieved from http://www.aberdeen.com/summary/report/benchmark/SuppPerfRisk_RA_BB_3941.asp.

3. P.R. Kleindorfer and G.H. Saad. Managing Disruption Risks in Supply Chains. *Production and Operations Management* 2005 Apr 1. Retrieved from http://www.allbusiness.com/company-activities-management/operations-supply/10570691-1.html.

4. D. Favre and J. McCreery. Coming to Grips with Supplier Risk. *Supply Chain Management Review* 2008 Sep 1. Retrieved from http://www.scmr.com/article/CA6591249.html.

5. D. Lock. International Purchasing: Selecting, Engaging, and Managing the World's Best Suppliers. *American Productivity & Quality Center* 1999 Mar 12. Retrieved from http://www.apqc.org/portal/apqc/ksn?paf_gear_id=contentgearhome&paf_dm=full&pageselect=detail&docid=100799.

6. R.M. Moncka, R.J. Trent, and R.H. Handfield. *Purchasing and Supply Chain Management, Third Edition* 2005. Mason, OH: South-Western Publishing; 216–220.

7. R.J. Duffy. The Future of Purchasing and Supply: Reaching Around the Globe. *Purchasing Today* 2000 Apr. Retrieved from http://www.ism.ws/pubs/content.cfm?ItemNumber=9727.

8. G. Hahn. Development Serves Customers Worldwide. *DSN Retailing Today: Connecting Northwest Arkansas Supplier Resource Quarterly* 2005 Fourth Quarter: 6.

9. S. Avery. Best Suppliers Will Do. *Purchasing* 2005 Aug 11; 134(13): 56–57.

10. H.L. Richardson. Streamlining the Supply Chain. *World Trade Magazine* 2003 Oct 1. Retrieved from http://www.worldtrademag.com/Articles/Feature_Art icle/0fa2e14ca8af7010VgnVCM100000f932a8c0.

11. M. Jayashankar and B. Tomlin. How to Avoid Risk Management Pitfalls. *Supply Chain Management Review* 2001 Jul 1. Retrieved from http://www.scmr.com/article/CA6457963.html.

12. J. Carbone. Suppliers Join the Design Huddle. *Purchasing Magazine Online* 2006 September 7; http://www.purchasing.com.

13. G.P. Fremlin. Careful Contracts Reduce Risk. *China Business Review* 2008 Jan/Feb; 35(1): 34–39.

8

LEVERAGING SUPPLY MARKET INTELLIGENCE

Never discount the important role that information plays within the risk management domain.

An often-repeated request of a supply manager is, "Where can I find information on suppliers?" Obtaining suitable market intelligence is an issue that confronts supply managers daily in their efforts to find, qualify, and use appropriate sources of supply.

The answer to this seemingly simple request for information has many aspects. First, a supply organization needs to identify the potential suppliers that exist for a particular commodity. Next, the organization must determine which suppliers are capable of providing the required goods and at what total landed cost. Then, it is necessary to narrow the supplier pool through a structured evaluation and selection process to arrive at a smaller set of supplier candidates. And, of course, a rigorous evaluation must occur to identify the final supplier/s. These factors, although complex enough on their own, are further complicated when suppliers are located in foreign countries. A rigorous evaluation process requires supply managers to obtain, analyze, and use supply market intelligence (SMI). SMI exists in many forms and places. No single source of intelligence is available.

This chapter approaches the subject of SMI by first defining the concept and then relating it to the development of supply strategies. Next, we present the uses, levels, and categories of SMI. Finally, many different sources of SMI are identified. Supply organizations that do not tap into the vast amount of information that is available are unnecessarily exposing their organizations to risk.

DEFINING SUPPLY MARKET INTELLIGENCE

SMI is the outcome of the process of obtaining and analyzing information relevant to a company's current and potential supply markets that has the objective of supporting effective decision making. SMI includes five elements:

- *Commodity profile information:* identifies the type and nature of a product or service, the manufacturing or service delivery process, and quality requirements or standards
- *Cost structure:* consists of the costs associated with capital investment, raw materials, manufacturing, quality, storage, transportation, duties, export control, inventory carrying, taxes, insurance, port of entry, supplier development, energy, overhead, and profit
- *Supply base information:* includes current and potential suppliers, their characteristics, and country location
- *Market information:* identifies supply and demand price drivers, capacity utilization, and other factors that determine price and availability for the commodities in question as well as the market size and predicted growth rate
- *Competitive analysis:* an assessment of buyer and supplier relative size and power, substitute products and services, other customers using the same sources of supply, their relative size and buying power, and other factors that influence buying leverage[1]

Determining the Right Supply Strategy

Before gathering SMI, it is necessary to determine the type of strategy a company should adopt given a specific supply requirement. This, in turn, influences the type, breadth, and depth of SMI that is required. (Chapter 10 elaborates on the concept of supply strategies.) Determining the type of strategy includes understanding a company's need for a product or service through spend analysis; the opportunities that exist to standardize the product; and the supply chain that currently exists to bring the product to the user. In addition, supply managers must understand the supply markets that exist, the competitive nature of these markets, and the strategies that best fit the supply requirement.

Portfolio analysis is a tool commonly used to determine the relative importance of an item (Figure 8.1). The use of portfolio analysis forces supply managers to segment their supply approaches and to recognize that one strategy approach does not fit all requirements.

Perhaps the most important reason for using portfolio analysis is its prescriptive nature. Once a supply manager or team quantifies the total spend for each commodity or category, the good or service can be positioned within the most

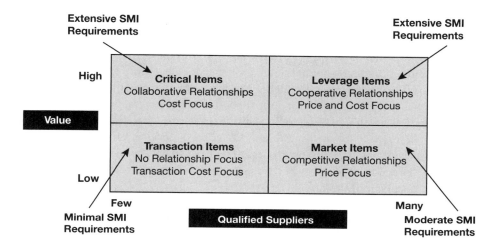

Items = purchased goods and services

Figure 8.1. Portfolio Analysis.

appropriate quadrant, which will help identify the type of supplier relationship to pursue; the intensity of the supply market information search; whether to engage in a win-lose or win-win negotiation and relationship approach; whether to take a price or cost analytic approach; the types of supply strategies and approaches that should work best given the placement of an item; the intensity of risk prevention and management approaches to take; and how best to create value across different purchase requirements. The effective use of a portfolio matrix, which is essentially a strategy segmentation tool, is one of the best risk management tools that we have in our arsenal.

An example of the application of sourcing strategy concerns an IT company located in the U.S. The IT company used portfolio analysis to determine what was thought to be the best sourcing strategies for its various needs. An IT help desk was determined to be less specialized or core to the business while other functions including Java 2 Platform and Enterprise Edition (J2EE) development were determined to be more critical. Where a specific requirement fell within the portfolio analysis helped determine how the work should be sourced and the level of information search and risk management that should take place. In this case, the company chose to source its help desk to the Philippines, but to retain its J2EE development on-site with joint venture partners. The following sections briefly describe each quadrant within the matrix:[2]

Transaction quadrant. The goods and services in the transaction quadrant have a lower total value with a limited supply market. Although many suppliers might be available for these items, the cost of a supplier search almost always outweighs the value of the search. Therefore, we say the supply market is actually limited. Miscellaneous office supplies, one-time purchases, magazine subscriptions to trade journals, and emergency tools needed at remote locations usually qualify as transaction items. Reducing the transaction cost of the purchase of these items is the primary way for supply professionals to create value here, usually through electronic systems or procurement cards. Any price analysis that occurs is cursory due to the low value of the good or service. In reality, supplier relationships are not even a concern here. The need to gather SMI here is almost negligible. Therefore, the items in the transaction quadrant are of minimal concern in terms of supply risk.

Market quadrant. The market quadrant includes standard items or services that are part of an active supply market; have lower to medium total value; feature many suppliers that can provide substitutable products and services with low supplier switching costs; and feature well-defined specifications. Commodity chemicals, fasteners, corrugated packaging, and other basic raw materials that do not have an unusually high dollar value or are not part of a leverage opportunity are logically part of this quadrant. Interestingly, market items are often sourced globally because they are easy to specify, many supply alternatives are available, and supply managers are not looking much past cost, quality, and delivery. As a result, the need for SMI does come into play. Even though these items are not critical and are not being sourced on a coordinated basis across a company, costly mistakes are still possible when sourcing these items, particularly when the sourcing occurs overseas.

Leverage quadrant. The upper right quadrant, or the leverage quadrant, includes those items for which consolidating purchase volumes and reducing the size of the supply base should lead to a range of benefits. The leverage quadrant features the extensive use of longer-term contracts. Examples of leverage items include any grouping or family of items whose volumes can be combined company-wide for economic advantage. Market quadrant items that are grouped into commodity families can be treated as leverage items. Because leverage items are often candidates for longer-term agreements, supply managers should engage in an intense information search. The development of longer-term contracts should lead to questions about cost, quality, delivery, packaging, logistics, inventory management, the supplier's financial health, and after-sale service, all factors that can affect supply chain performance. The need for SMI is intense for items and services in this quadrant. Although this quadrant will not have the most suppliers in terms of numbers, the dollar value of the leverage items should be high. Having fewer than 100 suppliers receiving 80% or more of total purchase dollars, often through leverage, longer-term agreements, is not unusual today.

Critical quadrant. The critical quadrant includes goods and services that consume a large portion of the total purchase dollars; are essential to a service or product's function; or where the end customer values the differentiation offered by the good or service. The critical quadrant also features fewer suppliers that can satisfy a purchaser's requirements, which often involves customization rather than standardization. At times a supplier is critical simply because it has a patent right to a good or service that the buying company must have.

The following example illustrates how one buying company has approached an item that truly is critical. In 2000, Boeing's board of directors approved the development of two longer-range versions of the popular 777. What makes this new plane unique is that Boeing only equips the longer-range 777s with General Electric engines. GE also shared in the plane's development costs and is now sharing revenue with Boeing from each plane sold, highlighting the special nature of the Boeing/GE relationship. No sane individual would argue against the notion that the engines are extremely valuable from a cost and performance perspective. Jet engines are also available from a limited supply base: Pratt and Whitney, General Electric, Rolls Royce, and a joint venture between GE and Snecma. It's impossible to overstate the importance of SMI as it pertains to critical items. The cost of making strategic errors within this quadrant can potentially threaten the well being of an entire buying company. What would the impact be on Boeing if GE could no longer supply 777 engines?

After completing the segmentation process, it is necessary to identify those items that are prime candidates for the gathering and use of SMI, particularly global SMI. As Figure 8.1 points out, SMI is particularly relevant for items within the leverage and critical quadrants.

USES, CATEGORIES, AND LEVELS OF SUPPLY MARKET INTELLIGENCE

SMI has varied uses. Supply managers essentially obtain and use SMI to identify those suppliers that can provide the necessary products and services, to consistent levels of cost, quality, and quantity, and that will enable the buying company to enhance its competitive standing. Supply managers also use this information to help prevent potential problems and surprises. Table 8.1 outlines the key uses of SMI.

SMI gathered under the categories in Table 8.1 will allow supply managers to make an informed decision regarding supply management issues. Collected on a regular basis, this information also allows supply managers to keep abreast of developments, including shifts and changes in demand and supply markets; the introduction of new products and technologies; the entrance of new competitors;

Table 8.1 Key Uses of Supply Market Intelligence

Type of SMI	Use of SMI
Commodity	To determine which commodities would benefit from global buying
Industry	To determine industries and suppliers within those industries, including capacity utilization and constraints
Competitive environment	To determine the competitive environment that exists by industry and supplier
Market forces	To determine the market forces at play that influence cost and pricing
Early warning signals	To determine early warning signals for supply market changes that affect availability, cost, price, or delivery
Suppliers	To determine the suppliers that exist and that can potentially supply a given commodity or service
Supplier capability	To determine those suppliers with the needed expertise to meet or exceed supply requirements
Supplier viability	To determine financial viability and continuity
New suppliers or new capabilities entering the market	To determine new suppliers coming into the market and/or potential new capabilities among existing suppliers
Levels/tiers of suppliers	To determine second- and third-tier suppliers that exist for a given commodity or service and their effect on the supply chain
Technology	To determine what new technologies will be available and the potential impact on supply and costs
Local laws and customs	To determine local laws and customs in potential supply countries and their potential effect
Trade barriers	To determine the implications of trade barriers that may be in effect
Customs and excise	To determine customs and excise requirements and duties that would apply and implications
Child labor laws and practices	To determine child labor laws and practices in potential supply countries and the history of conformance with or violation of these laws
Supply chain	To determine the supply chain that exists for a given commodity
Total cost	To determine total supply chain costs involved in outsourcing and for the development of cost models based on this information
Risk	To determine risk factors involved in sourcing from specific suppliers or countries and the potential effect if these risks occur

and changes to manufacturing processes. Insights gained from SMI help a supply organization adjust its strategies and tactics in a timely fashion. SMI should be gathered at different levels: the macro-environmental level, the country level, the industry level, the commodity level, and the supplier level.

Macro-Environmental SMI

The first level of information that a supply manager is interested in is the macro-environmental level. Macro-environmental level information includes market dynamics, world trade, demographics, political climate, economics, environment, and technology.

Market dynamics. Market dynamics refers to the interaction between forces of demand and supply and the pricing signals they generate. In most free markets, any significant part of market dynamics is beyond the control of any single company or group. At a lower level of detail, market forces are driven by the numbers of competitors in the industry, the supplier capacity that exists, customer requirements, the similarity or substitutability of products, and barriers to entry. In many cases, commodity prices are affected by market dynamics. In other cases, either when monopolies exist or the number of suppliers is limited, these market dynamics may apply to a lesser extent. A supply manager is therefore interested in the type and nature of the forces at work for various commodities and various geographies, so that he or she can determine what effect these forces are having on pricing and costs and how these forces shift over time.[3]

World trade. World trade is the global traffic in goods and services. According to the commonly accepted definition, trade can be by gift, barter, or sale. The balance of trade (introduced in Chapter 1) is the difference between the monetary value of exports and imports in an economy over a period of time. The volume and balance of world trade is important to the supply manager because this information indicates the available supply, costs, and cost shift for certain commodities, as well as the relative strength of the economy in various locations.

Demographics. Demographics are the selected population characteristics as used in government, marketing, or opinion research. Supply managers are particularly interested in the demographic information that applies to skilled labor and the growth or decline in this area for various geographies and countries. An area of interest for offshoring, for example, is Central and Eastern Europe because of lower labor costs. However, studies based on population data from the U.N. Population Division and the International Labor Organization Project indicate that the skilled labor force will shrink in this area over the next several decades,[4] which might drive up labor costs and make sourcing from this region a less attractive option.

Political climate. Political climate plays an important role in SMI. The relative political stability or instability of a country or region can affect sourcing decisions. In addition, supply managers are interested in government policies and support of free trade. Support of trade agreements, such as the North American Free Trade Agreement (NAFTA) and the General Agreement on Tariffs and Trade (GATT), might influence decisions to source within a certain area.

Economics. Economics includes the study of information relating to the production, distribution, and consumption of goods and services. Economics is tied closely to market forces and is of particular interest to supply managers because economic conditions in a specific area can affect the price of goods. Low or high capacity utilization can influence prices.[3] When capacity utilization is high, supply becomes more restricted and prices will rise (and vice versa). The macro-economy also plays a role. If interest rates rise in a country, then rates of return on investment for certain suppliers will affect the amount of capital available for investment. Shrinking labor markets can lead to cost increases and higher prices. Likewise, shortages of key commodities, or a glut of these commodities, can affect prices. Therefore, supply managers are interested in SMI that relates to economic conditions and market factors that will influence supply and demand and the effect that this has on costs and prices.

Environmental information. Environmental regulations can have an impact on a supply manager's decision to source from various geographies or countries. Many countries have strict laws in place to protect the environment that can affect the requirements for doing business. The level of investment required in ensuring that supply chain partners comply with environmental regulations and laws might lead to increased costs. In addition, certain suppliers in foreign countries could produce goods that when brought into another country might have an adverse impact on the environment. Therefore, supply managers require environmental SMI because this information could influence global sourcing decisions.

Technology. Suppliers in certain geographies and countries that do not have the current level of technology required for the efficient exchange and use of information will struggle to be part of an integrated supply chain. Supply managers must obtain information related to global technology that might impact the way business is conducted globally as well as the level of technology that exists within target geographies, countries, and suppliers.

How often to gather macro-environmental SMI. Macro-environmental SMI should be captured on an ongoing basis (weekly or monthly) because market forces shift continuously. Therefore, for a supply manager, being aware of what these shifts are and what effect they will have on commodity prices and availability is important. As currencies strengthen or weaken, for example, supply managers should be aware of the effect this will have on the currencies that are used to procure goods in various countries—information that can then be used as input when deciding what currency to use when making sourcing decisions. In addition, as supply and demand conditions change, the changes will tend to drive prices up or down. For example, a shortage in rubber over a period of time might increase the cost of tires. Changes to supply and demand for certain commodities can also be a leading indicator for increases or decreases in the prices of other downstream commodities or services. An increase in the price of oil, for example, will likely lead to an increase in supply chain logistics costs.

Country-Level SMI

A second level of SMI information relates to specific countries.[5] Country-level information is often a subset of the macro level with some additional topics included. Some economic and noneconomic SMI areas of interest at the country level include:

- Economic topics such as growth, regulatory bodies, the tax environment, level of employment, import and export levels, labor availability and costs, population size and trends, location of free trade zones, and countertrade requirements
- Cultural issues and levels of crime
- Logistics infrastructure, including the natural geography and size of country
- Safety of intellectual property
- Political climate and stability
- National holidays, working hours, and time differences

How often to gather country-level SMI. In the case of a critical global initiative, gathering SMI at the country level early on is important. Once a decision is made regarding the targeted sourcing country, SMI should then be updated on a regular, though not necessarily frequent, basis (perhaps monthly or quarterly). If updated monthly or quarterly, SMI at the country level can consider topics such as:

- Countries that are viable sources of supply
- Countries where costs are changing for the commodities currently being procured—by how much and why
- Countries where geopolitical changes are taking place—the effect this will have on the economy, the availability, and the costs of goods
- Countries where there is an increase (or decreases) in risk factors
- Countries where there are changes to employment rates—how this will affect the costs of goods being procured from that country

- Countries where new skill or technology developments are taking place

Industry and Commodity SMI

Industry and commodity SMI relates to the types, sizes, and relative strengths of industries that exist and the worldwide users and suppliers of commodities.[6] The critical information that supply managers require at the industry and commodity level include prices and pricing trends of commodities; substitution possibilities; primary producers and consumers within an industry or commodity; demand growth and capacity expectations; locations of suppliers and buyers; and capacity utilization.

How often to gather industry and commodity-level SMI. The nature of a commodity influences how often to gather SMI. Commodities that have a rapid rate of technological change, such as certain kinds of electronics, demand frequent collection of SMI. Industries and commodities that have a high percentage of suppliers under financial duress also require frequent SMI updates. Standard items characterized by active supply markets, or industries in which the rate of change is relatively slow, require fewer SMI updates. In some respect the frequency of SMI updates at the industry and commodity level is similar in concept to cycle counting parts. Anyone who has worked with a state-of-the-art inventory management system knows that treating every part or SKU the same is simply not feasible. Depending on a host of variables, some SKUs get counted weekly while others are counted every quarter or 6 months. Inventory control managers establish parameters that define the most appropriate cycle counting scheme. The same logic applies to commodity management. Some commodities require frequent SMI updates while others do not deserve the same level of attention. Best practice companies know the SMI update cycle for the industries and commodities they manage.

Supplier SMI

Supplier information comprises the next level of SMI and relates to the number of potential suppliers that exist, the products and services they provide, their location, relative size, and their capabilities. Supply managers are interested in information regarding a supplier's:[8]

- Management capability
- Financial strength and ownership
- Use of technology
- Labor relations
- Cost, quality, delivery, and cycle time performance

- Available capacity
- Environmental compliance
- Outstanding legal actions
- Protection of intellectual property

Referring to Figure 8.1, the need for SMI at the supplier level will be partly a function of where a supply requirement falls within the portfolio matrix. Not all supply requirements are created equally, including from an SMI perspective. Best practice companies understand the different types and levels of SMI data they need to collect.

How often to gather supplier SMI. Although considering SMI at a macro and industry level is important, these levels are often removed from the day-to-day operation of the supply organization. The same cannot be said for SMI at the supplier level. For example, at a time when Toyota thinks that at least 20% of its suppliers face the likelihood of bankruptcy, the need to gather SMI at the supplier level is almost real time. Supplier watch lists need to be developed and updated at least weekly. Supply managers should also be interested in acquisitions and mergers between suppliers and the effect this might have on supply markets and market prices. In addition to obtaining SMI about incumbent suppliers, supply managers must also obtain information about new suppliers entering the market (suppliers constantly enter and exit the marketplace for some items). A supply base that remains unchanged over an extended period often leads to complacency. SMI about new suppliers can help avoid complacency while maintaining some degree of competitive tension within the supply base.

SOURCES OF SUPPLIER MARKET INTELLIGENCE

Supply managers often wrestle with where to obtain SMI on global sources of supply. Although still not straightforward, many sources exist for obtaining SMI, and the task of locating these sources, largely due to the development of information databases and the Internet, has become somewhat easier for supply managers. This part of the chapter highlights some of the key sources of SMI.

Macro-Environmental SMI

Table 8.2 shows various websites that provide useful macro-environmental information. In addition to these sources, supply managers can find useful information that relates to the forces that influence supply and demand by referring to the producer price index (PPI). In the U.S., the PPI is a family of indexes that measures the average change over time in selling prices received by domestic producers of goods and services. These indexes are maintained by the Bureau

Table 8.2 Sources of Macro-Environmental SMI

	Website
Demographics	http://unstats.un.org/unsd/demographic/
Political	http://www.politicalresources.net/
Economic	http://www.econsources.com/EconSourcesPage.asp?PageID=5
Market dynamics	http://www.census.gov/epcd/www/97EC22.HTM
Trade	http://www.stat-usa.gov/tradtest.nsf

Source: Adapted from R. Handfield. *Supply Market Intelligence* 2006. Boca Raton, FL: Auerbach Publishing; 593.

of Labor Statistics and can be found at http://www.bls.gov. This website, which has recently undergone a radical redesign that makes it more user friendly, is an incredible source of free market intelligence. The site contains over 600 industry price indexes in combination with over 5000 specific product line and product category subindexes. The site also contains over 2000 commodity price indexes organized by type of product and end use. In addition, the website contains data on import price changes.

PPI indexes track commodity price movements month to month. By converting price increases into a percentage and comparing these percentages against the PPI, supply managers can determine whether any price changes they are experiencing with their suppliers are reasonable or not. Most developed countries will have their own version of this website. From personal experience, becoming familiar with the information these sites provide is well worth the reader's time.

Economic conditions also influence whether a market is favorable to a seller or buyer; therefore, a supply manager needs to be aware of current and forecasted economic conditions. A useful reference here is the website for the Institute of Supply Management (http://www.ism.ws), which shows pricing trends for various commodities. Other useful sources of SMI include industry-specific trade associations and journals as well as websites such as www.economy.com, www.marketshare.com, www.gartnergroup.com, www.ibisworld.com, and www.dismal.com.

Geographic and Country-Specific SMI

Many valuable sources of geographic and country-specific information exist. The National Trade Data Bank (NTDB) provides information on commercial guides by country, market reports, and other programs. The International Trade Library has a collection of over 40,000 documents related to international trade. Useful websites are http://www.stat-usa.gov/tradtest.nsf and http://www.library.ucsb.

edu/subjects/gov/statusa.html. Another source of SMI on this topic is the World Bank, which provides financial and technical assistance to developing countries for development programs such as bridges, roads, and schools. The stated goal of the World Bank is to reduce poverty. Information on the World Bank can be found at http://www.worldbank.org.

International trade associations also provide information. An industry association participates in public relations activities such as advertising, education, political donations, lobbying, and publishing, but its main focus is collaboration between companies. Associations might offer other services, such as producing conferences, networking or charitable events, and classes and educational materials. Many associations are nonprofit organizations governed by bylaws and directed by officers who are also members. A useful website is http://fita.org.

Additional sources of information can be found through the Standard & Poor's Country Profiles website, the Department of Commerce Trade Reports (http://www.commerce.gov), and the *Exporters' Encyclopedia and World Marketing Guide*. The material in the *Exporters' Encyclopedia and World Marketing Guide* is arranged geographically. For each country there is a country profile followed by marketing data; information on communications, transportation, business travel, and key contacts; and a summary of trade regulations and documentation requirements. Each edition also includes brief sections on U.S. ports; U.S. foreign trade zones; World Trade Center Association members; U.S. government agencies that provide assistance to exporters; foreign trade organizations; foreign communications; and general export and shipping information and practices. The website for the *Exporters' Encyclopedia and World Marketing Guide* is located at http://www.loc.gov/rr/business/duns/duns1.html.

Supply managers must also concern themselves with regulatory bodies around the world and the international laws and regulations that govern trade. Many regulatory bodies exist for specific industries such as the pharmaceutical, medical, and health-related industries, including international bodies such as the World Health Organization and the International Conference on Harmonization, as well as individual country-based regulatory bodies. An example of a country-based regulatory body is the Food and Drug Administration (FDA) in the U.S. Supply managers might find themselves dealing with many of these bodies, often acting independently from one another, when pursuing their global sourcing efforts.

Another concern of supply managers is international and country-specific laws. Examples of these laws in the U.S. include the Foreign Corrupt Practices Act, Anti-Boycott Legislation, and the Export Administration Act.[9] Information on these laws can be found at http://www.aimlink.com/linkslegal.html.

Industry and Commodity SMI

Information on industries and commodities can be found by using resource directories. International directories include *Moody's International Manual* and the *Market Share Reporter*, as well as industry-specific directories such as the *Textile World Blue Book*. Hundreds of these directories exist and can be accessed via the Internet.[10]

Principle International Businesses: The World Marketing Directory is another key source of information. This directory lists approximately 50,000 leading enterprises in 140 countries that are the largest employers worldwide. Included are mining, manufacturing, agriculture, forestry, fishing, power generation and distribution, construction, communications, transportation, financial institutions, insurance, real estate, and other service businesses and autonomous government entities and industries.

Marconi's International Register lists 45,000 companies that conduct business globally and lists commodities and products geographically under 3,500 headings. *The Encyclopedia of Global Industries* chronicles the worldwide history, development, and status of the most lucrative and high-profile industries. Each entry includes the size and economic impact of the industry; its organization and structure; its history and development; major countries and companies involved (including rankings); size and nature of the work force; and research. Some of the industries covered include aircraft, biotechnology, computers, Internet services, motor vehicles, pharmaceuticals, semiconductors, software, and telecommunications.

International Business Information includes international business publications; important new databases; company information sources; international accounting standards and practices; international marketing resources; disclosure requirements for major stock exchanges; export/import sources and information; and industrial and economic statistics.

Supplier SMI

One of the most important categories of SMI relates to global suppliers. Although many sources of information exist, the challenge becomes one of sifting through many sources and identifying the suppliers that can meet and exceed your performance requirements. This task seems especially daunting when confronted with the vast number of suppliers that compete on a global basis. In addition to the sources of information mentioned in the previous sections, several means and sources exist for locating and vetting new suppliers globally as outlined below:[11]

Intermediaries. Several avenues exist for locating and qualifying foreign suppliers using intermediaries:[11]

- *Trading companies:* Trading companies offer a comprehensive range of services, including locating and qualifying suppliers, performing product quality audits, and contract negotiations. A website containing a directory of trading companies in the U.S. and the UK can be found at http://b2b.tradeholding.com/default.cgi/action/viewcompanies/btypeid/3/btype/Trading_Companies. A list of trading companies in India can be found at http://explore.oneindia.in/industry/trading. Another website listing Chinese and Taiwanese product manufacturers, exporters, suppliers, producers, and trading companies is http://www.search-engines-2.com/country/chinese.html. A directory of Vietnamese trading companies can be found at http://www.eguidevietnam.com/VN/SEARCH/Trading+Companies/1.
- *Third parties:* Third-party assistance in locating and qualifying suppliers is available in the form of experts in the field who can act as purchasing agents or brokers on a commission basis. Agents and brokers are particularly useful when a company does not have the necessary foreign experience or presence. A directory of international shipping agents and brokers can be found at http://www.onelasvegas.com/wireless/ship_brokers.html. A directory of customs brokers and freight forwarders can be found at http://www.business.com/directory/transportation_and_logistics/intermediaries. In addition to the above, several third-party logistics firms, including UPS, FedEx, and DHL, provide customs brokerage and other related services.
- *Manufacturers/sales representatives:* Manufacturers/sales representatives can provide a useful source of information on potential suppliers. These individuals represent their companies in foreign countries.
- *Subsidiaries:* Subsidiaries of foreign companies located in the U.S. can provide support ranging from translation services to import merchant services. Links to business directories containing information on foreign subsidiaries operating in the U.S. can be found at http://www2.lib.udel.edu/subj/bsec/resguide/dirs.htm.
- *Commission houses:* Commission houses normally act as agents for foreign companies wishing to export goods and operate on a commission basis. Services provided include handling customs and shipping details. Links to local and international commission houses/agents can be found at http://www.kompassindia.com/directory-company-product/wholesale-distribution/commission-agents-570404-61240.html.
- *Import merchants:* If a supply manager is looking to buy a standard commodity, one option is to utilize an import merchant that handles

all logistical details, including customs clearance, currency exchange, and transportation.

- *Import brokers:* Import brokers bring potential suppliers and purchasers of goods together on a finder's fee basis. These brokers do not typically undertake any financial or logistics tasks or activities on behalf of either the buyer or seller of goods.

A remaining challenge for the supply manager is to identify reputable intermediaries with whom to do business. This information can be obtained by speaking with others who have used intermediaries through such avenues as trade shows, conferences, professional associations, and customers.

Trade consulates. Supply managers can obtain information from trade experts through trade consulates as well as by contacting embassies overseas to inquire about foreign suppliers. The U.S. Department of Trade provides another important source of information on foreign suppliers.[12]

Trade shows. Trade shows provide an opportunity for the supply manager to obtain information on a variety of suppliers in one location by commodity or industry. Hundreds of these shows take place every year in major cities around the world. Information on trade shows can be obtained by using business libraries that contain a directory of trade shows. An Internet search will provide the timing and location of these shows.[12]

Magazines and newspapers. Within the domain of supply management and supply chain management, various publications are available that are excellent sources of SMI. Several of these, such as *Business Week, Fortune,* and *The Wall Street Journal,* are ideal for providing timely information that relates to current affairs and the macro economy. Other sources are ideal for gaining insights into supply chain trends, strategies, practices, and supply markets. From personal experience, some solid publications include *Purchasing, Inbound Logistics, Traffic World, DC Velocity, Modern Materials Handling, Industry Week,* and *Supply Chain Management Review.* Each of these publications also has websites that allow users free access to their vast archives of data and information. With so much good information available, there is no excuse to be caught off guard.

Information databases. Normally proprietary, a supplier information database is kept in-company on suppliers that serve an industry. These supplier databases are normally populated by the procurement group. In some cases companies employ a full time staff to carry out this function.

Trade journals and directories. Most major industries have a group or council that publishes trade journals. These journals are often valuable sources of information regarding industry developments, new technologies, suppliers, and trends. In addition, trade journals exist for most industries that provide information on suppliers by country and by industry. Examples of these, beyond those mentioned previously, include *Dun's Asia/Pacific Key Business Enterprises, The Gulf Directory, Hoover's Masterlist of Major European Companies, Japan Company Handbook, Japan Directory, Kelly's* (a commerce directory for Great Britain), and *Major Companies of the Arab World.*[13]

Internet research. Apart from the websites provided above, a general Internet search can be revealing when looking for supply information. A word of caution, however, is in order here. Anyone who has done Internet searches (and that's likely everyone) has probably concluded two things: Internet searches pull in a great deal of "trash" that is not relevant to the primary search and the objectivity of the sites and information presented must always be assessed. Pay enough money and your company can be the first to appear whenever certain search terms are used.

Indirect sources of information. Indirect sources include contacts that a supply manager makes outside his or her organization, such as those made through professional associations, current suppliers for noncompeting companies, and customers.

CONCLUDING THOUGHTS

Understanding the changing dynamics of supply markets is a task that all supply organizations face. The responsibility for gathering and managing SMI depends on the size of the organization and the type and intended use of the data. Some companies have the luxury of employing full-time resources to manage critical commodity data, including the dissemination of this data to the appropriate users. In smaller companies, this responsibility should be part of a supply manager's normal duties.

An argument can be made that it is the responsibility of every supply organization to require its personnel to become more externally focused, which means obtaining information from technical and trade publications; conducting Internet research on the commodities for which they are responsible; talking with sales and other trade personnel; subscribing to third-party data sources; contributing regularly to data repositories; and making SMI a regular part of the supply management process. No matter how the gathering of this data is accomplished, ensuring that it is disseminated throughout the organization to those who can interpret and use it to support global initiatives is important. In fact, best practice companies have well-developed tools and processes to share SMI internally whenever it becomes available.

REFERENCES

1. C. Dominick. Buyers Ask: What Is Market Intelligence? *Next Level Purchasing* 2008 Feb 26. Retrieved from http://www.nextlevelpurchasing.com/articles/what-is-market-intelligence.html.

2. R.J. Trent. *Strategic Supply Management—Creating the Next Source of Competitive Advantage* 2007. Fort Lauderdale: J. Ross Publishing; 118-122.

3. R.M. Moncka, R.J. Trent, and R.H. Handfield. *Purchasing and Supply Chain Management, Third Edition* 2005. Mason, OH: South-Western Publishing; 346-347.

4. R. Das and E. Mendiratta. CEE's Dwindling Skilled Labor Supply: The Vagaries of Unfavorable Demographics. *Social Science Research Network* 2007 Dec 1. Retrieved from www. http://ssrn.com/abstract=1261946.

5. R. Handfield. *Supply Market Intelligence* 2006. Boca Raton, FL: Auerbach Publications; 175.

6. R. Handfield. *Supply Market Intelligence* 2006. Boca Raton, FL: Auerbach Publications; 586-617.

7. R. Handfield. *Supply Market Intelligence* 2006. Boca Raton, FL: Auerbach Publications; 205.

8. R.M. Moncka, R.J. Trent, and R.H. Handfield. *Purchasing and Supply Chain Management, Third Edition* 2005. Mason, OH: South-Western Publishing; 215-222.

9. R. Handfield. *Supply Market Intelligence* 2006. Boca Raton, FL: Auerbach Publications; 180-181.

10. R.M. Moncka, R.J. Trent, and R.H. Handfield. *Purchasing and Supply Chain Management, Third Edition* 2005. Mason, OH: South-Western Publishing; 309-310.

11. L. Krotseng. *Global Sourcing* 1997. West Palm Beach, FL: PT Publications; 40-42.

12. R.M. Moncka, R.J. Trent, and R.H. Handfield. *Purchasing and Supply Chain Management, Third Edition* 2005. Mason, OH: South-Western Publishing; 310.

13. R. Handfield. *Supply Market Intelligence* 2006. Boca Raton, FL: Auerbach Publications; 201-207.

PART IV.
PURSUING GLOBAL
SUPPLY MANAGEMENT
EXCELLENCE

9

MAKING THE CASE FOR GLOBAL SUPPLY MANAGEMENT

The hypercompetitive markets of today, more so than at any time in history, demand a continuous search for innovative ways to compete. Most executives will say that responding to competitive, customer, and financial market demands requires steady and sometimes dramatic improvements in cost, quality, delivery, cycle times of all kinds, and the development of new technologies. As we think about how to respond to a never-ending list of demands, the development of global strategies and processes should become an increasingly attractive but potentially risky option if not carried out correctly. The potential for high reward makes the business case for global supply management a strong one.

This chapter is the first of five that explore global supply management. Recall from Chapter 1 that global supply management involves proactively integrating and coordinating common items and materials, processes, designs, technologies, and suppliers across worldwide purchasing, engineering, and operating locations. The pinnacle of supply management, particularly as it is defined in this book, is an approach in which different worldwide sites and locations coordinate and integrate their activities and supply management efforts, under the guidance of strong centrally led leadership, within a cohesive framework. From a risk management perspective, global supply management offers an opportunity to achieve cost savings that are above and beyond those available from international purchasing; to eliminate costly duplication of effort; and to make better worldwide decisions because different activities and sites are coordinated under a single worldwide umbrella. The global supply management process can also expose a company to greater risk if global suppliers fail to live up to their performance expectations.

The first section of this chapter examines the need for a better understanding of global supply management. Next is an expansion of the international purchasing/global supply management model presented in Chapter 1. The third section makes a powerful case for pursuing sophisticated supply management strategies and practices. The chapter then concludes with the differences between companies that practice international purchasing and those that take a globally coordinated view.

THE NEED FOR A BETTER UNDERSTANDING

During the late 1980s and 1990s a great deal of research focused on various aspects of international purchasing. The growth in the topic of international purchasing related directly to the declining competitiveness of many U.S. companies along with the belief that international purchasing could help reverse this decline. A major portion of international purchasing research has addressed the benefits that U.S. companies should expect to attain from sourcing offshore as they battle aggressive and skilled foreign competitors. In particular, although most practitioners understood that the quest for lower prices seemed to be the primary driver and benefit behind international purchasing, academic researchers, in their customarily reactive fashion, spent a great deal of time validating what most practitioners already knew. Other research topics of interest during this period included calculating total cost savings vs. unit price savings; addressing the transactions cost associated with international purchasing; and various risk management issues.

After reviewing the research conducted during the 1980s and 90s, an obvious conclusion is the lack of any in-depth analysis concerning how global supply management should be pursued, along with the failure to identify the operational differences between international purchasing and global supply management. Although some observers have concluded that there is a need to develop global supply processes and strategies and to view global supply management as an important strategic process rather than a tactical tool, details concerning how to achieve this are few. Previous research also failed from a conceptual basis to differentiate between international purchasing and global sourcing or global supply management, resulting in the widespread interchanging of terms. A lack of detail concerning how to differentiate these terms or how to develop a more strategic orientation to global supply management became evident.

These shortcomings prompted two major research projects that were designed to increase our understanding of global supply management. The ideas and findings presented in Chapters 9 through 13 are the result of these two projects. Unless otherwise noted, all research findings presented in these chapters are from those two studies. We will not bore readers with reams of data and statistical evidence, but rest assured that the material presented here is well-supported empirically.

The first phase of the global supply research, conducted in the early 2000s by Robert Monczka and Robert Trent, investigated the critical success factors, benefits, progress, risks, methodologies, practices, and lessons learned from the development of global supply processes and strategies. This research included survey data from 162 predominately larger companies that were headquartered primarily in North America, although these companies managed worldwide operations and buying centers.

The second phase of the research included data from 167 companies. Although the second project investigated issues similar to the first study, the second project featured a greater number of European firms and stressed to a greater degree sourcing from emerging countries. Both research projects included respondents who were vice presidents, directors, or managers working at the corporate level rather than at the division or site level. In other words, the respondents were individuals who were knowledgeable about global strategy.

Along with extensive survey data, both projects also featured detailed site visits to several dozen leading companies. Site visits occurred across a wide range of industries, including the chemical, electronic, computer, consumer products, and transportation equipment industries. The research featured extensive face-to-face interviews with cross-functional team members, team leaders, sourcing and engineering representatives, executives and executive steering committee members, and others who were closely involved with global supply management. One result from both projects was the unmistakable differences in the practices, features, and results achieved between supply organizations that practice international purchasing vs. those that took a globally coordinated view of supply management. As will become evident, the business case for global supply management is a strong one.

EVOLVING TOWARD GLOBAL SUPPLY MANAGEMENT

Chapter 1 presented a five-level model showing the progression from domestic sourcing only to global supply management. What was not included in Chapter 1 was the percentage of companies that practice or expect to practice each sourcing level. Recall that the five-level model is divided into two segments for analysis. Levels II and III respondents represent the international purchasing segment, and Levels IV and V represent the global supply management segment. (Recall that

Level I	Level II	Level III	Level IV	Level V
Engage in Domestic Purchasing Only	Engage in International Purchasing as-Needed	International Purchasing as Part of Sourcing Strategy	Integration and Coordination of Global Sourcing Strategies across Worldwide Locations	Integration and Coordination of Global Sourcing Strategies with Other Functional Groups
	International Purchasing		**Global Supply Management**	
Current* 13.4%	21.3%	31%	18.1% + 16.1% = **34%**	
Future* 7.8%	7.8%	14.3%	15.6% + 54.5% = **70%**	
Expected Change** -42%	-63%	-54%	-14%	+238%

* Percent of companies operating or expecting to operate at a particular level.
** Expected change equals the percentage difference between current and future within each level.

Figure 9.1. International Purchasing and Global Supply Management Features—2000.

the term global sourcing is also used to designate these higher sourcing levels.) Comparisons between these two segments are quite revealing and will be presented shortly.

Figures 9.1 and 9.2 present data collected at two different points in time. Around 2000, slightly less than 35% of companies indicated they operated at either Level IV or V (see Figure 9.1). Interestingly, when the respondents in this sample projected where they expected to be in 3 to 5 years, almost 70% expected to be at Level IV or V. As we have learned, however, these projections were unrealistic. Making bold projections into the future is easy. Achieving those projections is another story.

Figure 9.2 reveals a real growth in the number of companies that perceive that they practice global supply management compared with the 2000 period (from almost 35 to over 50%). Furthermore, the future projections for this second group are not all that different from the 2000 time period. In 2000, 70% of respondents projected that in 3 to 5 years that they would be operating at Levels IV and V, while 80% in the later sample projected that they would be operating at Levels IV and V over the next 3 to 5 years. Because not everyone can or should operate at Level V, this might indicate that a steady state for operating at Level V might be between 50 and 60% of companies, although it is difficult to know for sure. As will be discussed shortly, the companies in these two studies were large,

Level I	**Level II**	**Level III**	**Level IV**	**Level V**
Engage in Domestic Purchasing Only	Engage in International Purchasing as-Needed	International Purchasing as Part of Sourcing Strategy	Integration and Coordination of Global Sourcing Strategies across Worldwide Locations	Integration and Coordination of Global Sourcing Strategies with Other Functional Groups

		International Purchasing		**Global Supply Management**	
Current* 8.4%	20.1%	18.8%	22.7% +	29.9% = **53%**
Future* 5.9%	6.5%	7.8%	20.9% +	58.8% = **80%**
Expected Change** -30%	-68%	-59%	-8%	+97%

* Percent of companies operating or expecting to operate at a particular level.
** Expected change equals the percentage difference between current and future within each level.

Figure 9.2. International Purchasing and Global Supply Management—More Current Data.

multinational organizations. These percentages will decline, probably drastically, for smaller and medium-sized companies.

Supply managers need to be realistic concerning what level will satisfy their unique requirements. Although most supply managers say they want to operate at Level V, and it is easy to look toward the future and boldly announce that is where you will be, many factors affect the appropriate level. Some of these factors include the intensity of worldwide competitive and customer requirements; the commitment of executive leadership; available skills and resources; the location of buying and engineering centers; the location of world-class suppliers; and the performance impact that global supply management can have. Supply organizations need to assess realistically the level at which they should operate and then identify at what level they currently operate. If a gap exists, then plans to narrow that gap must become part of the strategic planning process (something Chapter 10 addresses).

Supply managers must also recognize that their perception of global supply management will change over time. In fact, although most companies that practice global supply management today view it as a way to develop global rather than site-specific or regional supply contracts, supply leaders are moving beyond that relatively narrow perspective. Some supply managers rightfully view global supply management in terms of not only strategy development and contracts, but also as a way to develop best practices that become internal operating standards. Examples where supply organizations are beginning to converge on company-wide practices involve supplier evaluation and selection; strategic cost management; supplier development; measurement; and early supplier involvement. As mentioned earlier, process consistency rather than simply a set of global contracts might very well prove to be the most powerful benefit realized from global supply management.

REAPING THE BENEFITS OF GLOBAL SUPPLY MANAGEMENT

Reasonable to ask is why should anyone commit scarce resources toward a process as complex as global supply management? Fortunately, the argument to do that is quite compelling—and backed by some solid evidence. Simply stated, companies pursue global supply management because they expect to capture benefits that are not as readily available from less-sophisticated practices.

Perhaps the most revealing and interesting difference between the international purchasing and global supply management segments is the perception that each has regarding the benefits they realize from their worldwide efforts. Companies that engage in global supply management achieve an array of benefits at higher levels compared with companies that take a less-sophisticated sourcing approach.

Figure 9.3 presents these benefits sorted by the difference between the averages for the international purchasing and global supply segments. Companies that engage in global supply management say they realize every benefit they evaluate at a statistically higher level than those that engage in international purchasing. In fact, the overall average across all benefit areas is 30% higher for companies that practice global supply management compared with the overall average for the international purchasing segment. Sometimes we come across data that are so compelling that they cause us to quickly see the wisdom of a course of action. This is one of those times.

One benefit that both segments rate highly is the ability to achieve a lower purchase price or cost through worldwide sourcing (although the global supply management segment still realizes this benefit at a higher level). The initial benefits from international purchasing are usually price focused and are often available to a large degree from less-sophisticated international purchasing activities. However, it is the nonprice benefits that begin to separate these two groups. Certain benefits are simply not as available unless a supply organization has coordinated its supply activities globally. Better management of supply chain inventory, for example, is a benefit that global organizations enjoy at higher levels compared with companies engaged in international purchasing. Better management

Benefit	Level IV-V Average	Level II-III Average	Difference
Better management of total supply chain inventory	4.29	2.74	1.55
Greater supplier responsiveness to buying unit needs	4.47	3.08	1.39
Greater standardization or consistency of the sourcing process	4.25	3.01	1.24
Greater access to product technology	4.69	3.49	1.23
Improved supplier relationships	4.61	3.46	1.15
Greater access to process technology	4.54	3.46	1.08
Improved sharing of information with suppliers	4.10	3.04	1.06
Greater supplier involvement during product development	3.86	2.80	1.06
Lower purchase price/cost	5.98	5.04	0.94
Shorter ordering cycle time	3.61	2.76	0.94
Higher material/component/service quality	4.16	3.25	0.91
Improved delivery reliability	3.90	3.04	0.86
Improved environmental compliance	3.24	2.39	0.85
Greater appreciation of purchasing by internal users	4.25	3.44	0.81
Lower purchasing process transactions costs	3.67	2.87	0.80
Higher user satisfaction with purchasing	4.10	3.36	0.74

Scale: 1 = not realized; 4 = moderately realized; 7 = extremely realized.
Note: Average across all benefits = 3.2 average for Level II-III segment; 4.23 average for Level IV-V segment.

Figure 9.3. Differences in Benefits across Segments.

of supply chain inventory is critical given the emphasis that is now placed on managing inventory cost and investment. Who does not want to manage working capital better?

Another important nonprice benefit is greater access to product and process technology, an outcome that is particularly critical given the rapid rate of technology change that confronts many industries. As mentioned in Chapter 1, after cost reductions, access to technology is often a highly regarded reason for sourcing internationally. Other important benefits that are more readily available from global supply management include greater supplier responsiveness, greater sourcing process consistency, improved supplier relationships, and improved sharing of information with suppliers. Would any reasonable manager turn down these benefits if they were offered?

As hard as it might be to believe, let's say for a minute that your executive leadership is not yet convinced that a well-executed global supply model is worth the trouble. Is there anything else that might make the case for pursuing global supply management?

When executives are asked to rate the degree of similarity between their geographic locations and buying units, some interesting findings emerge. The global supply management segment rates some important areas as more similar across their operating units compared with the international purchasing segment, a similarity that is the result of taking a more coordinated view of supply management. Areas where the difference between the average similarity ratings for the global supply management and international purchasing segments is statistically meaningful (sorted in descending order by the largest to lowest average difference) include:

- Strategy development process
- Supplier assessment practices
- Purchasing or sourcing philosophy
- Current purchasing strategies
- Problem-resolution techniques with suppliers
- Contracting approaches
- Reporting level of purchasing/sourcing
- Similarity of purchase requirements
- Organizational reporting structures
- Supplier performance measures used
- Business ethics

Companies that engage in global supply management rate each of these areas as being more similar across their geographic regions and buying units compared with those that only engage in international purchasing. In the longer term, one of the most important outcomes from global supply management might be the consistency created by this process. Engaging strictly in international purchasing, which is typically an uncoordinated activity across worldwide units, does not lead to consistency across buying centers or sites. The items appearing at the top of this list all relate to sourcing approaches, practices, and beliefs. Again, what supply leader does not want to achieve this consistency, a consistency that goes a long way toward promoting the standard use of best practices and eliminating waste?

The performance differences between the two segments are unambiguous. These differences help explain why so many supply organizations want to evolve toward Levels IV and V. A lower-level approach to international purchasing just doesn't deliver the kinds of outcomes that effective global supply management delivers. Finding anything in this section that should discourage our interest in knowing more about global supply management would be difficult.

LINKING GLOBAL SUPPLY MANAGEMENT TO BUSINESS FINANCIALS

Instead of talking about the case for global supply management, showing the case for global supply management is probably better. Best practice companies can make the business case for global supply management in terms that executive leaders can appreciate. Supply leaders should be driven by a set of corporate metrics that are not at all functional. Whether we like it or not, finance might just become our new best friend as we work to show the financial benefits of global supply management. "Show me the money" is not just a line from a Tom Cruise movie.

An important part of making the case for any initiative involves showing the impact any resulting benefits have on financial performance, which means translating the performance indicators that are usually associated with functional areas (lower purchase prices, higher inventory turns, etc.) into indicators that grab the attention of executive managers. Indicators such as return on assets and investment as well as changes to working capital, cash flow, sales, and gross profit margins are always of interest to executive managers.

This section introduces a financial tool known as the DuPont model (also called the strategic profit model). Use of the DuPont model, as well as other financial tools, bridges the gap between operational procurement and corporate financial management. This tool shows how various balance sheet items and income statement components come together to affect a powerful financial indicator called return on assets (ROA). ROA is part of a family of ratios called *activity ratios*. Activity ratios measure how well assets are managed. Other families of ratios include liquidity, leverage, and profitability ratios. Some companies prefer to use RONA or return on net assets. For our purposes the differences between ROA and RONA are insignificant. Even if you do not think about these measures very often, rest assured the financial community is watching them closely.

Figure 9.4 presents recent data for a producer of semiconductors and chip sets. As Figure 9.4 shows, the company's financial health is positive, but probably not as strong as it could be. Let's present several scenarios that illustrate how global supply management could affect the corporate ROA metric.

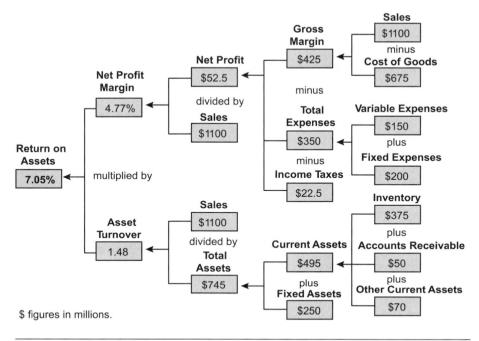

$ figures in millions.

Figure 9.4. DuPont Model Base Scenario.

Scenario 1: Reduced Purchase Costs from Global Supply Management

On any income statement is an innocent-sounding item referred to by various terms: costs of goods sold, cost of goods, cost of revenue, or cost of sales. Whatever term we use, this account includes all the costs that are incurred directly to produce products or services, including material costs to suppliers. This account also reflects any materials cost savings from integrated global supply management—what is more commonly referred to as the "tangible" benefits derived from the process. The DuPont model is ideal for evaluating the financial effects of tangible benefits. (*Note:* An Excel-based version of the DuPont model is a WAV feature of this book and may be found at www.jrosspub.com.)

What would be the effect on ROA if supply managers put in place a global supply process that reduced the costs of goods sold by 5%? (*Note:* Our example uses a 30% tax rate.) A 5% improvement in the costs of goods sold reduces this account from $675 million to $641 million. More importantly, this reduction improves ROA from 7.05% to over 10% (Figure 9.5), or an increase in ROA of over 40%! This increase in ROA is due to the increase in net profit margin that results from lower costs and a higher gross margin. Holding the other factors in

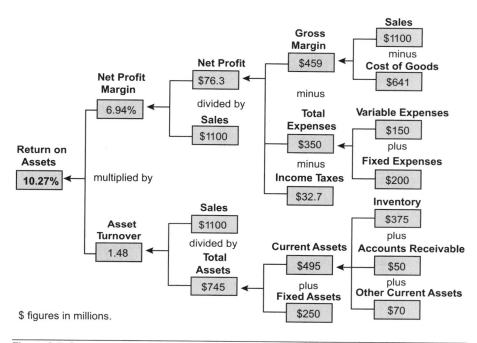

Figure 9.5. Scenario 1: Reduced Purchase Costs.

this model constant will likely understate the true impact of reducing the costs of goods sold. Lower material costs resulting from global supply management should lead to a lower total dollar value of inventory because lower prices reduce the unit value of the inventory. Lower unit value of inventory reduces the total amount of working capital tied up in the inventory account on the current assets section of the balance sheet, which will further benefit the ROA calculation.

Scenario 2: Reduced Inventory from Global Supply Management

As illustrated in Figure 9.3, better management of supply chain inventory is a benefit realized by companies that practice global supply management. Any effort to manage inventory more effectively, such as taking inventory out of the supply chain, will be reflected in the inventory turns measure. The inventory turns for Scenario 1 (2.93 turns) are arrived at by dividing sales ($1.1 billion) by inventory ($375 million) (see Figure 9.5). But is executive management all that enamored with inventory turns? Is this stuff out back spinning around? What really is the value of increased turns?

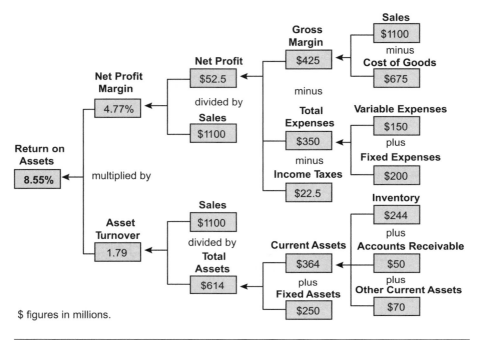

$ figures in millions.

Figure 9.6. Scenario 2: Improved Inventory Management.

This model is ideal for assessing the impact of inventory improvements on ROA. Let's assume that working more closely with global suppliers to better manage supply chain inventory, including faster material flow and consigned inventory, results in a 35% reduction in worldwide inventory. What effect does this have on ROA? The inventory account changes from $375 million to almost $244 million, which improves the ROA from the original 7.05% to almost 8.5% (Figure 9.6) or an increase in ROA of over 20%.

Scenario 3: the Best of Both Worlds

Although not shown in a figure, combining Scenarios 1 and 2 results in a new ROA of almost 12.5% or an increase from the original 7.05% of 77%! Is anyone singing "Happy Days are Here Again?" Besides illustrating the financial effect of global supply initiatives, the DuPont model is also ideal for estimating the impact of future efforts. Having the ability to perform *what if* analyses makes the DuPont model an essential part of a strategic planning process. The model is also ideal for evaluating the effects of simultaneously changing any of the accounts that appear in the ROA model. Supply managers must start acting like financial managers.

EXPLORING THE DIFFERENCES BETWEEN THE SEGMENTS

If global supply management can be as rewarding as we suggest, then why isn't everyone doing it? Three reasons quickly come to mind:

- Many supply managers do not understand global supply management as a concept. It's hard to implement something you don't understand.

- Many supply managers and organizations lack the vision, leadership, resources, and/or sophistication to coordinate their activities globally. Far too many procurement organizations are still reactive or maintain a lower position within the corporate hierarchy. Although each year the sophistication and reporting levels of supply organizations in the aggregate appear to be increasing, this increase is still moving at a methodical pace. Although saying you will soon operate at the highest global levels is easy, the reality of how complex it is to operate at these higher levels soon hits home.

- Not everyone operates at the highest global level simply because not everyone needs to operate at that level, which is especially true when we segment companies by size. Larger companies differ from smaller companies in terms of scope, complexity, and available resources. They are much more likely to have operations, including buying centers, that are worldwide rather than local or regional (scope), with more organizational levels covering a wider array of business and product lines (complexity). Corporate leaders often emphasize certain activities, including global supply management, partly just to manage a complex organization. Larger companies are also more likely to have greater access to the human and financial resources that allow them to put in place certain features. Identifying an appropriate sourcing level is an important part of the strategic planning process. The appropriate level does not necessarily have to be the most advanced level.

Simply making an argument for global supply management is not enough to be successful. The preceding sections merely increase our awareness that the case can easily be made for more advanced sourcing levels. The burden now shifts to understanding the nuances about how to make this shift happen. We must also appreciate what it takes to operate at the highest sourcing levels.

One way to appreciate how to operate at the highest levels is to more thoroughly explore the differences between companies that practice international purchasing and the companies that practice global supply management.[1] The differences are quite revealing, just as the differences in the benefits realized by the two segments are revealing. The following differences are the result of statistical comparisons between the international purchasing and the global supply management segments. Besides differing in the benefits that each receives from their efforts, the two segments also differ along some important fronts. (*Note*: The sections that follow are adapted from Reference 1.)

Difference 1. Companies that engage in global supply management are larger and more likely to have competitors that are multiregional compared with international purchasing companies. Although this finding should come as no surprise, companies that pursue global supply initiatives are clearly larger in terms of sales compared with those that engage in international purchasing. Larger companies are more likely to have worldwide production facilities, design centers, and marketing and sales activities. It should also be no surprise that the pursuit of global supply management opportunities becomes a fundamental extension of a larger company's sourcing philosophy. Competition also affects the sourcing response. Companies that pursue global supply management reveal they face greater competition from companies that are multiregional or global compared with the international purchasing segment. Most supply managers accept that extensive worldwide competition drives, at least partly, the progression toward global supply management. Size and the extent of competition are two predictors regarding whether or not a company will pursue global supply management.

Difference 2. Companies that engage in global supply management perceive their strategy implementation progress to be further along compared with international purchasing companies. An interesting question involves the perception each segment has about the progress of its worldwide strategy implementation. One would expect that the international purchasing segment would not be as positive about its progress as the global supply management segment. And in this case one would be right. Research participants have provided their perception regarding the progress of their worldwide sourcing strategy implementation. The international purchasing segment averages an implementation progress rating of 4.5/10, while the global supply management segment averages 6.23/10 (where 1 = no progress and 10 = total implementation). Both segments recognize they have a long way to go before they have a fully developed global organization in place, although the ones that practice global supply management know they have made greater progress. The international purchasing segment also appears to understand that it has not made all that much progress and that many sourcing opportunities are possible beyond what they are currently achieving.

Difference 3. Companies that engage in global supply management believe that performance improvement and cost reduction opportunities are more widely available from their efforts compared with international purchasing companies. This difference highlights the mindset that respondents in each segment have regarding worldwide improvement opportunities. The global segment is more likely to rate the improvement opportunities that exist from worldwide sourcing as being more extensive than the international purchasing segment. Companies that engage in global supply management are larger, which may indicate they have greater worldwide experience in general. They are likely to be predisposed to believe that performance improvements are more readily available from globalization. Another explanation is that global organizations are more likely to have experienced firsthand the improvements that are available from global supply management. An example supports this argument. A company that is rapidly gaining global supply experience has found that its site-based participants often have a performance improvement expectation that is limited by what they can attain from local or regional sourcing practices. Site personnel perceive that a 3% price reduction is quite an accomplishment (in reality most companies would welcome year-after-year incremental improvements, especially today). The potential improvements available from global supply management, which are often in the double digits, far exceed what these participants are willing to commit to or believe are possible based on previous experience. So what is the lesson here? Participants begin to recognize the performance differences between international purchasing and global supply management once they become part of the global process. The international purchasing segment has yet to experience the kinds of savings that will challenge any preconceived notions of historical improvement levels. These experiences logically affect the perception that each group has about the magnitude of potential savings.

Difference 4. Companies that engage in global supply management indicate that the development of global strategies is more important to their executive management compared with international purchasing companies. Given the definitional differences between international purchasing and global supply management, one can easily conclude that international purchasing is best described as a functional activity while global supply management is an organizational process. It should come as no surprise that centrally led leadership is critical to a process as organizationally complex and important as global supply management. And it should also come as no surprise that participants involved with global supply management believe that developing global supply strategies is important to their executive management. Global supply management does not happen without strong executive support. (Subsequent chapters will elaborate on the important role that executive leaders play during the global supply management process.)

Difference 5. Companies that engage in global supply management indicate they face more rapid changes to product and process technology compared with international purchasing companies. When asked to assess the annual rate of change faced across seven competitive factors—quality improvement; product and process technology development; price/cost reduction; new product development cycle times; responsiveness to customer improvement requirements; on-time delivery improvement; and overall customer service improvement requirements—the two segments rate each competitive factor the same except for one. International purchasers indicate their rate of product and process technology change within their competitive space is *stable to moderate*, while the global supply management segment indicates its rate of change is *moderate to dynamic*. Furthermore, the global segment indicates it faces greater competitive and customer pressure to introduce new product and process technology. Although cost improvements will always remain a primary driver behind worldwide sourcing activities, the need to manage product and process technology from a global perspective will drive some to pursue a more sophisticated sourcing level.

   Difference 6. Companies that engage in global supply management rely on a wider array of communication tools to support their worldwide efforts compared with international purchasing companies. Geographic complexity and extensive coordination requirements demand that global supply organizations rely more heavily on an extensive array of communication tools, including a higher reliance on groupware; video conferencing; web-based tools; and telephone conferencing at significantly higher levels compared with the international purchasing segment. Global coordination requires these companies to coordinate their activities and share information across worldwide purchasing and design locations, something that is not an issue in a less-coordinated environment. Examples of other powerful communication approaches used by global supply organizations include regular strategy review meetings between locations and joint training sessions involving worldwide team members. Project updates reported through an intranet, negotiation planning sessions, and the collocation of functional personnel to facilitate face-to-face interaction are also effective approaches. Systematic communication helps overcome the inherent complexities of coordinating a process that often involves participants from different continents. Any supply organization that expects to progress along the global supply continuum will need to invest in some serious communications technology. International purchasing efforts, typically focused at the site level, are usually not as complex in terms of communication requirements.

   Difference 7. Companies that engage in global supply management have in place more organizational features to support their worldwide efforts compared with international purchasing companies. A critical difference between the international purchasing and global supply management segments relates to how extensively each segment has put in place certain features to support their worldwide efforts (see Table 9.1). Best practice companies are not surprised by the kinds of features they must put in place to be successful. They know that having features that support their worldwide efforts is what they must do to capture the benefits from global supply management. Managers who are serious about elevating their supply management levels are urged to closely review Table 9.1, which identifies the features that must be in place to make global supply management a reality. The table also illustrates the profound differences in the scope and complexity between international purchasing and global supply management. If nothing else, Table 9.1 should provide a reality check about the range of features that global supply organizations put in place. Consider several items that show the highest difference between the two segments:

- Global organizations conduct regular strategy review and coordination sessions with worldwide procurement and other functional managers on a regular basis, a feature showing the largest average difference between the groups. Review sessions promote consistency by creating a common sourcing language and approaches that are coordinated at higher organizational levels. (Chapter 13 features a company that uses coordination and review sessions to support a supply organization that is scattered around the globe.)
- Global supply organizations are more likely to have access to the services provided by international purchasing offices (IPOs) (a topic featured in Chapter 3).
- A formal process exists for developing global supply management agreements (something that Chapter 10 addresses in depth).

The features in Table 9.1 (and subsequent chapters that elaborate on most of them) illustrate the very real differences between the international purchasing and global supply management segments. The issue becomes whether Levels II and III participants will have the commitment, resources, awareness, and expertise to put in place the features that characterize Levels IV and V.

Difference 8. Companies that engage in global supply management rate certain factors as more critical to their success compared with international purchasing companies. A variety of factors account for the differences in terms of their importance between the international and global supply management segments (see Table 9.2 for highlights). As with Table 9.1, please examine Table 9.2 very closely. In particular (and this is something that comes across in no uncertain terms), effective global supply management benefits from a centrally led or centralized structure. Global supply organizations have a higher-level CPO position or some other executive position who oversees the supply management process. This position is accountable for attaining significant results. Supply leaders also require the CPO to provide regular performance updates to the corporate executive committee and, on occasion, even to the board of directors. A weak or lower-level procurement organization guarantees that an evolution toward global

Table 9.1 International Purchasing and Global Supply Management Features

Feature	Global Supply Average	International Purchasing Average	Difference
Regular sourcing strategy review meetings with worldwide purchasing managers	4.64	2.54	2.10
Use of international purchasing offices	4.75	2.85	1.90
A formally established process for developing global sourcing strategies	4.88	3.01	1.87
Worldwide purchasing data bases or data warehouses	4.24	2.48	1.76
Development of global suppliers	5.04	3.27	1.76
Worldwide integration of technical design specialists, operations personnel, and sourcing personnel	3.75	2.10	1.65
Formal information sharing through electronic information systems across worldwide buying units	4.45	2.81	1.64
Coordinated sourcing strategy development efforts across regions	5.15	3.51	1.64
Use of cross-functional/cross-locational commodity management teams	4.96	3.55	1.41
Availability of electronic sourcing analysis tools available electronically	3.92	2.53	1.39
Centralized sourcing strategy development	5.15	3.89	1.26
Common worldwide part or commodity coding schemes	4.04	2.79	1.25
Worldwide supplier performance measures and measurement systems	4.22	3.00	1.22
Worldwide buyer/supplier executive councils	3.24	2.06	1.18
Post-selection site visits to suppliers	4.80	3.64	1.16
Pre-selection site visits to suppliers	4.94	3.84	1.10
Procurement engineers used for supplier visits	3.60	2.63	0.97

Scale: 1 = not used; 4 = moderately used; 7 = extensively used.

supply management will be slow and inconsistent. An organizational structure that features cross-functional teams, site-level participation in the process, and an executive mandate to source globally also show important differences between the segments. The availability of required information and data along with the ability to identify common requirements reveals the need to support the global supply management process with data.

Table 9.2 International Purchasing and Global Supply Management Critical Success Factors

Feature	Global Supply Average	International Purchasing Average	Difference
Centralized procurement structure	5.43	4.58	0.85
Suppliers who are interested in global contracts	5.92	5.08	0.84
Availability of information and data	6.20	5.57	0.63
Site-level participation during global contract development	4.90	4.28	0.62
Executive commitment or mandate to source worldwide	5.57	4.97	0.60
Ability to identify common requirements across buying units	5.86	5.26	0.60
Use of cross-functional teams to develop global strategies	5.66	5.10	0.56
Availability of suppliers with global capabilities	5.94	5.49	0.45
Ability to measure performance improvements from global sourcing	5.49	5.07	0.42

Scale: 1 = not a critical factor; 4 = moderately critical factor; 7 = extremely critical factor.

An example. The importance of globally capable suppliers and suppliers with an interest in global supply management contracts became evident after a visit to a producer of transportation equipment. From almost the first day that a European producer assumed ownership of a U.S. producer, both companies sought to leverage the purchase commonality between them on a global basis. In fact, this expected purchase commonality was one of the main factors behind the merger. Unfortunately, most original equipment manufacturers (OEMs) in the transportation equipment industry operate regionally, which the supply base is structured to support. Much to its disappointment, a majority of this company's global supply projects resulted in regional agreements and lower total savings due to a lack of global suppliers.

Some supply managers say that their suppliers are simply not willing to participate in global supply agreements due to the intense demands that globalization places on them. Although global supply management is often thought of as an internal process, support from external suppliers is a vital part of the equation. The strategy development process demands a realistic assessment of global supply markets and supplier capabilities (presented in greater detail in Chapter 10).

CONCLUDING THOUGHTS

Supply leaders should no longer view global supply management as an emerging philosophy. The pursuit of competitive advantage requires the development of processes and strategies that must become an integral part of our supply management efforts. The business case for integrated global supply management should not be in question today. Let's not waste time arguing for something we know to be good.

It is now time to move to the execution phase of this debate. The next four chapters explain in detail the importance of a formal process for developing global supply management strategies; the factors that define global supply management success; the characteristics that define a leading global supply management organization; and case examples featuring supply organizations that are pushing global boundaries. Although making the business case for global supply management is one thing, understanding the critical differences between international purchasing and global supply management, as well as understanding how to evolve *beyond* basic international purchasing, is an entirely different matter. After reading the next four chapters, there should be no excuse for not understanding how to capture the benefits from this complex yet necessary approach to sourcing. And there should be no doubt that global supply management offers the opportunity to better manage supply chain risk, another outcome that should be of interest to almost everyone.

REFERENCE

1. R.J. Trent and R.M. Monczka. International Purchasing and Global Sourcing—What Are the Differences? *Journal of Supply Chain Management* 2003 Fall; 39(4): 26.

10

DEVELOPING GLOBAL SUPPLY STRATEGIES

Although global supply management has not received the attention it deserves from executive leadership or the academic community, it will receive increased scrutiny as organizations search for new ways to compete. And because most supply organizations do not have well-developed global strategies in place, improvement opportunities are attractive and largely unrealized. Make no mistake about a very important point here. The core of global sourcing (and the larger domain of global supply management) is the articulation and execution of well-crafted strategies. If supply strategies are so essential to global success, then it makes sense to understand well the concept of strategy.

This chapter approaches global supply strategy from several perspectives. First a basic body of knowledge as it pertains to global supply strategies, including the importance of objectives and goals as well as the factors that create boundaries around strategy development, is presented. The next sections discuss the characteristics of effective strategies and the need to follow a structured approach when developing global strategies. The chapter concludes with the story of one company's awakening and journey toward global supply management. By the end of this chapter, readers should have a solid appreciation of the important interrelationship between a formal strategy development process, well-articulated strategies, and global supply management success.

UNDERSTANDING THE CONCEPT OF SUPPLY STRATEGIES

All functional leaders need to understand the concept of strategy and strategy development. Unfortunately, a strong argument can be made that supply managers have lagged in their development of strategies compared with other groups, particularly finance and marketing. Part of this is due to the reactive and often lower-level reporting status that exists in many purchasing organizations. Purchasing, a functional designation that some organizations no longer even use, simply reacts to requests for goods or services from internal customers. A clear indication that a supply management group has elevated its activities is the presence of well-thought-out and rigorous strategies that are often formalized through supply contracts. Increasingly these strategies must become global strategies.

Most individuals define *a strategy* as a longer-term plan. Although a plan is an important part of a strategy, for our purposes this definition is incomplete. A timeless definition views the definition of strategy, whether expressed or implied, as a conceptualization by organizational leaders of the long-term objectives or purposes of the organization; the broad constraints and policies that currently restrict the scope of the organization's activities; and the current set of plans and near-term goals that have been adopted in the expectation of contributing to the achievement of the organization's objectives.[1]

This is a fairly easy definition to summarize. An effective strategy essentially includes objectives, constraints, plans, and goals. The plans that are essential for carrying out any strategy are also called tactics. But having a vision about some global objectives is not enough. Executive leaders must also understand how to achieve that vision through action. Supply managers must clearly articulate their objectives, goals, and plans through global supply strategies.

Strategy development occurs at different levels. These levels, similar to a continuum, include corporate, business unit, functional, and departmental strategies:

- Corporate strategies define the businesses in which a corporation expects to participate and the allocation of resources to those business units.
- Business unit strategies are concerned with the scope of each business and its linkage with the corporate strategy. Strategies at the business unit level are also concerned with how a business unit achieves a competitive advantage. Increasingly, global supply strategies need to be a part of the business unit strategy level.

- Functional strategies define how the various functional strategies will support business level strategies as well as the strategies of other functional groups.
- Departmental strategies are the lowest strategy level and are a level of strategy that is not that applicable when discussing global supply management. These lower-level strategies, however, must recognize and endorse any global strategies that are in place.

The Importance of Strategy Objectives and Goals

One thing that should become evident after reviewing the definition of strategy is the important role that objectives and goals play within strategy. The problem when talking about the terms *objectives* and *goals* is they are often used interchangeably. A leading dictionary defines an objective as something toward which effort is directed. This definition goes on to say that an objective is an aim, goal, or end of action. This same dictionary defines a goal as an end toward which effort is directed and then tells us to see the word *objective*. Is it any wonder that we often use the terms interchangeably? Substitute the definition of one term for the other and it is highly unlikely the masses will rise up in protest. It just doesn't work that way. For our purposes, we want to draw some clear distinctions between the two terms. As they appear in this book, the terms *goals* and *objectives* are specific and different. They are not interchangeable.

When thinking about the differences between objectives and goals, it might be best to think of objectives as *aspirations* to be worked toward in the future. The major feature of an objective is that it provides broad direction, a direction that is often articulated by executive leadership. The key word here is *broad*. Objectives point organizational participants in a general direction, whether that direction deals with reducing costs, improving quality, enhancing the corporate image, or shortening cycle times, to name but a few possible directions. Goal setters use the broad direction provided by objectives to create specific achievements or accomplishments, i.e., the *goals* that must be realized by some future date. Ideally, goals align with objectives as articulated by supply management leaders. The bottom line here is that objectives drive goals, and goals make objectives actionable. It is difficult to overestimate the important linkage between objectives and goals within the strategic planning process.

Here is a non-supply example that illustrates in no uncertain terms how the difference between objectives and goals works. In the early 1960s, John F. Kennedy boldly proclaimed that the U.S. was going to send a man to the moon. If that statement had been all he said, we would have construed that his words related primarily to an objective. His proclamation was an aspiration that provided broad direction—space travel to the moon instead of pointing us toward

Mars or Jupiter or the sun. As some might recall, President Kennedy elaborated further on his strategic vision. He went on to say that we would accomplish this feat by the end of the decade and that we would bring this person safely back to earth (instead of leaving him there to perish). What the president did was to provide a strategic aspiration that was combined with a challenging goal. The rest, as they say, is history.

Also important is having an understanding of the distinction between goals that represent *activities* and those that represent *accomplishments*. Returning to the earthly world of supply management, reducing material costs and improving supply base quality by a specified amount, if achieved, represent tangible accomplishments. Conducting five Kaizen improvement sessions each quarter with suppliers is clearly activity focused. Although stressing activities over accomplishments is probably not in our best interests, most strategic planning processes feature both. The problem with activity-based goals is they often create a false sense of security. After all, prevailing wisdom tells us that certain kinds of activities are good, so performing those activities should naturally lead to good outcomes. We know this logic does not always hold true. Far too often we claim activities as victories while ignoring the essential need for tangible accomplishments. Global supply management is a tangible world that must deliver hard results.

Global Supply Strategy Constraints

All strategies, including global supply strategies, have internal and external constraints that create boundaries around what we can and cannot do. So, what is a strategy constraint? A strategy constraint is something that places a check or restriction on our ability to pursue some action. Certainly most people would assign a negative connotation to the word constraint. But in reality a constraint should have a neutral connotation, although admittedly something that constrains us is usually not viewed very positively.

Internal constraints. On the internal side, existing corporate policies and objectives are possible constraints that place boundaries on global supply strategies. For example, an emphasis on doing business with true global suppliers might conflict with a corporate policy that mandates doing business with smaller and disadvantaged suppliers. Because procurement is primarily a support function that serves internal customers, the strategic plans of other functional groups can also impact the global supply process. Additionally, the extensive use of longer-term regional contracts can constrain your global aspirations if a large percentage of expenditures is already tied to these agreements. Although this should come as no surprise, the internal constraint that might have the greatest effect on your global aspirations is the availability of critical resources. The development of global strategies inevitably requires financial resources, particularly for travel and living. For example, a commodity management team that performs site visits to suppliers will require budget support for travel and living. Operating an international purchasing office (IPO) will add a fair amount of overhead to the corporate cost structure. And access to individuals with the knowledge and skill who are capable of developing rigorous global strategies will remain a challenge for the foreseeable future. As mentioned in subsequent chapters, the shortage of qualified participants will continue to be a serious internal constraint facing most supply organizations. Another internal constraint includes negotiated labor contracts that contain restrictive language regarding outsourcing or agreements that prohibit suppliers from performing on-site services for the buyer.

   External factors. External factors can also affect the development of global strategies. For example, supply strategies are sometimes developed as a response to competitor actions. (Shouldn't we be sourcing in China if our direct competitors are sourcing in China?) Remember from Chapter 1 that economic factors impact supply strategies because of the increasingly global nature of supply markets. Currency changes, available capital, global interest rates, the forces of supply and demand, and worldwide growth all influence supply strategies. Another external factor includes domestic and foreign laws and regulations. For example, some countries expressly prohibit the use of consignment inventory, a popular approach used in North America when attempting to manage working capital. And let's not forget about the external demands that customers place on supply management. Many suppliers have grown because of the demands placed on them by their customers. A customer that expands its operations to Europe will influence how its suppliers form their growth strategies if the buying customer also expects the supplier to provide support within that region. And let's not forget that a primary objective of many supply alliances is to influence the technologies and strategies that suppliers develop in the future. Customer demands across all parts of the value chain influence supply strategies. Your customers influence your strategies, and your strategies influence your suppliers' strategies, and so on down the line.

   Several absolutes exist here: constraints create boundaries around our actions and, whether we want to admit it or not, all strategies are constrained at some point. Consider an example that illustrates the effect that constraints can have on global supply strategies. Boeing endorsed a model for its new Dreamliner aircraft that featured extensive outsourcing of entire systems to entities that the company called its global supply partners. Unfortunately, Boeing's union thought this model went a bit too far and went on a 52-day strike, a strike that cost $100 million a day in lost revenue and further pushed the first Dreamliner flight behind schedule. (Later in this chapter, we use an example to illustrate how one company realistically assessed the factors that would promote and the factors that would inhibit the development of global strategies. These factors then influenced the development of its global supply management process.)

Characteristics of Effective Global Supply Strategies

If an important part of global supply management involves the development of global strategies, then how do we know if our strategies are any good? The trick here is to recognize the set of characteristics that define effective strategies. Fortunately, experience and research reveal that effective strategies share some important characteristics. Effective strategies:

Are the result of an iterative process. Effective strategies result from an iterative process (involving different groups) that reflects the organizational rather than the functional nature of global supply management.

Match opportunities with resources. Effective strategies provide a proper match between opportunities and resources. Putting just about any strategy or plan down on paper is easy. But it's much more challenging to back up those strategies with resources, something that effective strategies routinely do.

Align with corporate objectives. Effective global supply strategies support and align with original corporate objectives. But they are not developed in isolation. They are drafted (at least partially) by those who are responsible for their attainment, which is a critical issue when seeking buy-in of a global strategy from site-based personnel. Too many corporate supply strategies receive a less-than-enthusiastic reception at individual operating sites or locations. Poor reception of a corporate strategy can become even more of an issue when the agreement is global in scope and involves suppliers that are totally new to the personnel who must rely on those suppliers.

Provide operational guidance. A critical feature of effective global strategies is they provide operational guidance to supply managers across an organization. In many ways the strategy development process helps establish a common understanding about the global supply process. (Chapter 13 features a supply organization that uses its global strategy development process to coordinate dozens of buying locations around the world.)

Are dynamic. Effective strategies are also dynamic and subject to review or change as conditions warrant, something that has really hit home over the last several years. Because most global strategies are formalized through longer-term contracts, supply managers must be vigilant in their efforts to manage or modify these agreements and always know when these contracts are due to expire.

Demonstrate performance results. Perhaps most importantly, well-executed strategies result in a wide range of performance outcomes that demonstrate that the global supply strategies are capable of providing new sources of corporate value. The performance outcomes from these strategies should be reviewed at the highest executive levels.

GLOBAL SUPPLY STRATEGY DEVELOPMENT

A primary characteristic of global supply management is the cross-functional nature of strategy development. In many respects global strategy development is an organizational rather than functional process. This statement is easy to make because our global sourcing research reveals that almost two thirds of companies say they extensively involve different functional groups during the development of their global supply strategies. Only 10% say that different functional groups are largely not involved when developing global strategies.

Integrated strategy development occurs in a number of ways. The use of commodity teams with a cross-functional representative is the most common approach. Integration can also occur through participation in a global sourcing steering committee or through strategy coordination and review sessions. Global sourcing research reveals that almost half of all companies rely on regular strategy coordination and review meetings that involve worldwide supply managers. Field visits reveal that many of these meetings involve other functional groups, particularly finance.

The development of global commodity strategies usually involves participants from different sites or locations, particularly when a small central group exists or the need for buy-in from different sites is essential to success. Global sourcing research also reveals that over half of all companies have representatives from different locations extensively involved during the development of global supply strategies. Almost a third say that representatives from different locations are somewhat involved in the development of global supply strategies. (Chapter 11 explores this involvement further.)

An issue related directly to global strategy development concerns the authority that teams or corporate sourcing managers have to develop contracts that operational sites must use. During the 1990s, compliance to contracts developed by commodity teams was often voluntary. In fact, many business units and sites used corporate contracts as benchmarks to compare against their own agreements. As a result, national suppliers (the agreements developed during this period were rarely worldwide) complained that they were not receiving the volumes they expected, which adversely affected the suppliers' cost and pricing structures and sometimes resulted in legal actions being taken by suppliers against their buying customers.

The issue of voluntary vs. mandatory contract compliance by sites and operating units is essentially a nonissue today. Research reveals that lower-level buying organizations and locations are required to comply with companywide purchase agreements at over two thirds of companies. Furthermore, supply leaders use their contract repository system as a means to verify and report local compliance to global agreements to executive management. Using this system to validate compliance is a global supply management best practice.

An important consideration when developing global supply strategies involves conducting something called *a spend analysis.* In our experience, supply organizations that are actively pursuing a global supply model have already accomplished two important tasks:

- They have segmented their total purchase requirements into commodity groups or categories.
- They have identified their total purchases across their commodities or categories.

We do not want to trivialize the effort required to accomplish these tasks. Even though the effort to segment and quantify total purchase requirements is usually extensive, do not underestimate the importance of these tasks when developing global supply strategies.

When identifying global supply opportunities, an important consideration is the determination of the percentage of purchase requirements that are available for sourcing *at that point in time.* The issue of whether global suppliers even exist usually comes later in the process. One supply leader calls the percent of a commodity that is available for sourcing globally as the "source-able" spend. (Referring to our earlier discussion of internal constraints, remember that some supply organizations that have actively pursued regional longer-term contracts might find that the volume that is available for global review is somewhat limited.)

Besides determining the "source-able" spend, another consideration involves the availability of global suppliers. One company's strategy development process involves a classification scheme to identify and then segment suppliers by their geographic capabilities. This designation helps when searching information databases for potential suppliers. In fact, any internal supply group at this company, whether it is involved with global supply management or not, can benefit from this classification when searching for potential suppliers. Although this system is far from perfect, especially because some suppliers might be difficult to categorize cleanly, this approach helps strategy development teams better understand supplier capabilities. This approach also makes the strategy development process more efficient. The classification scheme includes:

- *Local supplier:* A local supplier serves only a limited number of sites or buying locations (often only one) within a country. The database should include information about the country and the sites the supplier is capable of serving within that country.

- *Domestic supplier:* A domestic supplier can serve any location within a country. The database must note the country the supplier can competitively serve.
- *Regional supplier:* A regional supplier competitively serves the countries within a single region (e.g., regions such as North America, Latin America, Asia-Pacific, and Europe). Some suppliers might also serve only a portion of a region.
- *Multiregional supplier:* A multiregional supplier can competitively serve two regions.
- *Global supplier:* A global supplier can competitively serve at least three regions. In reality few truly global suppliers exist today.

A supplier does not have to own facilities in all geographic regions or countries to be designated a global supplier. The defining characteristic of a global supplier is whether the supplier can competitively support a country or region from its asset base. With that said, most suppliers find they have to "buff up" their assets and locations before they can lay claim to having true global supply capabilities. As an example, logistics providers often acquire other logistics providers to expand the services they offer and to extend their geographic reach. More and more industrial customers want "one-stop shopping."

A Leader's Approach for Developing Global Supply Strategies

Without question, virtually all supply leaders follow a defined or structured approach for developing global supply strategies. Most of the strategy attention in supply management to date pertains to developing contracts, which has now evolved toward a focus on developing global contracts that are almost always formalized with written agreements. Although contracts are a tangible output from the strategy development process, not all global strategy efforts involve the development of global supply contracts. For example, supply managers could develop strategies for increasing supplier involvement in product design, strategies for measuring supplier performance, or strategies for developing global information systems. Regardless of what kinds of strategies are being developed, research findings are clear: successful supply organizations follow a structured approach when identifying global opportunities and developing strategies. Global sourcing and supply represents the pinnacle of their strategic efforts and effective strategies are evidence of those efforts.

Companies that develop global strategies, or any strategy from a centrally led level, usually have some sort of process that involves a sequence of steps. The process might include as few as 5 steps or phases or as many as 16 (although the

Table 10.1 A Best Practice Global Supply Strategy Development Process

Step 1. Identify Global Opportunities
An executive steering committee identifies supply strategy development opportunities that offer the best return.
Step 2. Establish Strategy Development Teams
The steering committee creates teams with members from worldwide locations participating. The committee provides resources as required.
Step 3. Evaluate Global Opportunities and Propose Strategies
Teams validate the assumptions underlying the project; determine if qualified suppliers exist; verify current volumes and expected savings; evaluate current design specifications; and present preliminary supply strategy recommendations to the executive committee for review.
Step 4. Identify Internal Requirements and Develop Supplier Proposals
Strategy development teams prequalify suppliers and develop the RFP.
Step 5. Forward Proposals to Prequalified Suppliers
Teams forward proposal requests to six suppliers, on average, with responses expected within 6 weeks.
Step 6. Evaluate the Technical and Commercial Merits of Proposals
Teams perform a commercial and technical evaluation of supplier proposals and conduct supplier visits as required.
Step 7. Negotiate with Most Qualified Suppliers
Teams develop a negotiating strategy with improvement targets. A smaller team negotiates with suppliers at the buying company's U.S. headquarters.
Step 8. Award Contract(s) to Selected Supplier(s)
Information concerning the awarded contract is communicated throughout the company. The steering committee reports expected savings to executive management and finance.
Step 9. Manage Transition to New Contracts and/or New Suppliers
Load agreements into the appropriate corporate and contract management systems. Teams manage the transition if the supplier and/or part numbers change from previous agreements or designs.
Step 10. Monitor Supplier Performance and Review Expiring Contracts
Performance measurement systems assess supplier performance and validate savings. The contract repository system notifies supply managers of expiring agreements 6 months prior to expiration.

process that originally had 16 steps now has far fewer). Table 10.1 summarizes a process used at a leading supply organization to develop global contracts. The process in Table 10.1 is a home-grown process that has proven to be highly effective over time and is ideal for illustrative purposes. In our experience, no single approach or process is suited to all supply organizations when developing global strategies or agreements.

Process best practices. The process featured in Table 10.1 also contains some best practices that are not immediately obvious:

- Perhaps first and foremost, an executive steering committee takes an active role in overseeing this process and sponsoring global initiatives. (The clear relationship between executive support and global success appears in several places over the next several chapters.)
- Executive managers make budget funds available to support travel and living expenses for team members when they are developing supply strategies (removing the complaint from functional managers that supporting the process affects their budgets).
- The executive steering committee requires strategy development teams to meet specific milestones before the teams can proceed to the next step. Teams must present their progress to an executive steering committee on a regular basis as well as post their status on an intranet. Visible status reporting introduces a form of subtle control that ensures that the globalization process moves steadily forward. Please raise your hand if you enjoy standing up in front of an executive committee and making excuses for doing nothing over the last several weeks. It is easy to see why this requirement encourages team members to stay active.
- Lessons learned sessions are also conducted after the completion of each project to identify what went right and what went wrong. Lessons learned sessions also address ways to improve the development process, an endeavor that aligns nicely with an objective of continuous improvement. Results of the lessons learned sessions are summarized and communicated to other project teams electronically. Communicating lessons learned is a critical feature of a learning organization, something that most organizations are striving to become.

Some supply organizations create a structured approach from scratch that is specifically used for developing global supply strategies rather than extending previous development approaches, while other supply organizations simply adapt their existing commodity or regional strategy development process to include global opportunities. When an existing commodity or regional strategy is adapted, the global process usually places more emphasis on risk factors and total landed cost compared to the local or regional sourcing perspective. Also, logistical and communication issues often receive greater attention when emphasis is at the global level. Additionally, both the visibility that global strategies receive and the reporting level of strategy results should both increase compared with regional strategies.

Other supply organizations might lack the capability or the time to develop a global strategy process internally. When this is the case, these organizations often rely on consultants who specialize in global sourcing and supply. Several large consulting firms such as A.T. Kearney have made some serious money helping organizations develop global strategies following a defined process. Using consultants has the potential to speed up the development of a global strategy because consultants typically bring a structured approach to analyzing opportunities and developing strategies that has already been tested. Consultants can also offer databases of potential global suppliers and various tools to support the process. Each supply organization has its own opinion concerning home-grown processes vs. relying on consultant-driven programs.

Asking the Right Questions

The development of global supply strategies requires asking and then answering some important internal and external questions. Table 10.2 presents some of the more relevant issues to consider when creating a global supply strategy and agreement. The list of issues is quite extensive.

Some of the most important questions in Table 10.2 relate to supplier evaluation and selection. Without question an effective supplier evaluation process is central to global supply management. Far too many executives fail to recognize that the supplier evaluation and selection process is one of their most important corporate processes. When extending supplier selection to a global level, the process takes on almost exponential importance. Why might that be?

The time and cost involved with developing and then rolling out a global supply strategy can be eye opening. Using a team of cross-functional professionals to analyze a supply market can take months. And does anyone really want to select a global supplier without first performing a detailed site visit? What if a supplier will service your organization from ten different locations? Won't the selection team or representatives from an IPO want to see firsthand the capability of each location?

Central to global supply management is the concept of supplier switching costs. The development of a global supply strategy almost always results in someone doing business with a new supplier. Unfortunately, we are unaware of any cost accounting system that summarizes into a neat account the costs it takes to transition from one supplier to another. Although switching costs might have an intangible quality associated with them, they are nonetheless very real.

Take it as an article of faith that the switching costs related to global supply agreements can be extensive. For example, we know that the time required for

Table 10.2 Asking the Right Questions when Developing Global Supply Strategies

✓	Do we have a defined process to follow when developing global supply strategies and agreements?
✓	Does the global supply process have involvement or buy-in from operating sites and buying locations?
✓	Is the opportunity truly global or is it regional or local?
✓	Do we know how much we are currently spending for an item or commodity? Do we have the necessary data to evaluate this opportunity?
✓	How much of the total spend is currently restricted due to local or regional agreements?
✓	Do we know which suppliers are currently receiving our purchase dollars?
✓	What is the longer-term forecast for this item or commodity?
✓	What suppliers are potential candidates for global supply agreements? What are their financial strengths and performance capabilities?
✓	What are the geographic locations of potential suppliers? What are their shipping points?
✓	Are potential suppliers willing to share cost data to support total cost analyses?
✓	Are potential suppliers willing to share other information that is important to a longer-term supply agreement and relationship?
✓	What are the risks associated with different supply options? Have we developed risk management strategies?
✓	What other benefits besides lower price are we looking to gain from a global supply agreement?
✓	What value-added services, such as new product design support, do we want suppliers to perform?
✓	Do we know the unique requirements of our internal operating sites and buying centers? Have we factored these requirements into our strategy development plans?
✓	Are finance, logistics, and technical personnel part of the strategy development process?
✓	Do we have a plan to carry out a proposed strategy and manage any switching that occurs from one supplier to another?
✓	Do we have a plan for continuous improvement after reaching an agreement with a global supplier(s)?
✓	What are the key performance indicators that will apply to this global supply strategy and agreement?
✓	Do we have personnel assigned to manage a supplier agreement and relationship after the strategy reaches a steady state?
✓	Have we developed total landed cost models?

one company to analyze global supply markets, evaluate suppliers, negotiate a contract, and then transition the affected locations over to the new supplier was 21 months! Not getting the selection decision right the first time can be a long and painful process. A mistake here might affect every operating location and buying center. But don't worry! It's not like the affected locations will complain about the suppliers the centrally led team selected on their behalf.

Now it's time to illustrate the concepts presented in this chapter by featuring a company that endorsed a decentralized approach in virtually all aspects of decision making. Although a decentralized model was responsive to the needs of the individual operating sites, unfortunately the company's current supply management model failed to capture the benefits that global supply management offers. The following discussion highlights the story of how Dennison Chemicals developed a global supply management process to guide the crafting of global strategies. (*Note*: Dennison Chemicals is a fictitious name. The actual company requests that its name not be used. The company does, however, produce chemicals.)

DEVELOPING A GLOBAL PROCESS AT DENNISON CHEMICALS

Each operating facility that comprised Dennison Chemicals' worldwide network produced the same chemical compound that was used in hundreds of industrial applications. The problem, and herein lies the motivation for wanting to create a global supply process, was that each facility made its own purchase decisions for equipment, services, and materials. So duplication of effort and higher costs were inevitable with the company's supply management model.

Producing a semi-finished raw material meant that the laws of supply and demand affected pricing and profitability at Dennison. When demand exceeds supply, everyone starts thinking joyously about their year-end bonuses. When a surplus of supply exists worldwide, the mood becomes gloomier and the bonuses are not so inviting. Dennison's fortunes were also tied largely to the fortunes of the industrial customers it served as well as the amount of capacity that competitors brought to the marketplace.

After several slow years, it should come as no surprise that corporate executives at Dennison concluded that the time had come to better control their fate. This meant getting a better handle on costs to help get though periods when pricing was weak and gross margins became smaller. Two major initiatives emerged from this desire. The first involved a global engineering initiative that sought to standardize engineering requirements within capital equipment and facility services. The other involved the development of a global supply management process that would have linkage to the global engineering initiative. Table 10.3 summarizes in some detail Dennison's global supply process.

Process Absolutes

After deciding to pursue a global supply model, executive leaders at Dennison formed a high-level team to develop a process for crafting global supply strategies. Interestingly, because Dennison's corporate staff was so small (the corporate purchasing staff consisted of a total of three people), the team also included several recently retired executives who brought extensive knowledge of plant operations to the process and were able to represent the interests of the plants. Other members included the head of corporate purchasing, an engineering representative, and an external consultant who was retained to advise the team.

Early on, the process development team came to agreement about a broad set of "process absolutes," essentially the principles that would guide the development and eventual use of the process. (Developing a set of guiding principles at the onset is recommended to anyone who is charged with developing a corporate process that will have broad visibility.) The process absolutes included:

- The global supply process will be centrally led, but ownership of the process cannot reside only at corporate headquarters. Site-based ownership and involvement are essential for success.
- Global supply management will be an organizational rather than a functional purchasing process. Support from operations, finance, and engineering, particularly as members on global project teams, is critical to success.
- A well-defined process to guide strategy development teams must be developed, distributed, followed, and continuously improved upon.
- The process will succeed only if it has executive and cross-functional support from an executive steering committee with responsibility for overseeing the process and identifying global supply opportunities.
- Project teams will pursue at least three strategy development projects simultaneously, with each project having an expected duration of 4 to 6 months. Once a team completes a project, the completed project will be replaced by another project as identified by the executive steering committee, which will ensure that the process is a continuous one.
- Part-time strategy development teams will see the process through to contract agreement, at which time the contract owner will implement and manage the agreement and the supplier relationship.

Table 10.3 Global Supply Management Process Phases, Tasks, Deliverables, and Tools

Process Phase	Key Tasks	Required Deliverables	Available Tools
Phase I: Define Strategic Opportunities	• Define company business requirements (CFST) • Identify strategic supply management global opportunities (CFST) • Estimate rough savings and performance improvement targets (CFST) • Prioritize global opportunities (CFST) • Select opportunities to move to Phase II (CFST)	• Prioritized list of opportunities with estimated savings (CFST) • Selected opportunities to move to Phase II (CFST) • Quantified project timing and savings targets (CFST)	• SAP purchase reports • Global project prioritization template
Phase II: Establish Project Teams	• Create global project team charter (CFST) • Select core members and team leader and identify ad hoc members (CFST) • Identify team resource and training requirements (CFST) • Establish project team reporting method and frequency to steering team (CFST) • Communicate improvement expectations to project team (CFST) • Communicate team membership and responsibilities throughout the company (CFST)	• Identified project team resource requirements plan (CFST) • Completed project team charter (CFST) • Identified communication and progress reporting requirements (CFST)	• Team charter template • Assessment of individual tem member skills and capabilities • Team planning checklist
Phase III: Conduct Supply and Market Analysis	• Identify current contracts and sourcing strategies (PT) • Assess current supplier ability to satisfy global requirements (PT) • Perform a detailed supply market analysis (PT) • Identify potential suppliers not currently part of the supply base (PT) • Validate savings estimates and identify likely strategy level (local, regional, multiregional, or global) (PT)	• Validated and refined savings targets (PT) • Determined if opportunity is global (PT) • Approval to move to Phase IV (CFST)	• Current supply/market analysis template • Listing of secondary information resources

Phase IV: **Formulate** **Global Supply** **Strategy**	• Survey internal customer to identify requirements (PT) • Qualify supplier candidates using RFI's (PT) • Finalize contractual issues and requirements (PT) • Further refine performance improvement targets (PT) • Complete strategy recommendation summary (PT)	• Strategy recommendation summary (PT) • Approval to move to Phase V (CFST)	• Supplier prequalification template for RFI • Total cost index (TCI) supplier analysis template • User contract requirement template • Strategy recommendation template
Phase V: **Implement** **Global** **Strategy**	• Develop, send, and analyze supplier RFPs (PT) • Perform site visits as required (PT) • Identify negotiating team member (CFST) • Develop and communicate to the executive steering team the supplier negotiating strategy (NT) • Conduct negotiations with supplier(s) (NT) • Review proposed agreement with the legal department (NT) • Load contract into contract repository (PT) • Develop contract roll-out plan (PT and NT) • Begin contract roll out (PT) • Establish the supplier's key performance indicators (PT)	• Written contract negotiation strategy (NT) • Signed global agreement (NT) • Contract and strategy roll-out plan (NT, PT)	• Sample RFP cover letter • Total cost RFP analysis template • Contract negotiation planning template • Site visit assessment guide • Contract templates • Currency risk management guidelines • Key performance indicator template • Roll-out planning checklist
Phase VI: **Review** **Performance** **and** **Continuous** **Improvement**	• Identify process and project lessons learned (PT, CFST) • Disband project team and transfer roll out and supplier management responsibility to supplier relationship manager (CFST) • Identify internal and external continuous improvement opportunities (PT, supplier relationship manager)	• Lessons learned document available for electronic distribution to other teams (PT, CFST) • Continuous improvement plan (SRM)	• Continuous improvement planning template • Lessons learned template

Note: Information in parentheses represents ownership for an item; CFST = cross-functional steering team, PT = project team, NT = negotiating team, SRM = supplier relationship manager.

Global Facilitators and Inhibitors

The steering team at Dennison first undertook a realistic assessment of the forces that would *inhibit* and those that would *facilitate* the development of a global process; then they began the development of global strategies. (Remember from earlier in this chapter that the point was made that strategies, including the process that guides their development, *always* face constraints of varying severity.) The facilitating factors included seven similar operating facilities; operating sites and purchasing personnel that reported to the same corporate executive; facilities that were responsible for meeting the same set of financial performance indicators; and a fully implemented ERP system in place. On the negative side, Dennison's decentralized operating structure and culture were not supportive of a process that usually required centrally led decision making and change; the operating sites were extremely diverse geographically with no purchasing integration between them; and minimal integration occurred between purchasing and engineering. The following discussion elaborates on these factors.

Seven similar worldwide facilities (positive). One challenge with diverse corporations is that the areas of overlap might not be great enough to justify taking a more coordinated view of worldwide sourcing and supply management. For example, a consumer products company with over 100 diverse operating units decided that in terms of direct materials, the sparse similarities between their units did not justify a coordinated or centrally led approach to worldwide supply management. Instead, this company focused on developing common processes, systems, and contracts for facility services. But lack of similarity was not the case at Dennison. Each Dennison facility engaged in primarily the same operating business, meaning that a great deal of commonality offered a great deal of potential global opportunities. Similar equipment, service, and material purchases across each unit made the argument for global supply contracts almost a no-brainer.

Worldwide facilities and purchasing reporting to the same executive (positive). The procurement group and the operating sites at Dennison reported to the same executive position at corporate headquarters. Having these different groups report to the same executive is a positive feature because this inidividual was the driving force behind globalization. This single executive had the authority to make his global vision become a reality without worrying about conflict between the functional groups that reported to him or conflict with other functional corporate executives.

Sites accountable for meeting a common set of corporate performance indicators (positive). Each operating site was responsible for achieving the same set of corporate performance indicators. The process development team viewed this as a strong positive. Having a comparable set of indicators made it easier for the team to convey the business case for global supply management. The development team could also show the site managers how expected savings would affect their personal performance indicators, particularly EVA.

A fully implemented ERP (positive). A fully implemented ERP allowed project teams to easily retrieve data about purchases, suppliers, and expected volumes across the operating sites. The development team expected this capability to reduce data collection and analysis by several weeks compared with earlier systems.

A decentralized operating structure and culture (negative). As mentioned earlier, Dennison allowed its sites to make key decisions, including supplier selection decisions. Clearly a global supply process would shift some decision-making rights away from the operating managers. Because global supply management requires a strong central group, the development team was concerned that any attempts at central control or coordination would conflict with the corporate culture.

Extremely diverse facility locations (negative). Dennison maintained operating sites in the U.S. (two sites) and one each in France, Great Britain, Brazil, China, and Australia. Although each facility produced the same chemical compounds (something that works in the favor of developing a global supply process), four issues caused concern within the development team:

- The geographic dispersion among the locations raised questions about logistical issues.
- Several locations operated in countries with restrictive import and export trade rules.
- At least one site generally resisted anything that came from the U.S. corporate office (we will let you guess which one).
- The global project teams would discover that few suppliers with true global capabilities actually existed.

Minimal purchasing integration between facilities (negative). Purchasing personnel who were spread across the facilities had no history of ever working together. This situation would likely be an issue when project teams included representatives from the various operating sites. Furthermore, would operating site personnel have the ability to visualize a supply network that is now regional or global rather than local?

Minimal integration between purchasing and engineering (negative). During development of the global supply process Dennison simultaneously pursued a global engineering initiative that sought to standardize engineering specifications and production processes between facilities. The corporate expectation at Dennison was that the global supply teams would eventually support this initiative. Furthermore, the development team expected the global project teams to be cross-functional with strong support from the engineering community. To date these two groups had no strong awareness of one another.

Small corporate purchasing staff (negative). A decentralized operating culture coincided with a small corporate purchasing staff, which meant few available resources at the corporate level to support the development of the global process. (As a comparison, a company of comparable size in terms of sales, but in a different industry, that also pursued a global supply model had 30 personnel in its corporate purchasing group.) Supply organizations in this position simply must become more creative in how they obtain the resources necessary to develop and then gain benefits from a global supply process.

Any organization that plans to pursue a global supply model should realistically perform a self-assessment. To not do so increases the risk that reality will provide some really nasty surprises when attempting to develop global processes and strategies.

Dennison's Global Supply Process

Like most organizations that start a global supply management journey, the formal process developed at Dennison focused primarily on developing global contracts—what we referred to as global sourcing. The objective at Dennison was to capture material savings and develop worldwide contracts as quickly as possible.

The process required about 3 months of discussion before it was presented to executive management for approval. Table 10.3 includes key phases, the tasks associated with each phase, the required deliverables, the various tools to support each phase, and what group has ownership of the various tasks and deliverables. Not all of the tools were available at the time the process was developed. This set of tools was what the development team believed would support each phase.

The process in Table 10.3, like the others presented throughout this book, includes some best practices that are worth emulating. In fact, supply managers at Dennison included many best practices that they had observed elsewhere—in particular, the intensive role that an executive steering committee plays within the process was critical to their success. The process also recognizes the importance of project teams. Every effort is made to address any issues that can affect success, including the development of a team charter so others do not challenge the team's authority to act. Recognition that the composition of a project team and a negotiating team might sometimes be different reinforces the important role that negotiation plays when crafting global agreements. Making continuous improvement a formal part of the process is absolutely essential.

CONCLUDING THOUGHTS

This chapter has some important objectives:

- To draw a strong link in the reader's mind between the articulation of formal global strategies and global supply management success
- To ensure that the reader does not underestimate the importance of a formal process when crafting global supply strategies

The second objective is so important that it appears in various forms in subsequent chapters.

At this point, we should be well versed regarding the business case for global supply management (Chapter 9) as well as understanding the importance of a formal process for developing global supply strategies. So, where do we go next? Chapter 11 presents a set of critical factors that define the difference between global supply management success and failure. Each factor is supported by research findings, reinforcing our confidence about their importance even more.

REFERENCE

1. R.F. Vancil. Strategy Formulation in Complex Organizations. *Sloan Management Review* 1976 Winter; 17(2): 1–18.

11

FACTORS THAT DEFINE GLOBAL SUCCESS

Desiring to pursue the highest levels of global supply management is not a matter of snapping your fingers and hoping that good things will magically happen. If it were that simple just about every purchasing group would be a world class global supply organization. And we know that's not the case. Rather than happening magically or by accident, excellence at the highest global supply management levels is the result of carefully executed plans by individuals who know what they are doing. They know what must be done to ensure success.

This chapter presents a set of critical success factors—factors that allow readers to better understand what it takes to make global supply management a reality. Paying close attention to these factors, which research reveals all relate to some very desirable outcomes, defines the difference between global success and failure. Chapter 12 translates many of these factors into a general set of characteristics. These characteristics provide a profile of what an ideal global supply management organization looks like.

GLOBAL SUPPLY MANAGEMENT SUCCESS FACTORS

Table 11.1 lists a set of factors that are critical to global supply management success. Each factor has a positive relationship to the outcomes that we want from our global efforts (outcomes that Chapter 9 outlined in some detail). Refer to these factors when thinking about what to focus on as your organization develops its global vision. In particular, pay close attention to the first three factors—access to qualified personnel; a formal and well-defined global process; and certain

Table 11.1 Global Supply Management Critical Success Factors

Critical Success Factors
➤ Access to qualified personnel
➤ A formal and well-defined global process
➤ The right organizational design features
➤ Ability to measure global savings
➤ Availability of real-time communication tools
➤ Systems that provide access to critical information
➤ Awareness of global suppliers
➤ Availability of suppliers with global capabilities
➤ Operations, manufacturing, and internal customer buy-in
➤ Preselection supplier visits

organizational design features. Although each factor presented in Table 11.1 is important to some degree, if we could only select three factors, these three would be at the top of the list.

Access to Qualified Personnel

One theme that consistently emerges when working with leading companies is the important relationship between access to qualified personnel and global success. In fact, when companies are asked to identify the most important factor that contributes to their global success, access to personnel with the right knowledge, skills, and abilities is at the top. But, guess what? When asked to rank the seriousness of problems that might affect global success, a lack of qualified personnel emerged as the most serious of a dozen potential problems. Respondents also identify different skill and ability levels across geographic locations as an important concern, something which can be an issue when forming cross-locational teams to develop company-wide supply strategies.

An inability to recruit qualified personnel can be a difficult barrier to overcome for several reasons:

- Most companies have procurement organizations that do a decent job of tactically managing transactions and material flows across a supply chain, but the knowledge and skills required at a global level differ dramatically from those required for day-to-day operational purchasing.
- Site-based individuals might favor familiar supply sources, a condition known as home market bias, when an awareness of global suppliers is required.

- Global supply management usually requires close collaboration between engineering and procurement. Unfortunately, a level of mistrust, often created by different objectives, knowledge, and skills, sometimes characterizes the relationship between these two groups.

Taking someone who is comfortable at a local level and placing him or her in an environment that demands global awareness can be a rude awakening. It's not that these people are unintelligent. It has more to do with placing people in an environment that is alien to them.

So what types of skills and abilities are required for the global supply management process? Unfortunately, if we were to ask ten experts to list the knowledge and skills that define supply professionals today, we likely would get ten completely different lists!

The following knowledge and skill set is based on focus group research with leading companies. Some skills are so taken for granted, such as the ability to communicate well, manage conflict, and demonstrate ethical behavior, that we will not elaborate on them. Ideally, global supply management participants have the ability to:

- Take a strategic rather than an operational or transactional view of supply management
- Manage nontraditional procurement areas, including services
- Manage critical supply relationships worldwide
- Understand strategic cost management rather than basic price analysis
- Work virtually and across time zones and cultures
- Understand the global supply management process and its objectives
- Be comfortable with using, and perhaps even developing, electronic sourcing and contracting systems
- Understand statistical analysis and fact-based decision making
- Work cross-functionally and cross-locationally
- Negotiate and manage global contracts
- Maintain an unbiased worldwide perspective

Staffing a global process with personnel with the right skills will likely require the development of high-potential individuals, the recruitment of talent from other functional groups or companies, and the recruitment of promising college graduates. Detailed and regular assessment of employee knowledge and skill sets must also occur, along with providing training tailored to the needs of individual employees. Companies might also have to build relationships with leading academic institutions. All of these things are done to satisfy one primary objective—ensuring that qualified participants are available to support global supply management.

Access to the right people is magnified in importance as companies take a global view of supply management. Mistakes or errors in judgment can have far-reaching consequences. Do not take this factor for granted or assume that qualified human resources are readily available.

A Formal and Well-Defined Global Process

Chapter 10 presented the importance of a well-defined global process within the context of developing global strategies. That chapter also presented several examples of the steps that companies follow when using their processes to craft global agreements. Similar to access to individuals with the right knowledge and skill set, never underestimate the important relationship between a formal and well-defined process and global supply management success.

When global supply managers are asked to identify the most important differences between their least and most successful worldwide efforts, they are adamant that their most successful efforts followed a well-defined approach or process. These individuals are also adamant that their least effective efforts did not follow a well-defined approach or process. Without question the development of a well-defined and adhered to process is a global supply management best practice. The findings are so clear in this regard that any arguments against this statement are an exercise in futility.

Organizing work around processes makes sense for a number of reasons. And these reasons apply quite well to global supply management. In fact, proponents of total quality management understand quite well the value of developing and then following defined processes. Well-developed and well-understood processes accelerate learning as participants across a company become experienced with applying a defined framework. Furthermore, processes can "build in" best practices that enhance the likelihood of success. (Chapter 10 presented a strategy development process and pointed out the various best practice features built directly into the process.) Processes are also repeatable, which helps ensure consistency. And, perhaps most importantly, organizations can document, measure, and continuously improve their processes. At a theoretical level there is a great deal to like about processes.

Taking a process view also helps organizations manage the conflicts or trade-offs that inevitably occur across a value chain, including across geographic locations. The activities that make up a process almost always cross functional and often organizational and geographic boundaries. Not all that much of the work that really matters today is vertical or functional in scope. Therefore, a process orientation must have as an objective the seamless movement of work and information across different groups. Assuming a process perspective also helps geographically diverse locations and units to adhere to a single process or approach rather than developing, and probably suboptimizing, individual approaches. Even decentralized organizations should benefit from the use of consistent processes across their decision-making units.

The Right Organizational Design Features

Various organizational design features directly support global supply aspirations. Organizational design, too often an afterthought that elicits a big yawn, is a broad term that refers to the process of assessing and selecting the structure and formal system of communication, division of labor, coordination, control, authority, and responsibility required to achieve an organization's goals.[1] Important design features that directly support global supply management success include centrally led decision making supported by strong executive leadership; the use of cross-functional teams to develop global strategies; an executive steering committee to oversee the process; international purchasing offices; and strategy review and coordination sessions. Ironically, a topic that often receives minimal attention consumes the most pages within this chapter.

Centrally led decision making supported by strong executive leadership. Whether we like it or not, global supply management is a process that is best managed from a centrally led level, and that means the presence of strong executive leadership. The terms *centrally coordinated* or *centrally led* do not necessarily indicate the presence of a large corporate procurement staff. In fact, the presence of a large central staff is sometimes of concern to operating or business units as they think about loss of control, longer-decision making times, and a bureaucracy that is far removed from where the day-to-day activity occurs. Central coordination can occur across regions, business units, sites, and other functional groups through various design features that have little to do with a massive physical presence of people residing at a central location.

The emphasis on centrally led or centralized sourcing governance, coordination, and decision making is evident today. Consider the following statistics, which reveal the extent to which companies adhere to center-led or centralized authority and governance:

- Almost 60% of companies say their overall business unit is structured and governed centrally; 39% say the business unit is decentralized with some coordination; and only 2% indicate their business unit is decentralized.

- Over 51% of companies say supply strategy decisions for their business units are now made from a worldwide perspective; 33% take a regional perspective.
- Over 70% of companies indicate that purchasing and supply management decision-making authority is centralized or highly centralized.

Intense pressure to reduce costs brought about by increased global competition is something that separates this current focus on central control from previous periods. And this focus is not likely to shift back toward decentralization any time soon. Most companies recognize that they cannot indiscriminately raise prices for finished goods. This situation demands the coordination of supply activities and the consolidation of purchase volumes in an effort to minimize total supply costs. The challenge becomes one of effectively coordinating and leveraging worldwide supply requirements while still remaining responsive to the needs of business unit and operating sites.

Planning and execution levels are often different within a centrally led supply model. In fact, just talking about having a strong centrally led effort is only half of the story here. We know that site-based control of operational activities is also an important consideration. A model that is becoming increasingly common is to separate strategic activities, which are often associated with planning, from tactical activities, which include carrying out various decisions or tasks.

Figure 11.1 shows how one leading supply organization separates centralized and decentralized responsibilities. This company divides responsibilities into strategic and tactical. This model implies both reporting and physical separation. Separating strategic and tactical groups makes sense for several reasons:

- The skills required to support strategic and tactical thinking are vastly different.
- Few people can operate comfortably in a strategic and a tactical environment or switch easily between one mode and another.
- Operational or tactical activities must be satisfied first in a decentralized model, leaving less time for longer-term planning and strategy development.
- Decentralized models feature minimal coordination and often the suboptimization of strategies, procedures, and operating best practices across worldwide locations.

The separation of responsibilities should be clear. Centralized activities usually include developing category or commodity strategies; negotiating and establishing contracts; locating potential supply sources; evaluating and selecting company-wide suppliers; managing important supplier relationships; and managing supplier development and early involvement activities. Responsibilities

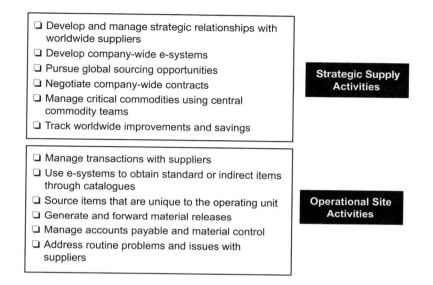

Figure 11.1. Separating Supply Management Responsibilities.

that generally remain decentralized include executing schedules and inventory plans; expediting goods and services; issuing releases or purchase orders; planning inventory levels; and developing requirements schedules. When pursuing a model that separates responsibilities, care must be taken to avoid the perception that two classes of employees now exist or that one group is better or more important than the other.

The importance of strong executive leadership is also an important part of a model that best supports global supply management. It's hard to imagine achieving your global objectives without an executive leader who has the skill, authority, and resources to translate a global vision into reality. An executive leader is often a chief procurement officer, but engineering and finance executives can also assume leadership roles in promoting a coordinated approach to worldwide sourcing. Companies that realize performance advantages from their global supply efforts have a higher-level executive officer who has accountability for global results.

The executive leader responsible for global success should make regular strategy and performance review presentations to the CEO and even the board of directors. One study found that having a company's CPO make regular strategy and performance presentations to the president (or CEO) correlated highly with an organizational design that helps companies achieve their supply objectives.[2] This is accountability at the highest corporate level.

The visibility and resources that come with having an executive position that is on par with other functional executives are critical. Because every functional group can argue the need for having a higher-level executive position, supply management executives must make the business case regarding why they should have a senior executive with resources that are on par with other functional executives. A successful global supply management process that demonstrates consistent results helps make that case. (Refer to Chapter 9 for information about how to make a business case that supports global supply management.)

Not all companies are comfortable with a centrally led approach to sourcing. When this is the case, executive managers should use their organizational design as a way to coordinate global activities without having to group purchasing professionals in a central location. These companies will maintain some purchasing activities at a decentralized level, particularly those involved with day-to-day materials and supply management, while creating organizational models that feature coordinated discussions between business units or operating locations. Rest assured, however, that the findings are clear regarding the relationship between centrally led decision making and global supply management success.

Use of cross-functional teams. Companies that pursue global supply management actively use teams, groups, and executive committees to develop strategies and to coordinate worldwide supply management activities. So just how widespread is the use of teams and groups? Around 80% of companies have implemented or partially implemented the use of cross-functional and/or cross-locational global supply management teams. (*Note*: Cross-locational teams are comprised of personnel from different locations.) The use of cross-functional teams to develop worldwide strategies correlates well with many of the performance outcomes we seek from global supply management. Although the use of teams is widespread, executive managers are encouraged to use global teams selectively and with careful attention to the issues that affect successful teaming. The use of teams as a design feature will remain popular, but a clear connection between teaming and higher corporate performance is not guaranteed. For example, relying on cross-locational teams to develop global strategies presents a number of challenges that central commodity management teams or regional teams might not encounter:

- Perhaps foremost, cross-locational teams often operate virtually, making communication and coordination tools critical to success. In fact, it is not unusual for team members at some companies to never meet face-to-face. These teams rely on web-based meeting tools, such as WebEx or Web Meeting, to coordinate team activities. When teams do meet face-to-face, the process is expensive and time-consuming.

- Cross-locational team members might favor suppliers from their respective regions when analyzing global supply markets, which could challenge team effectiveness. Identifying potential global suppliers, particularly in emerging regions such as China or India, can be difficult. Most companies are familiar with their local or domestic suppliers, but much less familiar with worldwide sources. At times team members have a degree of comfort with existing suppliers that can border on complacency.

- Cross-locational teams often have team members who do not appreciate the magnitude of the savings that are available for their sites or business units from global supply agreements, which affects their willingness to establish aggressive savings targets. For example, a site representative might perceive a 3 to 5% price improvement as being significant (many sites would welcome such savings today), but global agreements often result in savings of 20% or higher! Site-based representatives who participate on cross-locational teams might have a difficult time, at least initially, visualizing and committing to double-digit savings.

Executive managers should plan for and use teams selectively, always keeping in mind the barriers to the effective use of teams as well as the factors that affect team success. Regardless of the quality of the participants, global supply management is going nowhere if the participants lack the time to commit to the process. One study of cross-functional sourcing teams found that time was the least available resource from a listing of ten resource categories.[3] This study also found that the availability of time correlated the highest with effective teams when compared with all other resource categories. In other words, teams that had the time to pursue their tasks were more effective, on average, than those that did not have time. The importance of time is especially true for global supply projects because most companies use teams to support their global efforts. The question becomes how to make a scarce resource such as time more readily available to global participants.

Executive steering committee. The formation of an executive steering committee or council to oversee global supply management is an important way to show commitment to the process. For example, the steering committee at a leading electronics producer clearly reflects a commitment to globalization. This committee includes the vice president of research, the vice president of supply chain management, the corporate controller, the vice president of marketing and sales, and the vice president of information technology. Each committee member is responsible for championing a global project that relates to a major purchase category. During a recent planning period, the CEO, to whom the

✓ Prioritize and select global supply opportunities

✓ Sponsor a global team

✓ Solicit new global opportunities from around the company

✓ Provide required resources

✓ Remove barriers confronting global project teams

✓ Communicate, educate, and advocate the need for a global supply management process

✓ Meet with project teams on a regular basis to update and review in-process projects

✓ Develop team charters

✓ Validate and report the success of global initiatives

✓ Identify and appoint project team members and leaders

✓ Ensure linkages exist with new product and technology teams

✓ Establish project objectives and broad improvement goals

✓ Revise, review, and improve the global process as required

✓ Manage post-project lessons learned sessions

Figure 11.2. Executive Steering Team Roles and Responsibilities.

steering committee reports regularly, stated that the development of a global supply process was one of his primary initiatives. This pronouncement quickly resulted in support from functional managers, including a willingness to take on steering committee responsibilities. (Chapter 12 presents this example as a global best practice.) Figure 11.2 highlights the responsibilities of an executive steering committee at a leading company. As Figure 11.2 illustrates, this committee engages in some serious work. This figure serves as a guide for anyone who wants to identify the kinds of activities that an executive committee should engage in as it pursues its global supply initiatives.

International purchasing offices. A design feature that does not receive much attention among practitioners or academics involves the use of international purchasing offices (IPOs). IPOs are a formal part of organizational design and are expected to increase in importance as the scope of global supply management expands. Rest assured that progressive supply organizations have established IPOs in the geographic areas that are central to their supply success. (Chapter 3 discussed the value and role of IPOs in detail.)

Strategy review and coordination sessions. Global supply leaders should also promote the use of strategy review and coordination sessions. Strategy review and coordination sessions, which can be face-to-face or virtual, attempt to align different participants from around the world with a common global vision. (A company featured in Chapter 13 is a leader at using these sessions to create a common set of global objectives.)

These features are certainly not the only ones that can be put in place. They are, however, the ones that are expected to have the greatest impact on how well global objectives are attained. Do not take for granted that an existing organizational design is necessarily the right one for supporting a demanding set of improvement objectives.

The Ability to Measure Global Savings

At times it seems that the need to measure and report the savings achieved from global supply management comes across as self-serving. (Don't most of us have a psychological need to tell everyone in our company what a great job we are doing?) Unfortunately, the legitimacy of the claims regarding procurement savings is oftentimes challenged. After all, if procurement is saving so much money, where did it all go? Did the savings somehow evaporate before they reached the bottom line? This issue only gets worse as we migrate to the global level.

Supply leaders must have measures and systems that validate the real value of global supply management. Without an ability to show objectively the impact these supply initiatives have on corporate indicators, including bottom line performance, the benefits and the story behind global supply management often remain untold. Do not discount the importance of this topic. (Chapter 9 presented various ways to report the financial benefits of global activities.) Consider the following examples:

A consumer products company. An executive vice president at a well-known consumer products company maintains that one of his group's greatest failures is an inability to report the savings from his staff's global supply efforts to his CEO. Early on during the development of global supply strategies, the procurement group developed several methodologies to record savings by locations, projects, and contracts. The procurement group forwarded these numbers to the finance group for validation and eventually reporting, budgeting, and planning purposes. Unfortunately, the finance group did not think that validating the numbers was good use of its time so it declined to participate. Internal debate continues today about how best to report the true savings from globalization. As an aside, this experience did nothing to promote a better working relationship between procurement and finance. We are confident that the active involvement of the finance group within the supply management process is a best practice.

A worldwide industrial components producer. Frustration over the involvement of finance is completely the opposite at a worldwide producer of industrial components. Supply managers have developed an IT system, with finance group involvement, that provides visibility to all kinds of information that supports worldwide sourcing. A key feature of this system is its ability to capture all expenditures for direct and indirect items. After capturing a transaction, the system compares every price paid against a pre-established baseline price. Company-wide transactions over a 12-month period are captured, compared against baseline prices, aggregated across commodities and locations, and reported to executive management. Most importantly, the finance group signs off on the validity of the figures reported through this system.

Reporting the savings from global supply initiatives usually requires meeting three key requirements:

- Having a system that captures data from around the world (something that a later section discusses in more detail).
- Having the active involvement of the finance group. If you plan on "showing the money," then it makes sense to have the money people on your side.
- Having a higher set of metrics—metrics that show the impact of these global initiatives on corporate performance indicators. Traditional purchasing indicators are not going to work in a global environment.

The Availability of Real-Time Communication Tools

Global processes and initiatives cannot be successful without ready access to communication tools, particularly when participants are located across geographically dispersed locations. Virtual teams are becoming increasingly common within the global supply arena. For example, a team leader at a major producer of medical systems that relies extensively on global commodity management teams has never met a third of her team members. In fact, she does not even know what some team members look like.

Excelling in having ready access to communication tools requires state-of-the-art communication tools that allow real-time sharing of information and the coordination of global activities. Supply organizations that rely extensively on real-time communication tools are more likely to realize a wide range of desirable performance outcomes, particularly in the areas of an improved supply management process and better inventory management. Real-time communication tools include web-based meeting software, electronic mail, video conferencing technology, telephone conferencing, and face-to-face meetings. The link between state-of-the-art communication tools and a set of desirable global outcomes means that supply management leaders must not ignore this important factor.

Systems that Provide Access to Critical Information

Hard to imagine is a successful global supply project that does not provide its participants with access to complete, reliable, and timely information. If systems are available to make this information available, then the process should flow that much better. (Global projects can be a real data hog.) Examples of relevant information include a listing of existing contracts and suppliers; reports on supplier capabilities and performance; projected worldwide volumes by commodity or category; information about potential new suppliers (including their global performance capabilities); internal customer requirements; and common requirements across buying units.

A key resource that supports global strategy development is access to relevant and timely data. During the early days of aggregating purchase volumes, spending 6 months simply trying to identify total purchases for a commodity was not unusual. Now, almost two thirds of companies (and these are primarily larger companies) say that relevant data such as the total spend for a commodity, the total volume requirements, and the different volumes across internal locations are available for important goods and services on a worldwide basis. Only 12% indicate they lack the necessary access to the required data for important goods and services. The remainder says that the required data are somewhat available.

Although some companies still struggle from a lack of relevant worldwide data, other companies have developed information systems that they rapidly find to be an indispensable tool. For example, a Midwest enterprise found that a sourcing and contracting system helped reduce data collection time for a certain commodity from 40 days to 1 day and overall strategy development costs by 95%. The widespread development of enterprise resource planning systems that include a suite of supply chain applications makes access to data less of a constraint compared to just a few years ago.

Perhaps the most important feature of whatever kind of system that is being used is its ability to capture all expenditures across operating units with comparisons against benchmark prices. These systems should also serve as a contract repository. As contracts come closer to their expiration dates, supply managers receive an automatic notification about the need for reviewing and reestablishing global agreements as required, a best practice feature of these systems. Expiring agreements should come as no surprise. How many contracts are renewed automatically because the contract owner did not plan for the contract's renewal?

Another powerful feature of sourcing and contracting systems is their ability to identify common purchase requirements across buying units. Although it seems obvious that identifying common requirements across buying units affects global success, the reality is that many companies continue to struggle with this task. For example, an energy company that has different IT and coding systems across its vast array of worldwide locations committed 6 months to simply trying to determine what it purchased in total and then identifying what each operating unit purchased by commodity grouping. Supply managers eventually had to ask suppliers for help identifying what the company had purchased.

Not unusual for larger companies is growth through mergers and acquisitions. Although the newly combined units often have similar purchase requirements, they rarely have compatible contracts, systems, or material coding schemes. In fact, for companies that engage in global supply management, after social culture and laws, part numbering and coding systems have the lowest degree of similarity across operating units. We conclude that having a common part-coding scheme is not essential, but having the ability to identify common requirements or material groupings across buying units is critical.

As noted earlier, global supply management demands vast amounts of data and information, making the systems that provide that information a real asset. One way to ensure that participants have access to that data is through the development of a data warehouse and other systems that make information available on a worldwide basis. A data warehouse is a collection of integrated, subject-oriented databases designed to support a specific function. A database is a large collection of data organized especially for rapid search and retrieval. In a data warehouse, each unit of data is relevant to some moment in time and contains atomic data and lightly summarized data.[4] (Atomic data represent the lowest level of process analysis data stored in a data warehouse.) Effective sourcing and contracting systems feature easy access to the right kinds of data.

A supplier information management (SIM) platform is an example of a system that will increasingly support global supply management. SIM 10 (developed by Aravo Solutions of San Francisco) is an on-demand tool that creates supplier dashboards that are loaded with supplier information. The system pulls together information from diverse systems and also incorporates third-party data and supplier-provided information. These data are then summarized into a centralized master data repository for easy access through supplier dashboards by anyone around the world with the need to know. Information technology is only expected to grow as a great enabler of global supply management.

An Awareness of Global Suppliers

Very much related to accessing critical information is the need to have a specialized type of information—information about potential global suppliers. Identifying potential global suppliers, particularly in emerging sourcing regions such as China or Eastern Europe, can be challenging. Most companies are familiar with their local or domestic suppliers, but are much less familiar with worldwide sources, particularly in more obscure regions of the world. And, as discussed earlier, most companies usually have sites that have a high degree of comfort and loyalty to their existing supply base.

One way to gain insight into worldwide suppliers is through RFIs (or requests for information). An RFI is a process to collect information about the various capabilities of potential suppliers. At one leading company, RFIs involve generic questionnaires that ask global suppliers about their sales, production capacity, quality certification (such as ISO 9000), familiarity with the buyer's business, and major customers. An RFI also includes a signed introductory letter from a corporate executive that outlines various global supply goals.

One leading manufacturer of transportation equipment has put an extensive RFI process in place to collect data and information about its potential global suppliers. Using a database of worldwide suppliers purchased from a third party (supplier databases are available from a number of sources), the project teams use RFIs to gather detailed supplier information. Project teams can use these RFIs to provide volume estimates to suppliers. They can also tailor the RFIs to meet the specific needs of the category or segment under review. It is not unusual for this equipment manufacturer to forward 400 to 500 RFIs during a global supply project, depending on the project's complexity. The supply managers view the RFIs as an important source of information and the first major filter in the global process. Using RFIs has also helped to overcome the regional biases and preferences that were affecting the equipment manufacturer's global projects. Although data collection about potential suppliers has involved an intensive work effort, these RFIs have forced the manufacturer's teams to consider previously unknown supply sources. (Fortunately, the amount of digital information that is readily available about supply sources should make an awareness of potential sources less of an unknown.)

The Availability of Suppliers with Global Capabilities

Achieving higher levels of globalization, at least as it pertains to global contracting, is difficult when only a few suppliers with global capabilities are available. For example, several years ago, an executive at a major electronics company stated that although global supply management was a worthwhile pursuit, the reality was that few *truly* global suppliers existed in his industry, which forced his company to pursue primarily a regional supply model.

For our purposes, we define a global supplier as one that has the ability to competitively satisfy a buyer's *worldwide requirements* in terms of design, cost, quality, delivery, etc. The designation of global supplier, however, does not necessarily mean that a supplier has operations all over the world. The important relationship between global suppliers and global supply management success becomes evident when examining the aftermath of a merger between a U.S. and European manufacturer.

From almost the first day that the European producer assumed majority ownership of the U.S. producer, both companies sought to leverage the commonality between them on a global basis. In fact, a primary argument put forth to financial analysts prior to the merger was the expected global synergies between the companies, particularly in procurement and engineering. But, unfortunately, most suppliers in the industry lack global capabilities or are structured to compete regionally.

Most original equipment manufacturers (OEMs) in the U.S. company's industry operate regionally, which the supply community is structured to support. Although the European supplier, for example, might have a regional representative or business unit in the U.S., the global decision-making authority or knowing how to shift from a regional to a global perspective at the supplier might not be clearly understood. The U.S. supplier representative is also likely accustomed to making regional decisions, but not accustomed to relying on or working with the European corporate office to make global decisions (and vice versa).

Much to management's disappointment, the lack of globally qualified suppliers has resulted in more regional rather than global agreements. The savings from the supply management process are about half the average savings at companies that develop global agreements with truly global suppliers.

Even suppliers with true global capabilities might not have an interest in participating in global agreements. Consider the case of a company that operates worldwide facilities that produce similar products.

A key objective during each global supply project is to identify suppliers that can competitively satisfy the material requirements of each facility. By entering the sourcing market as a single customer, the buying company expects suppliers to provide uniform standards, specifications, consistent quality and logistical service, and uniform pricing to every internal location. The supply managers also expect suppliers to maintain worldwide electronic linkages with each of the buyers' locations. Furthermore, this buying company expects double-digit price reductions compared with previous agreements, which may be difficult for suppliers to accept or support. The demands placed on global suppliers often far exceed those required of local or regional suppliers and deter some suppliers from participating.

It should be obvious by now that global supply management works best with global suppliers.

Operations, Manufacturing, and Internal Customer Buy-In

Given the importance of having global supply management as a centrally led process, a major concern is gaining buy-in to new suppliers, contracts, systems, and processes from operating and site-based personnel. Although this issue is not as great a concern as it was just a few years ago as operating sites become more familiar with their company's global objectives, a lack of buy-in to the global process and any resulting contracts still can present hurdles. But it's a safe bet that because of the nature of the global process that some locations will have to use new suppliers or make changes to the way they operate. So the acceptance of change will continue to be an important issue.

Involving users or operating personnel in a global process has two dimensions:

- Involving users at buying centers and possibly even internal operating sites or using locations
- Involving nonpurchasing functions such as marketing and engineering

But why should users and other interested parties have a voice or involvement during the development of global agreements or globally standard processes? First, local sites must agree to use any selected suppliers so it makes a great deal of sense to gain buy-in to any agreements or changes. Second, site personnel are a supplier's true customers so it's important to represent their interests throughout the development process.

How to involve internal users and customers is a complex question. And different models exist to gain their involvement. One leading supply organization designates an individual to represent the interests of multiple sites and to act as a liaison between global project teams and operating centers. Another model features an executive steering team that represents internal groups. In this model, functional executives represent the needs of various groups, such as operations, marketing, and engineering, and steering team members communicate with regional or local managers during global analysis.

Another creative way to involve users is to provide them with the ability to specify their requirements through an electronic contract template. In this approach, sites convey their requirements (perhaps for delivery, service, or warranty) electronically to a commodity or negotiating team. Negotiators consider these requirements when crafting a global agreement and might include an addendum that addresses the requirements of specific sites.

Also possible is creating global project teams comprised entirely of site personnel (although few supply organizations appear to endorse this approach). In this approach, the only support provided by a central group involves training, data, and budget support. A variation of this model features a single member from the corporate level, often acting as a project coordinator or leader, who works with participants from buying centers or sites.

Regardless of the model used, gaining buy-in to worldwide agreements is essential for ensuring that operating sites support the process and accept new suppliers. Particularly important is avoiding the creation of an "us vs. them" mentality that features competition between a centrally led group and the operating locations.

Preselection Supplier Site Visits

The pursuit of the highest levels of global supply management makes supplier evaluation and selection decisions considerably more complex and important. Given the performance demands placed on global suppliers, and the extremely high cost of switching suppliers after selection (remember that global suppliers usually receive longer-term agreements that can take a year or more to craft), the use of site visits to evaluate a supplier's capabilities is an important part of the global process. Site visits, however, require a major commitment of personnel and time, cross-functional support, and a budget for travel and living expenses. Visits to more than one supplier might also occur because site visits often determine the short list for final negotiations. Additionally, global suppliers almost always provide material from more than one shipping point or facility, which adds more complexity because buyers must evaluate multiple supplier locations.

Given the important relationship between site visits and doing business with the right suppliers, it is easy to see why supply leaders rely on IPOs to support this part of their global process. When a team visits a supplier, the team should evaluate a potential supplier's financial condition, global capacity, logistical networks, supply management practices, process capability, willingness to work with the buyer, and technology innovation. In short, the team should perform due diligence by acting as if it were buying the supplier rather than buying the supplier's capabilities. It's quite easy to discount or even avoid site visits, but in the long run a lack of rigor during supplier selection will have serious repercussions. The cost of making worldwide site visits is high, but the cost of making poor decisions is even higher.

CONCLUDING THOUGHTS

The factors described in this chapter will, on average, differentiate successful from less successful global supply organizations. If this chapter has come across as somewhat prescriptive, then we have succeeded in what we intended to do. Why guess about the tangible things that need to be done to take advantage of globalization when the legwork about these things has already occurred?

The success factors presented here are not the product of an overly creative imagination. They are the result of extensive data collection from hundreds of companies and interviews with leading supply management executives. Basing actions on supported logic will go a long way toward reducing the risks faced when undertaking an initiative as bold as global supply management. Supply organizations face enough risk during the normal course of their operations. Why make life harder?

REFERENCES

1. G. Hamel and C.K. Pralahad. *Competing for the Future* 1994. Cambridge, MA: Harvard Business School Press; as referenced in D. Hellriegel, J.W. Slocum, and R.W. Woodman. *Organizational Behavior* 2001. Cincinnati, OH: South-Western College Publishing; 474.

2. R.J. Trent. The Use of Organizational Design Features in Purchasing and Supply Management. *Journal of Supply Chain Management* 2004 Summer; 40(3): 4.

3. R.J. Trent and R.M. Monczka. *Cross-Functional Sourcing Team Effectiveness* 1993. Tempe, AZ: CAPS Research.

4. W.H. Inmon, J.D. Welch, and K.L. Glassey. *Managing the Data Warehouse* 1997. New York: John Wiley & Sons; 365–366.

12

CREATING A WORLD CLASS GLOBAL ORGANIZATION

Imagine being able to visit many different supply organizations, each of which is well along on its path toward global maturity. Imagine further that because of these visits you are able to walk away with an idea or two that was unique and valuable. And think how great it would be if you could compile these ideas into a package that describes a super global supply organization. Imagine no more. The time has come to articulate what a super global supply organization looks like.

The first sections of this chapter describe the characteristics of a leading global supply management organization. These characteristics are the result of dozens of visits to progressive companies across a broad range of industries. The second part of the chapter describes in more detail a variety of best practices observed at leading supply organizations. These practices reveal some of the innovative ways that leading supply leaders use to take a global vision and turn it into a global reality.

CHARACTERISTICS OF A SUPER GLOBAL ORGANIZATION

An obvious conclusion after reading earlier chapters is that many organizations have aspirations of progressing toward more advanced supply management levels. And many of these organizations should have these aspirations. A logical question then becomes what are the characteristics that describe global supply

Table 12.1 Designing a Super Global Supply Management Organization: Essential Characteristics

Executive Leadership
• An executive position has the authority and ability to translate a global vision into reality.
• Executive leaders work to gain participation and support for the global process and agreements from cross-functional groups and individual sites.
• Executive leaders recruit qualified cross-functional and/or site-based participants to be part of global project teams.
• Global supply leaders make strategy presentations to the executive committee and, on occasion, to the board of directors.
• Cross-functional leaders participate actively on a global steering committee or council.

Process
• A well-defined and understood process is in place that requires participants to establish goals, meet process milestones, and report progress to executive leaders.
• An executive leader or steering committee reviews and proposes process improvements as required.
• Global agreements are managed, reviewed, and reestablished as required.
• Lessons learned sessions are conducted at the conclusion of each project with findings distributed to worldwide participants.

Resource Commitment
• A wide range of information is made available to global participants, including forecasted volumes at each site; volumes by commodity or purchase category; current supplier performance; comparisons of actual prices to baseline prices, and data on potential suppliers.
• Executive leaders identify and make available critical resources, including budget and qualified participants, to support global initiatives.
• The global process involves individuals who have the ability to take a global rather than local or regional sourcing perspective.

Information Technology
• Contract repositories store global agreements and provide warning about expiring agreements.
• Data warehouses provide access to required data and information on a real-time basis.
• Support documents, guidelines, templates, and project updates are maintained on a company-wide intranet.

Organizational Design
• Cross-functional project teams are responsible for the detailed analysis of global opportunities and the development of strategies and agreements.
• A formal executive steering committee or council identifies high-potential global opportunities and oversees the global supply management process.
• An executive position is responsible for the success of a centrally led global process.
• IPOs support global supply requirements within specific regions, including site visits to prospective suppliers.
• Supply management personnel are (1) collocated with technical and marketing personnel during design and development projects and (2) linked organizationally to the appropriate global project or commodity teams.

Table 12.1 (continued) Designing a Super Global Supply Management Organization: Essential Characteristics

Measurement
• Finance representatives agree on methods to validate savings from global initiatives, including how to establish baseline prices and compare aggregated savings against preestablished targets.
• Supply representatives meet regularly with executive leaders to review savings from existing agreements and expected savings from in-process activities.

• Measurement systems support the calculation of:
  o Company-wide savings realized and expected-to-be realized from global agreements
  o The impact that global initiatives have on corporate financial measures (ROI, ROA, EVA)
  o The return on investment for individual projects
  o The impact that global suppliers have on site and buying location performance indicators

Communication and Coordination
• Project teams meet regularly, either face-to-face or electronically, to coordinate efforts and to update project status.
• Strategy review and coordination sessions occur between functional groups and across sites and buying locations to ensure understanding, alignment, and buy-in to global initiatives.
• Project teams report progress to executive leaders on a regular basis.
• Advanced communication and coordination tools are available, including audio and video conferencing technology and web-based meeting and collaboration tools.
• Information and global project updates are posted on a company intranet.

management excellence? And how can we benchmark ourselves against what this organization looks like?

Detailed visits with industry leaders have helped us identify a set of characteristics that describes a super global supply management organization. The ultimate characteristic, of course, is the generation of improvements that provide a steady stream of tangible returns. The ability to show results is what makes global supply management a results-driven process rather than an activity-centered process.

Table 12.1 presents a set of desirable characteristics that cluster into seven areas: executive leadership, process, resource commitment, information technology, coordination and communication, organizational design, and measurement.[1] Although few, if any, supply organizations demonstrate a majority of these characteristics, the profile in Table 12.1 serves as a guide when mapping out your global plans. This profile can also serve as a useful benchmarking tool.

Executive Leadership

We already know from earlier discussions that it's hard for a process as complex as global supply management to become a reality without having the involvement of an executive champion who has the ability to translate a vision into practice. In fact, one of the first questions asked when beginning early evaluations of a company's global capabilities is who will be the senior executive responsible for success?

Evidence is also quite clear that leading companies recognize the importance of having a higher-level individual who can communicate the global vision and then be accountable for its success. Laggard companies have not quite grasped this concept and often have difficulty identifying a specific individual who is responsible for promoting globalization. But having a formal position with an impressive title is not what is important here (although that does help capture the attention of other functional leaders). Rather, it is the *authority* and *resources* that come with a position that is on par with other functional leaders that matters.

One leading supply organization has demonstrated its commitment to global supply management by creating a formal position that is best described as a "sourcing czar." This man, a well-respected engineer with over 25 years of experience, works closely with an executive steering committee to prioritize global supply opportunities while also overseeing the process. He recruits team members, allocates budget to specific projects, helps teams establish improvement targets, meets with project teams weekly to update projects, and looks for ways to constantly improve the global supply management process. Perhaps most importantly, he is a highly respected individual inside and outside the supply management organization.

Executive leaders must be unwavering in their commitment to globalization, a commitment which can happen in many ways. For example, leaders can support the development of a well-defined global process; make staff and budget available to support global project teams; promote site and plant-level participation and buy-in to global activities and agreements; and stress the importance of global supply management to non-sourcing groups. In short, these leaders demonstrate their leadership and commitment through *action*, not talk.

A Well-Defined Process

As Chapter 10 noted, no single approach or process model exists to guide global strategy development or to oversee global supply management (and if a single super process does exist we have yet to find it). But after studying the processes that leading companies follow when pursuing their global agenda, it is possible to reach some macro-level conclusions. Even though five leading organizations might have five different approaches for pursuing global opportunities, effective global processes share some important features. It is these features that are noteworthy:

- The process must be widely communicated and understood. This communication can occur, for example, through strategy coordination sessions, something that supply leaders do quite well. The process then becomes the foundation for pursuing global supply management.

- Effective global processes have a designated owner, such as an executive or a steering committee, who has responsibility for reviewing and improving the process.

- The process approaches global agreements, which are tangible output from a defined global process, as a beginning rather than an end state. Global contracts are continuously managed, reviewed, and reestablished as required.

- An effective global process allows executive leaders to practice what Takeuchi and Nonaka term *subtle control* by requiring global participants to provide regular updates to executive management and to achieve stringent milestones.[2]

- Lessons learned sessions are conducted at the end of each project or major activity and results are forwarded to global team members and leaders. Lessons learned sessions involve asking questions about what went right; what went wrong; what was encountered that was unanticipated; what can improve the process; and what can be done differently during subsequent projects?

Even though the process might differ in structure and steps, effective global supply management processes should include all of the features just described.

Resource Commitment

A set of important but often-overlooked variables includes the resources that can promote or interfere with the translation of a global vision into effective practices. The availability of needed resources has the potential to separate marginally performing from exceptionally performing global organizations. The question then becomes which resources are likely to be the most critical to global supply management success?

Figure 12.1 presents a comprehensive resource set. Although any resource category can affect a global supply initiative, the resources that are usually the most critical are executive commitment; access to qualified participants; required

Job-Related Information
The information and data required to support global analysis and performance

Materials and Supplies
The routine materials and supplies required to support global activities

Required Help from Others
The services and assistance needed from others external to project teams but within the organization

Time Availability
The amount of time that participants can commit to global activities

Executive Commitment
The overall support that executive management exhibits toward the global process

Tools and Equipment
The specific tools, equipment, and technology required to support the process

Budgetary Support
The financial resources, not including salaries, required to support global team and tasks

Team Member Task Preparation
The personal preparation and experience of those who are part of the global process

Work Environment
The physical aspects of the work environment

External Participation
The support that customers and suppliers provide when involvement is beneficial

Figure 12.1. Global Supply Management Resource Categories. (Source: Adapted from L.H. Peters, and E.J. O'Connor. Situational Constraints and Work Outcomes: the Influence of a Frequently Overlooked Construct. *Academy of Management Review* 1980; 5: 391–397.)

services and help from others; time; budget; and information. Supply leaders recognize the importance of these resources and ensure that they are available before global initiatives even commence.

Adequate time. Having the time required to commit to global endeavors is an important but often overlooked resource. The availability of time remains an important concern because most organizations rely on team members who often already have other job responsibilities. Availability of time might not guarantee a team's success, but an absence of time will almost certainly guarantee less than optimal performance.

Help from outside. As with any process that relies on teams, availability of help from resources outside the team is often critical. Outside help might involve legal help when reviewing contracts; technical help when evaluating supplier proposals; regional help when evaluating suppliers; or site help when collecting data or securing buy-in to proposed strategies. The project team becomes the core group and those who are external to the team are formally identified as as-needed resources. A best practice is to identify the individuals who must support a global initiative even before forming a project team.

Budget funding. One leading company provides a travel and living budget at the time a global strategy development team is formed to alleviate the concerns of functional managers who are reluctant to use their budgets to support team expenses.

Information availability. Leading companies take the time to develop data warehouses and contract repositories to ensure that all participants in a global supply initiative have access to timely and complete data (a topic the next section addresses).

Information Technology Systems

It seems intuitive that data and information are vital to global supply management, but the reality is that some companies often struggle in this area. As already discussed, many companies grow through merger and acquisition, and although these newly combined enterprises often feature similar requirements, they rarely feature compatible contracts, systems, or part-numbering schemes. Industry leaders address this need for compatibility by creating global data warehouses that rely on common coding schemes for easier aggregation of worldwide requirements. The systems should also serve as contract repositories that provide advance notification of expiring regional and global agreements. Having the ability to perform a global spend analysis is likely just a dream without access to data and systems.

An important observation by the authors after working with dozens of supply leaders is that not having a common part-numbering scheme probably isn't a game-breaker, but it is critical to have a *classification scheme* that places similar requirements into commodity families, categories, or groupings. Leading companies assign a commodity or category code to every major item and service that is purchased by their business units. They also identify the most logical level for sourcing that item—whether it is local, by country, by region, or on a global basis. Easy access to information is essential when analyzing global opportunities.

Besides data warehouses and contract repositories, leading supply organizations rely extensively on web-based systems and intranets to make information seamlessly available to worldwide participants. For example, a company that is recognized for its creative use of information technology has placed a wide range of global support documents on its intranet. These documents include an on-line manual that describes the global supply management process; a global strategy development template; a contract terms and conditions checklist; a report that identifies the status of completed, in-process, authorized, and future global opportunities; a RFP (request for proposal) template; and currency risk management guidelines. This system also allows participants anywhere in the world access to information about approved suppliers.

Underestimating the role that information systems play within a global supply network is a serious mistake. Information technology has become the great enabler.

Organizational Design

As also discussed earlier, organizational design can be such a mundane topic that it often gets overlooked or taken for granted—an oversight that can have serious consequences, particularly because we know that having the right organizational features in place is vital to global success. (Chapter 11 presented the design features that are especially important to success so there is no need to repeat them here.)

The organizational design features that are selected should directly support your global supply objectives. (Recall from Chapter 10 that objectives are really nothing more than aspirations.) So if your objective is to gain better insight into the requirements of internal customers, then the collocation of supply personnel with other functional groups or their involvement on new product and demand planning teams will be important. Having an executive who reports one or two levels from the chief executive officer will support an objective of providing higher visibility to the global supply management process. A supply organization that would benefit from having a physical presence in different regions will also establish international purchasing offices (IPOs). A strong organizational design directly supports your most important global objectives.

Measurement

Progressive supply organizations give serious thought about how they will validate and report the savings achieved from global activities. (Reporting is usually to executive and site-based managers.) This validation usually involves the direct involvement of a finance group that has the authority to verify that actual prices are lower than a prior base price or are better when compared to market prices. Furthermore, progressive organizations, also with the active support of a finance group, report the impact these savings have on measures that capture the attention of executive leaders—measures such as return on assets (ROA) or improvements to working capital and cash flow. Taking this validation/reporting process one step further, progressive organizations also show how the savings from global agreements affect the financial performance indicators at individual sites, which helps create buy-in to the process from site locations (a factor that we know is critical to global supply management success).

Progressive supply organizations also rely on measurement to promote process consistency. Instead of reinventing a methodology for evaluating potential suppliers, buying locations can use assessment criteria and measures that are consistent company-wide, with local adaptation as required. Evaluating supplier performance can also occur using a common scorecard system that includes a defined measurement process and set of metrics. The benefits derived from measurement should be broader than simply aggregating cost savings.

Communication and Coordination

The dramatic increase in communication complexity clearly differentiates global supply management from international purchasing. Global participants are often located around the world, making real-time and face-to-face interaction difficult. Furthermore, participants might speak several languages and adhere to different business practices, cultures, and laws. When global participants are asked to identify the most important differences between their least and most effective sourcing efforts, they say their most successful efforts featured well-established approaches to communication and coordination while their less successful efforts lacked such approaches. Progressive supply leaders know they must address the communication and coordination requirements demanded by global supply management.

Operating at the pinnacle of global supply management requires a variety of approaches to manage communications. Examples include regular strategy review meetings; joint training sessions involving worldwide team members; regular reporting of project updates through an intranet; and state-of-the art video conferencing technology. A common approach for coordinating team efforts is to rely on scheduled conference calls, usually on a weekly basis. The inherent complexities of globalization demand systematic methods to overcome the barriers presented by distance and time differences.

Any company that has mastered even a simple majority of the characteristics presented in Table 12.1 will be hard to beat, at least as it pertains to global supply management effectiveness. Supply managers should use Table 12.1 to evaluate their progress by noting any deficiencies and developing plans to close any gaps. The items in this table are not the product of an overly creative imagination. They are the result of extensive site visits and interviews with leading supply managers who each provided a nugget or two of wisdom. It is time to put these little nuggets to work for you.

GLOBAL SUPPLY MANAGEMENT BEST PRACTICES

This section presents in more detail some best practices that support global supply management. We could present dozens of best practices, but the following provide a sampling of the ways that supply leaders support their global efforts.

By no means do these practices comprise a complete listing, but they do point out the intensity required to operate at the highest global supply levels.

Best Practice: Supporting Global Supply Management at the Highest Corporate Levels

Because global supply management is an organizational rather than a functional process, it seems logical to conclude that support from the highest organizational levels will go a long way toward making the process successful. And that is exactly what happened at a high technology company located in the eastern U.S.

The CEO at the company elevated the importance and visibility of the company's global supply process by publically stating that successfully launching a global supply process was one of his three *primary* corporate objectives. Publicly stating the importance of developing a global supply strategy (which quickly affected the business plans of the nonprocurement groups) helped ensure that the development process was supported throughout the corporation. The culture in this company is one in which major initiatives are successful when executive commitment is present.

Global supply management at the company also received executive support in other ways. At a quarterly business meeting, the chief procurement officer presented a formal overview of the process to worldwide managers. Other managers subsequently viewed a videotape of the presentation that described the global process in detail. The CEO also forwarded a memo to all salaried personnel announcing the need to support global supply initiatives.

The corporate structure included a high-powered executive management committee that included the company's top 12 executives. The vice president of purchasing reported monthly to this committee, further illustrating the visibility (and accountability) that the global process receives.

With executive support like this, it should come as no surprise that the global supply process is showing tangible results at this company.

Best Practice: Using Cross-Functional Teams to Support Global Supply Management

Using teams to support a purchasing and supply initiative is a common occurrence. But using a team approach does not mean that the teams are guaranteed to be effective or that they are certain to arrive at solutions that are better than those developed by other forms of organizational design. Rest assured, however, that the use of teams is not going away anytime soon.

Cross-functional teams play an integral role in managing the global process at a respected chemical company. At this company, an executive steering committee is responsible for identifying global supply opportunities and then chartering project teams to pursue those opportunities. Project teams include an assigned team leader and a facilitator who are expected to commit half of their professional time to team activities. The leader and facilitator report directly to the executive steering committee.

Team membership includes representatives from engineering, finance, purchasing, and various stakeholders. (Stakeholders might be a facility representative or someone from an international procurement group.) Purchasing directors, as well as the executive steering committee, also spend considerable time securing the involvement of members from outside the purchasing group. Outside involvement is essential to success because team members generally commit about 25% of their professional efforts to team activities. Although we can shout from the rooftops that global supply management is an organizational rather than functional process, engineering and finance directors are still being asked to part with some very valuable resources. And global supply leaders know they cannot take this support for granted.

Executive management expects project teams to perform a variety of tasks as they develop their global strategies, which in this case are finalized through formal supply agreements. These project team tasks include identifying the strengths and weaknesses of the various buyers and sellers in the marketplace. The teams also have the authority to redefine the initial goals that were established by the executive steering committee. During the project, the teams identify potential suppliers; manage the RFP process; finalize the criteria and weights used during supplier evaluation; make selection decisions; and negotiate a final agreement.

The level of empowerment granted to project teams is a key part of this process. Team members have the authority to make strategy decisions rather than simply making recommendations. External research reveals that groups and teams with external decision-making authority are more effective, on average, than teams that are simply asked to make recommendations that are then passed along to others.

Best Practice: Continuously Identifying and Reviewing Global Opportunities

An important part of global supply management involves identifying those opportunities that offer the potential for the highest payback.

Shortly after two major transportation equipment providers merged, attention turned to identifying global synergies between the two entities, partly to help justify to financial analysts the arguments for the merger. Searching for global commonality within procurement and engineering became an obvious opportunity area.

Taking a global perspective resulted in this newly formed company dividing its product line into six major groupings. (Electrical components and engines, for example, were two of those major groupings.) Using personnel drawn from the U.S and Europe, a combined team next divided total spending into two broad categories. One category was termed "relevant spend," which included all purchases within a major group. The second category was termed the "source-able spend." To be part of the global process, at least 70 to 80% of the relevant spend in a category had to be source-able. Some items might be committed to existing contracts and therefore could not be addressed or a design might be undergoing engineering changes that prohibited a global review.

After completing product segmentation and spend analysis, 27 global supply projects across the 6 major groupings were identified. (Project teams now apply this segmentation and strategy development approach to indirect purchases.) Executive leaders then formed cross-functional teams that pursued nine global projects simultaneously (known as a wave). Each project lasted 6 months with each team pursuing three global projects simultaneously, so three teams in a wave pursued a total of nine projects. After several years, the project teams reviewed the entire product structure and associated contracts. After completing the waves, which saved over $20 million annually, the teams shifted to reviewing the global contracts that were now ready for a second review and renewal. Supply managers found that continuously identifying and reviewing global opportunities created an intensity that helped ensure global supply management did not become the latest "flavor of the month."

Best Practice: Retooling the Supply Management Workforce

Without question, global success requires individuals who have the right knowledge, skills, and abilities to be active participants. Research evidence supporting this point should not even be the subject of debate.

A U.S. company that has historically operated in a comfortable regional market found itself facing intense global competition as it expanded its buying and selling operations worldwide. Avoiding a competitive disadvantage required employees who were capable of taking a global view of suppliers and supply markets, which unfortunately was a challenge here. (When a buyer in Tennessee thinks international purchasing means buying from a supplier in Ohio, it becomes evident that some workforce retooling might be in order.)

One area where the workforce needed retooling was the sourcing and supply group, a diverse organization with over 300 people. The vice president of strategic sourcing recognized the need for supply personnel to shift from a reactive, short-term, operational perspective to one that created value at the highest levels.

As a result of her vision, the supply management organization created a series of training courses that all supply personnel attend.

The curriculum, developed with the help of external educators, examined the topics where supply management professionals should be proficient. A sample of the training areas included cycle time management; process mapping and control; cross-functional/cross-locational teaming; supplier selection, management, development, and integration; supply strategy development; forming and managing suppler alliances; supplier quality management; longer-term contracting; strategic cost management; international purchasing; and supply chain changes and trends.

During the training sessions, participants worked in groups to present improvement ideas that related to class material, some of which had already become working initiatives within the supply management group. Employees also had to demonstrate their competency by taking a case-based midterm and final exam. Executive management recognized that achieving future competitive advantage required supply personnel who were at the forefront of mastering new knowledge and skills.

Overestimating the importance of the human element as it relates to global supply management success is difficult.

Best Practice: Providing Time to Pursue Global Opportunities

Anyone who has participated in a project in which the objective was to develop a global supply contract understands quite well how time consuming the process can be. The need to collect, analyze, and organize data from worldwide suppliers can be exhausting, particularly if the project is in addition to regular job responsibilities (which is often the case).

A progressive industrial company recognized that pursuing global opportunities across its procurement and design centers was going to be a time-intensive process that would challenge team members. In response, supply leaders at this company created a full-time business analyst position to manage the time-consuming tasks required within the company's nine-step strategy-development process. Each global project team had a business analyst assigned to the team to support it. Management at the industrial company also viewed the analyst position as a way to develop high-potential individuals. The position served somewhat as an on-the-job training assignment before the analyst progressed to managerial responsibilities.

Analysts are central to the success of the RFI (request for information) and RFP (request for proposal) processes. They compile and send RFI and RFP packages to suppliers; track and report response rates; submit data from suppliers into a database; and follow up with those suppliers that are late with their submissions.

A business analyst also serves as the point of contact for suppliers by answering any questions they have or by forwarding their inquiries to an appropriate team member.

A key responsibility of an analyst involves maintaining a software database developed specifically to support the global project teams. The analyst inputs the sourcing categories and subcategories that a team is evaluating into the database; establishes RFI and RFP records; and loads individual part numbers as they are received from engineers located in different design centers. The software provides a report that compares a supplier's quote to the best quote received.

The analyst also has responsibility for recording and reporting all data collected throughout the process. This individual attends team meetings and is present at supplier negotiations to provide information or data as required.

The availability of time is often the resource in shortest supply when cross-functional teams pursue their responsibilities. It is a simple fact of life that the most effective teams have the time necessary to pursue team activities. The lesson here is clear—global supply management is usually supported by teams, and these teams must have the time to perform the process effectively. Creating the business analyst position alleviates the burden of time-consuming and often mundane tasks.

Best Practice: Making Globalization Work within a Decentralized Culture

At this point, it should be obvious that global supply management is a process that is best coordinated at a centrally led level. But what do you do if your company is highly decentralized with dozens of different operating units that report into different profit and loss groups?

A well-known company made a strategic decision, due to limited commonality between its businesses, not to leverage direct materials across its diverse operating units. Upon closer inspection, however, corporate leaders concluded that the failure to coordinate the purchase of indirect items was working against their corporate interests.

To overcome the inefficiencies associated with a decentralized and regional sourcing model, corporate leadership established a Strategic Sourcing Council, which was headed by the corporate vice president of purchasing. Council membership included the vice president of corporate strategic sourcing; the director of process excellence; the director of Asia-Pacific sourcing; worldwide commodity directors; the director of strategic sourcing information; and the four chief procurement officers from the profit and loss groups. (To say this is a high-powered group is a gross understatement.)

This council meets monthly to evaluate the indirect purchasing categories that offer the largest payback from a more coordinated global perspective.

Specifically, the council's role is to agree on various supply strategies; identify where to focus team efforts; determine who should lead any worldwide projects; and develop the capabilities of its 600 worldwide purchasing professionals.

The decentralized culture that prevails here is one in which affiliates or operating units do not have to comply with company-wide agreements. The Strategic Sourcing Council spends considerable effort seeking input from the operating sites before proceeding with a global project. Typically, the chief procurement officers (CPOs) of the four profit and loss groups assess their initial interest in a global opportunity. If these executives believe an opportunity is promising, they survey the interest of the company's purchasing directors, a group that is quite powerful. If enough of the directors show an interest in the project, then a team is formed to pursue the opportunity. At this point, interest does not necessarily mean commitment. However, purchasing directors must state their intentions to commit to any subsequent agreement once RFPs are forwarded to suppliers. Project teams have to provide a reliable forecast to the suppliers.

Purchasing directors meet at corporate headquarters twice a year for a general meeting and business overview with the Strategic Sourcing Council. The chief procurement officers also meet separately with the purchasing directors, a part of the process in which detailed analysis occurs on proposed supply projects. Examples of worldwide projects this council has sanctioned include mill supplies, temporary personnel services, janitorial services, air travel, and hazardous waste disposal. Supply leaders estimate their global supply activities save $200 million a year in real savings (not cost avoidance). The Strategic Sourcing Council expects to address capital requirements such as compressors and generators, as well as facility services.

This section has provided a handful of best practices that illustrate how leading supply organizations back up their global visions with action rather than talk. As these examples make clear, globalization is so much more than buying from foreign suppliers. It is an organizational process that requires nurturing and support combined with innovation and commitment.

CONCLUDING THOUGHTS

Global supply management is a never-ending process of improvement and renewal. To believe otherwise invites the possibility of stagnation and decline. Appreciating the characteristics and best practices that typify leading supply organizations, which is the primary objective of this chapter, will help ensure that your supply group captures the benefits that an effective global process has to offer. Chapter 13 presents in detail what three leading companies are doing to capture these benefits.

REFERENCES

1. R.J. Trent and R.M. Monczka. Achieving Excellence in Global Sourcing. *MIT Sloan Management Review* 2005 Fall; 47(1): 24.

2. H. Takeuchi and I. Nonaka. The New New Product Development Game. *Harvard Business Review* 1986 Jan/Feb; 64(1): 137–147.

13

LEARNING FROM GLOBAL SUPPLY LEADERS

When thinking about the state of global supply management, the reality is that few supply organizations operate at the highest levels as defined throughout this book. Furthermore, the description of the highest level today will surely be modified tomorrow. Not so long ago using commodity teams to make buying decisions, replacing shorter-term contracts with longer-term contracts, and reducing the size of the supply base were leading-edge practices. And although many companies still need to do a better job at many of these practices, they are no longer considered leading edge.

This chapter discusses three companies whose global supply practices are worth understanding. The first company features a supply organization that has progressed from emphasizing worldwide contracts to one that features process consistency across its worldwide buying centers. The second case highlights a company that is at the forefront of communicating and coordinating a global supply vision across buying centers located in dozens of countries. The chapter concludes with describing a supply organization that has transitioned from a regional perspective to a truly global supply management organization.

EVOLVING TO THE HIGHEST GLOBAL LEVEL AT AIR PRODUCTS

The discussion in this section builds on the Air Products example presented in Chapter 1. As a review, Air Products, a leading industrial gas producer headquartered in the eastern U.S., operates air separation facilities worldwide.[1] (This case is based on extensive interviews with company executives and is a modified version of a case that appears in Reference 1.)

Over the last 15 years, industrial buyers increasingly viewed industrial gases as commodity items, which, along with intense global competition, created extensive downward price pressures. Although industrial gas prices have recovered somewhat over the last few years, the need to manage costs remains a timeless pursuit for Air Products.

Historically Air Products has operated in an engineer-to-order environment, which resulted in a great deal of engineering and design work being customized to each new air separation facility. Newly designed and constructed facilities were largely engineered without considering previous designs or leveraging commonality across design and procurement centers in the eastern U.S. and the U.K. Historically, even if the U.S. and Europe centers required a similar or even the same item (which was often the case), or designed the same facility in terms of its physical process and technology, each facility had components and equipment developed separately by engineers and procurement personnel who did not coordinate their efforts. As a result, design specifications differed unnecessarily due to a lack of coordination.

Executive management concluded that Air Products must pursue standard designs and off-the-shelf products on a global basis. A corporate objective was to enter the global marketplace as a single, integrated company. A major action taken to support this objective was the internal development of a coordinated global supply process—called the global engineering and procurement process (GEP).

Global engineering and procurement now focuses on opportunities that are identified by an executive steering committee. Each new production facility (built as a stand-alone plant or built onsite to feed a customer's plant with industrial gases) involves an extensive analysis between the U.S. and U.K. design centers to identify areas of commonality, standardization, and synergy in procurement and design. Cross-functional teams with U.S. and European members work jointly to develop common specifications and contracts that satisfy each center's needs while supporting future replacement and maintenance requirements.

As a result of the GEP, worldwide design and procurement centers have better aligned their strategies between themselves and with corporate business strategy. The GEP at Air Products has been so successful that its participants have been formally recognized by the CEO. This process provides a new source of competitive advantage to a company that operates in a mature industry.

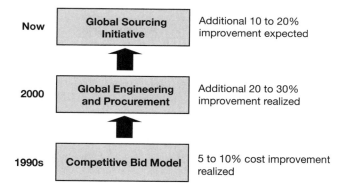

Figure 13.1. The Evolution of Supply Management at Air Products.

The Global Sourcing Initiative—the Next Generation of Globalization

Although the GEP represented leading-edge thinking at its introduction, competitive demands, along with a need for continuous improvement, are now driving the development of the next generation of global supply management, an evolving process that Air Products calls its global sourcing initiative (GSI). The GSI is defined as "a strategic process for procuring equipment, materials, and services that provides competitive advantage in the markets and geographies that we serve. This includes searching for, identifying, qualifying, and bidding/awarding business to suppliers who offer the lowest total evaluated cost on a global or regional basis." A primary objective of this process is to create consistency across worldwide buying centers. It is not about writing global contracts, which more aptly describes the GEP process; it's about supporting the sourcing of engineer-to-order (ETO) items that are part of the global engineering and procurement process.

The GSI provides a framework that complements rather than duplicates or eliminates other sourcing approaches. In fact, the executive steering committee that supports the global engineering and procurement process is the same committee that supports the global sourcing initiative. Each steering committee meeting now features updates on the GEP and the GSI processes. Figure 13.1 depicts the evolution and incremental savings from three sourcing perspectives.

GSI is a "front end" process that different groups use to identify, screen, and qualify promising new suppliers. It is a process that recognizes the importance of supplier selection on a worldwide basis. With a set of tools developed specifically for the GSI, this process recognizes the need to identify leading supply sources wherever they exist. Although the process is centrally led, worldwide sites play an

Table 13.1 The GSI at Air Products

Process Step	Definition	Available Tools	Data to Input
IDENTIFY	Buyer-initiated search for suppliers that have the potential to supply a specific requirement	Internet, *Thomas Register*, and trade journals	Name, address, telephone number, e-mail and website address, and commodity
SCREEN	Buyer-initiated data-gathering effort to validate supplier potential, including commercial review and initial technical assessment	Screen template, Z-score risk calculator assessment tool	Financial data, sales volume, D&B rating, manufacturing capabilities
PREQUALIFY	Buyer and commodity leader obtain and evaluate data to technically assess supplier capabilities for a given commodity prior to making a possible site visit	Prequalification checklist, commodity-specific template	Labor skill sets, IT capabilities, work processes, commodity-specific technical information
QUALIFY	Buyer and commodity leader validate prequalification data to allow for Air Products sites to bid the supplier with risk management plans; award business if the supplier provides a proposal that conforms to the technical and commercial requirements of a specific bid opportunity	Commodity-specific template, site visit guide (if necessary)	Informational needs determined on a commodity-by-commodity basis to fully qualify a supplier
APPROVE	Supplier is technically and commercially acceptable and used successfully on a previous project	Purchase order	Project close-out report

integral role when identifying needs and participate in the screening, qualifying, and approving of suppliers.

Table 13.1 summarizes the process that underlies the GSI: identifying, screening, prequalifying, qualifying, and approving suppliers. A major output from this process is a worldwide approved supplier list that is available to buyers and sourcing teams for use when developing critical and high-priority commodity strategies. Executive leaders expect the GSI to deliver new value across three major areas:

Strategic supplier relationship management. Developing collaborative relationships with key suppliers is an important corporate objective. These suppliers often have global capabilities and provide a high level of value-add, particularly in technology areas.

Support critical and high-priority commodities. The GSI steering committee works with internal business units to identify a high-priority "hot prospect list" that offers the potential for worldwide improvement. A cross-functional team is then assigned to identify and qualify new sources. Part of the output from this part of the process includes a database containing approved suppliers.

Developing product- and country-specific supply strategies. A GSI objective involves developing local sources with the ability to support country-specific expansion strategies, such as in China. At a minimum, Air Products expects to target local suppliers who have the capability to evolve into regional or even global suppliers.

Expected Performance Outcomes

Supply managers at Air Products are clear about their longer-term expectations. As with any major global initiative, the expected benefits are extensive and wide ranging:

- Supply managers expect the GSI to support a "one-company" supply process that provides maximum focus and efficiency across all buying centers and operating units.
- Supply managers expect this initiative to result in a company culture that values, recognizes, and institutionalizes a willingness to use new suppliers combined with a willingness to pursue new supplier development.
- The initiative is expected to support the corporate business strategy by accelerating the development of new facilities in low-cost countries by relying on local suppliers who are evolving globally.
- Lower prices are an expected outcome as current suppliers recognize that they might lose business if they do not accelerate their rate of performance improvement. Nurturing longer-term relationships with strategic suppliers, however, is still important.
- Better management of supply risk is a high expectation.

Making the GSI Work

A process as advanced as the GSI cannot become a reality without a set of process enablers. Air Products has committed extensive resources to ensure its global engineering and procurement process is successful, including a well-defined process; a committed staff; information technology support; and an executive steering committee with responsibility for overseeing the process. A full-time IT person has been assigned to support database design and input requirements. The willingness of Air Products to use web-based information technology to support its sourcing processes is clearly a supply management best practice.

A web-based knowledge management system serves as a repository of supplier information, including whether a supplier is qualified or approved. A *qualified supplier* can receive bids or proposals, but does not have a performance record with Air Products. An *approved supplier* is one that has consistently demonstrated high performance as an Air Products supplier.

Personnel from around the company add information to this database. Internal users have the ability to search the database for potential suppliers using commodity and design codes. The database also contains links to third-party information, such as Dun & Bradstreet reports, *Thomas Register* listings, and trade journals. Participants at any level or location can use this database to support supplier selection decisions.

One of the more innovative web-based features is a risk management tool that calculates Z-scores. The Z-score, developed by Edwin Altman, is a measure that predicts a supplier's financial health 2 years from the point of the data. A Z-score combines selected balance sheet and income statement data to numerically score a company's financial health. Buyers use Z-scores as a preliminary screening tool when evaluating potential suppliers. Sourcing managers can also use Z-scores to evaluate periodically the financial health of current suppliers. Besides the Z-score, the GSI process requires participants to identify nonfinancial risks and develop risk mitigation plans.

Although almost every enterprise with worldwide operations wants to pursue greater globalization, the reality is that many lack the understanding, size, capability, or willingness to achieve the more advanced levels. As Air Products recognizes quite well, globalization demands vision and leadership, a well-defined process, qualified participants, a supportive organizational structure, a focus on risk management, and extensive data and information technology support. The process must also support consistency on a global basis rather than simply taking a contract-to-contract sourcing approach. Perhaps most of all, the globalization process is one of never-ending improvement.

COORDINATING SUPPLY MANAGEMENT ACROSS MANY COUNTRIES

A common theme among leading companies is that a global supply process benefits greatly from a strong center-led or centralized structure and leadership, a

topic that other chapters have stressed. But what if your organization has historically maintained a local or regional focus with operations spread across dozens
of countries? Is it realistic to expect this type of organization to pursue a centrally
led global supply model? Let's look at how one U.S. consumer products' producer that spends over $6 billion annually with 7,000 direct and 20,000 indirect
suppliers manages its global efforts. (This case is based on extensive interviews
with company executives and is a modified version of a case that appears in
Reference 1. The company requests to remain anonymous.)

What makes this organization unique is that even though it has sourcing and
production operations in over 80 countries and sells in several hundred countries,
the diverse operating units have actively aligned their activities with a common
set of objectives, mandates, key initiatives, deliverables, practices, specifications,
and performance indicators. In other words, worldwide coordination and align-
ment is actively pursued even though most efforts are focused largely at the country and regional level. Even the name of the corporate sourcing group reflects a
focus on integration—the Global Materials, Logistics, and Sourcing Group.

The emphasis on local and regional decision making in this organization
directly counters many other supply organizations that are recognized for their
global prowess. Geographically diverse locations—and the organization's locations are about as diverse as one can get—rely on a set of common business
objectives and mandates; a seven-step strategic sourcing process; and common
information systems and data warehouses. Figure 13.2 presents the business
objectives and mandates that executive supply leaders have established for all
regions and locations to follow. This company is also known for its effective use
of strategy coordination and review sessions to align its worldwide operating
units with a common corporate vision. (Remember that earlier chapters referenced the importance of these sessions.)

Executive management expects its sourcing groups at all levels to help fund
and drive corporate growth. Funding growth occurs primarily through the development of supplier relationships that provide cost savings, while driving growth
occurs primarily through relationships that feature integration and innovation.
Let's take a closer look at how this all works.

Segmenting Worldwide Opportunities

The company segments its direct purchases into three primary levels when evaluating worldwide opportunities:

- *First level:* The first level relates to true global items, which are
  sourced at the corporate level using a seven-step strategic sourcing
  process. Although directors at the corporate level have few direct
  reports, they work closely with directors and managers located

throughout the world through a matrix-type organization when developing company-wide agreements. These regions and sites have responsibility for generating material releases and issuing purchase orders against centrally led negotiated contracts. Responsibility for paying suppliers also rests with the divisions or sites.

- *Second level:* Second-level sourcing features a reliance on lead buyers. A lead buyer represents the interests of various locations within a region for items that do not have a global application. The lead buyer is increasingly becoming an attractive design feature among larger, more diverse corporations as a bridge between globally sourced items and locally sourced items.

- *Third level:* The third sourcing level involves items that are unique or sourced strictly at a local or site level.

A corporate group manages high-dollar and critical items while regional centers handle noncentrally coordinated goods and services. Raw materials which are purchased in large quantities are obvious candidates for central coordination. Many other items, particularly packaging supplies, are obtained at a regional or local level. This segmentation approach is a supply management best practice.

A Seven-Step Strategic Sourcing Process

Sourcing leaders have developed a seven-step process that involves the finance group (another best practice; illustrated in Figure 13.3). Again, the importance of a defined process comes through in no uncertain terms. Involving the finance group early in this process centers on the need to identify and eventually validate the savings that must be achieved. It also recognizes that reviewing contracts late in the process leads to minimal value-add from the finance group. (The indirect sourcing group also applies this process when evaluating worldwide opportunities.)

The strategic sourcing process in Figure 13.3 is an example of developing common processes and approaches that apply to the corporate level as well as across different regions and locations. This process is used not only when developing company-wide strategies, but also when developing regional or country-specific strategies. Local representatives are involved directly when developing regional and global strategies. This is critical because we know that site involvement affects the success of global initiatives by ensuring buy-in to agreements that move beyond a country or region.

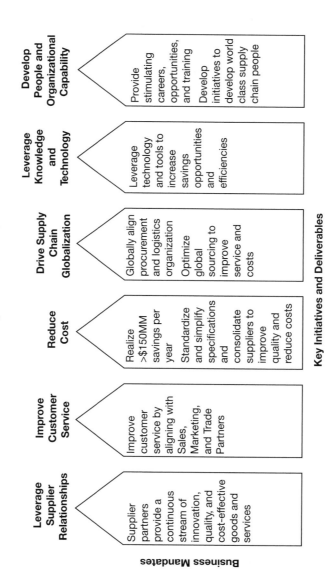

Mission: Provide a significant competitive advantage by being the best global procurement and logistics organization in the world

Objectives: Drive corporate growth; fund corporate growth; be the best place to work

Leverage Supplier Relationships	Improve Customer Service	Reduce Cost	Drive Supply Chain Globalization	Leverage Knowledge and Technology	Develop People and Organizational Capability
Supplier partners provide a continuous stream of innovation, quality, and cost-effective goods and services	Improve customer service by aligning with Sales, Marketing, and Trade Partners	Realize >$150MM savings per year Standardize and simplify specifications and consolidate suppliers to improve quality and reduce costs	Globally align procurement and logistics organization Optimize global sourcing to improve service and costs	Leverage technology and tools to increase savings opportunities and efficiencies	Provide stimulating careers, opportunities, and training Develop initiatives to develop world class supply chain people

Business Mandates

Key Initiatives and Deliverables

Figure 13.2. Global Materials, Logistics, and Sourcing.

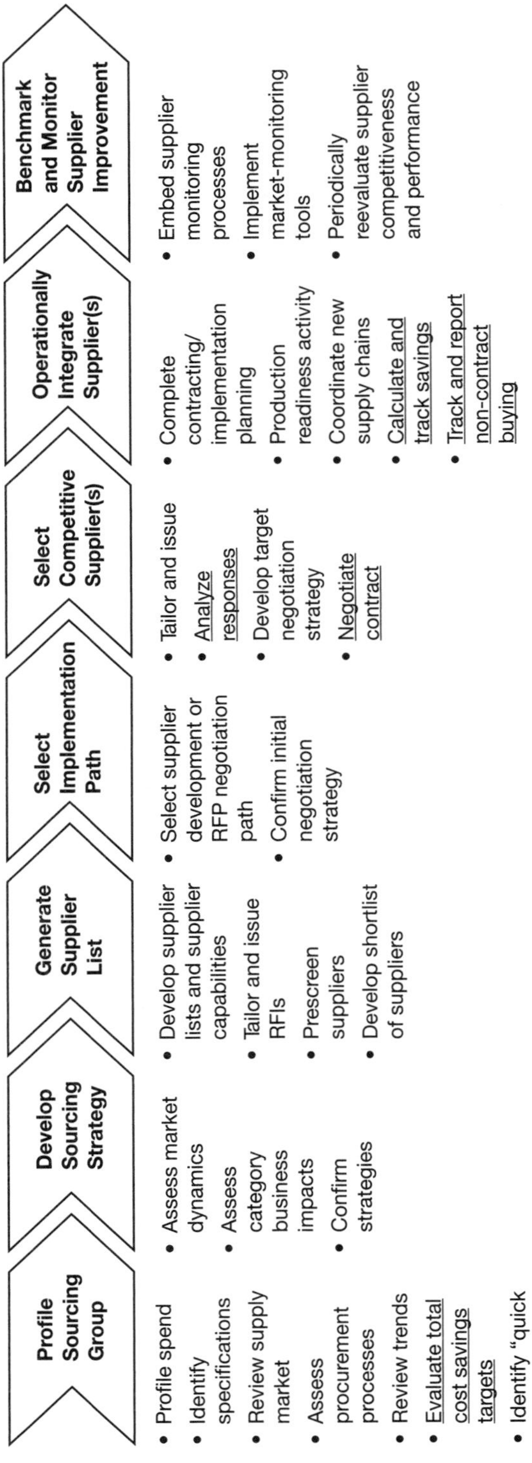

Profile Sourcing Group	Develop Sourcing Strategy	Generate Supplier List	Select Implementation Path	Select Competitive Supplier(s)	Operationally Integrate Supplier(s)	Benchmark and Monitor Supplier Improvement
• Profile spend • Identify specifications • Review supply market • Assess procurement processes • Review trends • Evaluate total cost savings targets • Identify "quick hits"	• Assess market dynamics • Assess category business impacts • Confirm strategies	• Develop supplier lists and supplier capabilities • Tailor and issue RFIs • Prescreen suppliers • Develop shortlist of suppliers	• Select supplier development or RFP negotiation path • Confirm initial negotiation strategy	• Tailor and issue • Analyze responses • Develop target negotiation strategy • Negotiate contract	• Complete contracting/implementation planning • Production readiness activity • Coordinate new supply chains • Calculate and track savings • Track and report non-contract buying	• Embed supplier monitoring processes • Implement market-monitoring tools • Periodically reevaluate supplier competitiveness and performance

Note: Underlined items involve the finance group.

Figure 13.3. Strategic Sourcing Process.

Global Systems Support

Another way that divisions and locations in this organization are aligned is through the use of systems technology. A global ERP system provides visibility to worldwide contracts for direct and indirect items. This technology enables the identification of direct and indirect items and commodities across divisions that have worldwide application. All six geographic divisions that form this company are now part of a common ERP system.

Supply managers have also developed a worldwide packaging and specification system that provides visibility into prices; real-time price comparisons; supplier expenditures; and worldwide usage. Prior to having this system, most packaging groups had no formalized packaging specification process. Do not underestimate the importance of providing timely packaging information to a global consumer products' producer.

The packaging and specification system also supports the development of packaging cost models by individual country. Software was developed that breaks out package build-up costs at every major supplier. This software supports making decisions from a total cost perspective. A business team spent 2 years developing the costing software, which requires regular factor updates. Fluctuating exchange rates, for example, require updating of the cost model on a frequent basis.

Suppliers understand that cost modeling is critical for doing business with this organization. Supply managers and cost engineers in one country can now model the cost of doing business with suppliers in other countries. This has helped reduce not only total packaging costs, but also the total number of suppliers that are maintained as sourcing groups increasingly search across borders for suppliers. Participants appreciate quite well the power of an information-enabled global process. Managing even the simplest tasks can be overwhelming if the value of information tools and applications is ignored.

Making Globalization Work—Some Examples

The following discussion describes how three very different corporate materials management groups at the organization are each pursuing their vision of global supply management.

Corporate leaders identified three areas—packaging, fragrances and flavors, and raw materials—as offering enticing opportunities for some great returns because each of them consumes some serious money. With over 10% of annual revenues being spent on packaging materials, for example, it does not take a rocket scientist to figure out that packing was one area that might benefit from new thinking.

Packaging

Before taking a company-wide approach to packaging procurement, the buying centers suffered from (please be seated so you're not too shocked here) a proliferation of packaging sizes, materials, and smaller, country-based suppliers. Although proponents of decentralization make some good arguments to support their beliefs, one argument they cannot make is that decentralization helps control all types of proliferation.

The corporate packaging director has few direct reports, but he interacts extensively with divisional directors worldwide through a matrix organizational structure. He maps out procurement packaging strategies and solicits new ideas from around the world. Packaging strategies and innovations are now extensively coordinated across geographic divisions.

Several times a year, divisional packaging procurement managers meet to review a list of improvement opportunities, develop packaging strategies, and identify the country or region that will lead each initiative. One example of an improvement opportunity involves packaging tubes. At one time, the various buying centers purchased 27 different diameters of package tubes. Today, six diameters satisfy the company's entire worldwide requirements. Simplification is a primary objective of the lean supply chain.

One of the corporate packaging director's primary objectives is to develop closer relationships with a smaller group of packaging suppliers, particularly in developing countries. A tangible outcome of these better relationships has been an increased willingness by some suppliers to invest in new plants to support business opportunities in new countries or regions. Qualified suppliers can also receive funds to begin operations. Interestingly, few longer-term contracts are used to obtain packaging materials, a clear departure from the practices of most organizations. Having fewer longer-term contracts allows enhanced flexibility to reconfigure the supplier network as needed.

Some decisions related to packaging occur at the corporate level while others occur at lower levels, which is consistent with the segmentation model discussed earlier. This company still maintains an informal corporate culture with a fair amount of autonomy at the regional, country, and site level. For example, each site has an individual who is responsible for package engineering. If a site sees an opportunity to work with a supplier that already supports another location, the inquiring site can contact that location to develop material shipment schedules.

Fragrances and Flavors

Most products developed by the company require fragrances and flavors. Local and regional control of fragrance and flavor development, however, has resulted in a proliferation of suppliers, fragrances, and flavors. The prectice has been for suppliers to work with their local contacts only, and even the internal compounding centers around the world did not communicate with each other. No ingredients for flavors and fragrances are produced internally, but all compounding (finishing) is performed in-house. Again, it's no big surprise that supply managers recognized the need to change how they manage this important purchase category.

Historically each subsidiary managed its own development and sourcing of fragrances and flavors. But a more coordinated approach now features the director of fragrance and flavors sourcing working extensively with the corporate Global Business Development (GBD) group to establish a worldwide fragrance and flavor strategy for each product category. The GBD group also works extensively with Research and Development (R&D). For example, a central group now identifies new fragrances and flavors and then works with GBD and R&D to develop the fragrance or flavor. The central group also performs extensive cost modeling.

As is done in each materials group and division, extensive strategy and product coordination occurs. New product forums are conducted three times a year with the participation of the director of fragrance and flavors sourcing. Six times a year technology grid reviews which involve the corporate sourcing director are held for each product category. Additionally, each region conducts reviews that are attended by the corporate director of fragrance and flavors. Top fragrance and flavor suppliers participate in an annual technology review meeting with product category managers. Extensive use of coordination sessions to manage fragrance and flavors development is a central part of the global process.

The company has also created a system that tracks every fragrance development project. Fragrance development occurs primarily in one of two ways: proactively through interaction between GBD and R&D and responsively through submissions from the regions. Regions can submit a "global brief" for a fragrance via the corporate system that initiates a trigger for corporate involvement. Local sites, however, can still select the fragrance that is best suited for local tastes. With supplier involvement and corporate support, the time required to identify an appropriate fragrance has been reduced from 11 to 6 weeks.

Before taking a centrally coordinated view of fragrance development, the company had built a portfolio of almost 900 fragrances. Now less than 500 fragrances comprise the worldwide portfolio. Perhaps even more dramatic, the worldwide supply base has been narrowed from 30 to less than 5 fragrance suppliers. Although the reduction in flavors has not been as dramatic, similar efforts to rationalize the flavors portfolio are well underway.

In addition to requiring less time to identify an appropriate fragrance, what other tangible outcomes have resulted from the rationalization process? Current agreements with the top fragrance suppliers feature a higher level of mutual trust and commitment; generalized rather than detailed contracts; shared assets; and joint development of new fragrances. Additionally, the closer relationships stress joint strategy and technology planning sessions, the development of joint performance measures, and greater risk and reward sharing between the parties. For those who are responsible for managing fragrance contracts, life smells sweeter.

Raw Materials

Of the three corporate materials groups featured in our discussion, the group that manages raw materials is the most centrally coordinated. The raw materials group centrally manages 26 major items that have been selected based on their total worldwide spend, availability, and if suppliers can provide material competitively across the globe. Although a central group is responsible for negotiating agreements for these global items, representatives from the various divisions help develop supplier requests for quotations (RFQs). Technical representatives are also involved when developing material specifications. The central group is also responsible for developing models that identify the total landed cost of obtaining raw materials across different locations and regions (a topic covered in Chapter 4). Logistics plays a major role in this cost analysis—and given the pressures that supply chains are under today, logistics should only intensify in importance. The close relationship between supply management and logistics management is another best practice.

A primary objective of the raw materials group is to optimize the number of specifications for raw materials. For example, at one point, silica had 12 different specifications. Now, the target is to have three worldwide silica specifications. Each item that is managed globally requires a plan to simplify the procurement process and to reduce (i.e., "commonize") specifications. Suppliers are involved in evaluating the feasibility of simplifying specifications. Although the process of reviewing specifications is not formally defined, participants understand this objective and the steps for reviewing specifications. Simplifying specifications aligns well with the business mandate of reducing costs.

A second objective of this group is to apply a similar set of best practices across each operating location—no small challenge considering that operating sites are located in 80 countries. Furthermore, conducting business in some regions is more difficult compared with others. African countries, for example, require extensive documentation to complete a transaction. As with the other materials groups, the raw materials group relies extensively on communication and coordination sessions that involve representatives from worldwide locations.

During the sourcing process, the logistics activities associated with obtaining raw materials are an important consideration. Given that the global materials director reports to the vice president of global materials, logistics, and sourcing, it should come as no surprise that logistical issues at both ends of the supply chain receive serious attention when developing global raw material agreements. (Previously the logistics group considered only the movement of outbound finished goods.) Once a logistics contract is in place, electronic review sessions involving representatives from the various divisions take place quarterly to identify continuous improvement opportunities.

The discussion of this case shows how a diverse organization, which traditionally focused at the country and regional level, has successfully taken a globally coordinated view of its worldwide operations. Even when a country or region continues to maintain responsibility for items that are not part of a centrally led effort, managers work to align their divisions with a common vision and common objectives and processes. Supply managers strive to maintain the best of both worlds—responsiveness at the country and regional level while capturing the benefits offered by global supply management. Perhaps we *can* have our cake and eat it too!

DOING IT LIKE THE TEXTBOOK SAYS AT WHIRLPOOL

Whirlpool, a brand that most of us recognize, is a major manufacturer and marketer of home appliances. With $20 billion in annual revenue, 73,000 employees, and 73 manufacturing and technology centers worldwide, the company boasts an impressive portfolio of brands that includes Whirlpool, Maytag, Amana, KitchenAid, and Jenn-Air. Whirlpool also makes a large number of Kenmore appliances.

Not all that long ago, Whirlpool was a $3-billion enterprise that focused its manufacturing and selling operations largely within North America. Through internal growth and an aggressive acquisition strategy, Whirlpool has become one of the world's largest appliance makers. Moving from a regional producer that competed against a familiar array of brands, Whirlpool now competes against global competitors with names such as Samsung, LG, Electrolux, and Bosch. But pursuing a global supply model was not something that Whirlpool executives just happened to feel like doing in their spare time. It was a competitive necessity that now demands constant attention.

Although Whirlpool's growth at the corporate level is impressive, equally impressive are the steps that supply leaders have taken to become a premier global supply organization. Whirlpool is organized primarily at the regional level with strong coordination across regions (Figure 13.4). Each region has a fully staffed procurement organization. In total, Whirlpool has 750 sourcing professionals located around the globe. The procurement group in Europe, for example,

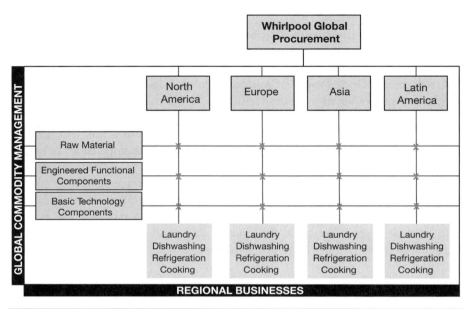

Figure 13.4. The Global Supply Organization at Whirlpool.

consists of 150 people, 50 of which are in Eastern Europe. Part of the responsibility of each region is to support centrally managed global commodity teams.

Our analysis describes what Whirlpool is doing to stay at the forefront of global supply excellence. After reading this discussion, it should become obvious that Whirlpool is pursuing a global supply management model that includes all the right things. (The authors would like to thank Thomas Egan, vice president of supply at Whirlpool, and his worldwide staff for their generous support in the development of this analysis.)

It Starts with Strong Central Leadership

At the heart of Whirlpool's supply management organization is a strong central leadership team that endorses global commodity management. Annually the company spends over $9 billion in direct spending and $4 billion in indirect spending. What is impressive is that fully two thirds of the direct purchases are placed into commodities and coordinated at a centrally led level. These commodities consist primarily of raw materials and standard or functional items that have commonality across regions and product lines. Examples include steel, resins, chemicals, copper, aluminum, and zinc. Other centrally controlled items include wiring controls, motors, pumps, and cooling systems. The remaining purchases are managed at the regional level, although supply managers continually evaluate the mix of items that are managed between the levels.

Some indirect coordination also occurs at a centrally led, global level. (In fact, the indirect side of procurement went through a similar process as the direct procurement side did to identify global opportunities.) A good example here involves ocean freight. Each region participates in an annual process in which carriers bid on 2200 transportation lanes. By using a standard process, Whirlpool has been able to identify a reduced set of multiregional and global carriers.

The central staff determines the commodities that are managed globally. A primary objective here is to interact with suppliers who can operate on a worldwide basis and have the potential to offer Whirlpool a competitive advantage, particularly in design and technology support. As products continue to become more sophisticated and cost-reduction pressures never go away, Whirlpool expects these suppliers to become an integral part of the company's success.

Sourcing leaders are held accountable for three key metrics:

- Sourcing productivity improvements (year-over-year cost improvements)
- Improvements to working capital (a metric that most supply leaders have on their short list). (Recall from Chapter 9 that companies that coordinate their supply management activities globally rate more highly their ability to better manage inventory compared with companies that engage in international purchasing.)
- Supplier quality and performance

Whirlpool's CPO meets monthly with the CEO and the executive committee to review supply performance. (Remember that having a CPO conduct periodic strategy and performance presentations to the CEO or president is one of the most critical features that identify an effective supply organization.) The reporting process also creates tremendous pressure to achieve a steady stream of performance improvements. Regular reporting by the CPO to the CEO is a best practice that characterizes Whirlpool's global supply organization.

Whirlpool's centrally led efforts focus on three areas of organizational leverage: a global management structure, including the extensive use of global commodity business teams; a global management footprint; and global processes and systems. Figure 13.5 illustrates the features that comprise these three areas. The following sections describe some of these features and others from interviews with executive managers.

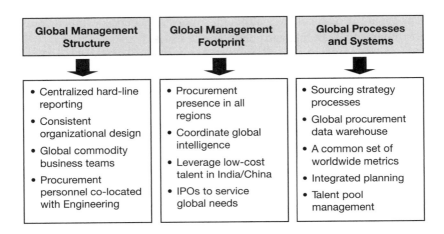

Global Management Structure	Global Management Footprint	Global Processes and Systems
• Centralized hard-line reporting • Consistent organizational design • Global commodity business teams • Procurement personnel co-located with Engineering	• Procurement presence in all regions • Coordinate global intelligence • Leverage low-cost talent in India/China • IPOs to service global needs	• Sourcing strategy processes • Global procurement data warehouse • A common set of worldwide metrics • Integrated planning • Talent pool management

Figure 13.5. The Global Supply Organization at Whirlpool.

Using Global Commodity Business Teams to Get the Job Done

Commodity business teams are responsible for developing Whirlpool's supply strategies. Personnel at the company's buying centers around the world are tasked with supporting these teams, which include full-time commodity managers. Business teams follow a strategy development process that features four key phases (a process that is modified slightly for teams that manage indirect items). Again, the presence of a defined global process makes another well-earned appearance in a discussion of best practices. These commodity business teams are responsible for performing a "deep dive" into their commodity and supply market every 3 to 5 years, although strategy reviews occur more frequently.

Commodity teams assume some important responsibilities. Each team is responsible for meeting with Whirlpool's different businesses to understand their goals and needs in a process that is described as intensely collaborative. These teams are also responsible for supporting Whirlpool's product development initiatives. Global risk management is also a responsibility of these teams. Each team has access to services that provide financial information about suppliers. Commodity teams also interact with corporate personnel who are responsible for commodity hedging, which senior leaders describe as a best practice within the supply group. Hedging involves items such as copper, aluminum, zinc, nickel, natural gas, and diesel fuel.

Across U.S. industry, the use of commodity teams as part of the formal organizational design has been around for a while. The reality is that teams are an accepted part of most organizations. (Recall from an earlier discussion of organizational design effectiveness that centrally managed teams are an integral part of just about any leading supply organization.) After the CPO making presentations to the CEO or president, having teams that develop and implement company-wide supply strategies along with cross-functional teams that manage the procurement and supply process are the two next most important features that describe an effective supply organization. For good reason, commodity management teams, as well as new product development teams that include procurement and supply representatives, have become an indispensable part of the global supply management model.

There is nothing startling about the use of teams today, but the ability to use these teams globally is still evolving. The sentiment among supply managers at Whirlpool, however, is that the commodity business team concept with active support from regional personnel has passed the test of time. Although using teams is no longer a unique practice, it has certainly been a consistent practice that helps Whirlpool achieve its global supply objectives.

Establishing International Purchasing Offices

When sourcing in emerging supply markets, Whirlpool and other producers face comparable challenges. A major part of Whirlpool's global management footprint now includes the use of international purchasing offices (IPOs) to support a global objective of finding the best and the lowest-cost sources of supply. Whirlpool relies extensively on its IPOs to find and develop suppliers; to perform preselection site visits; and to represent the supply organization during supplier negotiations. (Chapter 3 discussed in no uncertain terms the important role that IPOs play when sourcing around the world. Chapter 3 also detailed the primary responsibilities of IPOs, a model that is fairly consistent across companies.)

In 2002, Whirlpool opened its first two IPOs, which were both located in China. The main IPO was in Shanghai with a staff of 50, while a second IPO was located in Shenzen with a staff of 15. The effort in China started with basically a "blank sheet" because Whirlpool had no real presence in China before that time. A relatively new IPO is now located in India. It has a staff of five that supports Whirlpool's supply efforts in that region. Near-term plans include opening a purchasing office in Vietnam, although the final form for that office is still being debated.

For most companies, starting an IPO presents a fairly common set of challenges:

- Obtaining the right leadership and capabilities to staff the office—For Whirlpool, an IPO requires individuals who have knowledge of the appliance industry as well as a thorough understanding of Whirlpool. Among larger companies, as the use of IPOs grows, competition for local talent becomes more intense, something that can increase IPO labor costs.

- Transitioning to new suppliers that are located in emerging countries, particularly China—The transition period requires careful management during supplier switching.
- Operating an IPO when changing exchange rates and other factors alter the economics underlying the IPO.

Even minor economic changes can alter the business model for IPOs located in specific regions. Consider the currency rate. For many years, the currency rate was not a concern in China because the Chinese government pegged its currency to the dollar at a fixed rate. Now, however, the Chinese government allows the yuan to float more freely, a change that has altered the economics of doing business in China. Movements in the currency markets can quickly undermine an IPO's economic model.

Supply leaders at Whirlpool are now in the position of speaking from experience when they look at the evolution of their IPOs. And what have they learned? These supply leaders say they should have worked with technology people at Whirlpool earlier when using IPOs to identify Chinese suppliers. Early on, the search for suppliers resembled a model that "pushed" suppliers onto the product teams and manufacturing centers: the IPOs helped locate suppliers in emerging markets and then pushed them onto engineers. Engagement has now evolved more toward a "pull" approach that features early on engineering involvement to identify the needs of key internal customers.

Component Architecture Management Teams—a Bold, New Initiative

At Whirlpool, one of the most exciting initiatives underway involves a global "attack" on component proliferation and waste. To accomplish this, Whirlpool forms what it calls component architecture management (CAM) teams. The primary objective of this intensive process is to remove complexity and redundancy from product and component designs. And while the teams are pursuing this objective, they will use the initiative as an opportunity to refresh their global commodity strategies. CAM teams represent a large chunk of the work that is now occurring outside the normal flow of supply management.

The initiative to attack component proliferation and waste involves something called rationalization. In a relatively short period, engineering and sourcing leaders expect to rationalize the components within all 52 of the company's commodity categories. Rationalization refers to any effort that tries to find the right mix and number of something to maintain. For Whirlpool, rationalization involves a search for the right mix and number of components needed to support worldwide production requirements. While rationalization does not have to mean "fewer choices," often we have too much of something (too many suppliers, too many distribution centers, too many part numbers, etc.). As an example that is typical at Whirlpool, across its design and manufacturing centers, engineers have designed 150 different water valves for dishwashers. Most observers would agree that there might be an opportunity to take this number down a notch or two. Whirlpool's goal is to reduce the number of water valves worldwide to 40 or 50.

Whirlpool CAM teams include four major functions: procurement, engineering, technology, and global consumer design. Suppliers are also part of the CAM activity, particularly to provide the data attributes of the components. The process brings sourcing, engineering, and suppliers together in an environment that one senior leader describes as being "joined at the hip." A desired outcome is to create a cultural change that requires personnel to justify why Whirlpool needs another variation of a part rather than justifying why there are so many.

The timeline. A pilot project that validated the component rationalization process started in July 2007. The formal kickoff for the initiative occurred in November 2007, with the first full wave of teams commencing in January 2008. Whirlpool established around 20 CAM teams with plans to methodically but aggressively address all 52 commodity groups. At the commodity level, CAM teams have 16 weeks to analyze their opportunity before delivering an executable plan for rationalizing product components.

The review process starts with a blank sheet of paper and determines how many variations of a component or design are needed. The entire process to rationalize all components and materials managed at the central level is expected to take several years. A series of company-wide workshops are also being offered so that everyone understands the component rationalization process.

A formal sign-off process is in place that puts a CAM project in the engineering project system. The formal tracking and documentation that goes along with component rationalization lends credibility to the process. The initiative has senior management visibility, which adds that much more pressure to demonstrate results. Senior managers are confident that this process will lead to major returns and believe that what they are doing in component architecture is another example of a best practice.

The expected financial improvements from this process are staggering. Whirlpool expects to realize $1 billion annually in direct material savings, a figure which does not include any accounting for cost avoidances, improvements to product quality, or reductions to product development cycle times from having component designs available for reuse. Although these types of benefits should be significant, they are also difficult to quantify, which is the primary reason that the finance group is part of the core leadership team that oversees this process.

The rationalization process is something that most companies should undertake on a regular basis. Any company that has not effectively coordinated its design centers or has grown through mergers and acquisition (the case with Whirlpool) should not be surprised to find it has too many suppliers and too many designs. Having too many parts and designs can also be the result of a syndrome that we call "engineers gone wild," which refers to the tendency of technical groups to overdesign or create new designs even when previous applications are available. In this syndrome, every new design must be the latest and greatest masterpiece. The next component design is that engineer's Mona Lisa.

Teams must have access to good data before anything can be done within component architecture. Whirlpool readily admits it has room to improve in the area of information technology systems—not surprising because Whirlpool has grown rapidly through acquisitions. (And everyone knows that when one company buys another, the transition to a newly integrated unit is swift and easy, particularly because both companies usually have the same processes, part numbering schemes, suppliers, designs, and systems. We need to talk if you actually believe any part of the previous sentence.) Although Whirlpool has a data warehouse, senior executives admit gaining visibility to supply and part data given the differences across the units and brands that make up the worldwide product portfolio has been challenging.

The rationalization process also taps into what should be a primary objective of any global supply chain—standardization. Standardization means "to conform to something that is a model or ideal example" (i.e., the standard). A failure to standardize usually leads to wasteful duplication of effort that fails to promote best practices. What is the value of five design centers designing what is essentially the same component? The answer: likely no value, but plenty of duplicate costs. During product design, extensive use of custom or newly designed components when standard or previously designed components are available is wasteful. What is the value of every purchasing center developing its own IT system, supplier scorecard methodology, or supplier development program?

Standardizing across a broad array of areas is the wave of the future. It is time to declare war on global complexity.

Supply Chain Improvement Initiatives

Another Whirlpool initiative involves working directly with suppliers to improve their lean capabilities. Whirlpool has done a good job internally with lean, something that supply leaders want to extend to suppliers through a concerted effort to promote lean based on the Toyota Production System model. The company has even gone so far as creating a lean group within procurement to work directly with suppliers. This group identifies critical manufacturing projects within Whirlpool and then looks upstream to identify improvement opportunities related to those projects. The group also searches for issues with suppliers in areas such as quality and delivery. Each of Whirlpool's geographic regions is responsible for identifying specific development opportunities

Another example of supplier development involves using a European program called Operational Excellence (or OPEX). OPEX is Whirlpool's version of Six Sigma that also includes suppliers. The main features of this program include suppliers attending the same training sessions as Whirlpool personnel and pursuing supplier quality certification. To date over 13,000 internal participants and personnel from 400 suppliers have been trained through the OPEX program.

Senior mangers know that Whirlpool must constantly search for internal and external best practices. On the internal side, senior managers maintain that the involvement of procurement on new product development teams is a best practice worth emulating. Co-locating procurement personnel within engineering and technical groups is also a best practice. This model is ideal for gaining a better understanding of internal customer needs, faster problem resolution, and the development of trust-based relationships.

On the external side, Whirlpool needs to more formally pursue supplier involvement opportunities. A supply model that features an extensive reliance on a smaller set of global suppliers will increasingly look to those suppliers for design and engineering support. Although suppliers are involved in design and other projects, too often this involvement is ad hoc rather than systematic. Supply managers and engineers are beginning to develop technology and product roadmaps that identify early on those areas that will benefit from true supplier integration. Early involvement will be a primary feature that defines Whirlpool's future supply management model.

CONCLUDING THOUGHTS

The companies featured in this chapter know they can never rest on their laurels. This trait is something that helps create an environment in which leaders are *never* content to sit back and react to the events that happen around them. What is leading edge or unique within global supply management today will not look all that special tomorrow. So, although we have a good idea about what defines global supply excellence right now, the big question is what will define global supply excellence tomorrow? Chapter 14 will help define this future state.

REFERENCE

1. R.J. Trent. *Achieving Excellence in Global Sourcing* 2007. Tempe: AZ: CAPS Research.

PART V.
LOOKING TOWARD
THE FUTURE

Chapter 14. Defining the Future State

DEFINING THE FUTURE STATE

At this point, it should be obvious that a solid body of knowledge exists about what defines an effective global supply organization. And we are comfortable in our understanding of what the world of global risk and supply management looks like right now. A logical question becomes what will this world look like over the next 3 to 5 years? With that question in mind, this chapter presents some predictions that have a decent likelihood of happening.

PREDICTIONS RELATED TO GLOBAL SUPPLY MANAGEMENT

The predictions in this section extend our discussion of global risk and supply management. To make a prediction is to simply *foretell* on the basis of observation, experience, or scientific reason. And while the following predictions are based on observation and experience, not to mention extensive data, one never knows for sure about anything when looking toward the future. This is especially true in uncertain times. The usual disclaimers apply whenever predictions are the featured subject.

Prediction: Companies that are less proficient at global supply management will stress the development of four enabling areas. Something to remember is that most supply organizations do not have in place well-defined global sourcing and supply processes. Achieving the kinds of improvements presented in Chapter 9 remains largely unrealized. An organization cannot pursue more sophisticated supply management approaches, however, without focusing on four key enablers, something that supplier managers are increasingly realizing. These enablers are the development of measurement systems, including total cost of ownership systems; access to qualified personnel who have the ability to view the supply network from a worldwide perspective; a supportive organizational design; and information systems technology.[1] The reason we are confident that supply organizations will stress these four areas is because supply managers have said this is the case. As part of our global sourcing research, companies were asked to provide responses to: "What are the most important changes at your company that would enable global sourcing and supply to deliver significantly superior results?" An analysis of over 300 responses revealed that most responses fell into the following areas:[2]

- Developing effective organizational structures, governance, and teaming
- Establishing effective worldwide e-sourcing and supply systems
- Improving measurement and data
- Enhancing human resource acquisition, development, and retention

These areas create the foundation for global excellence. For many companies, future success demands a strong emphasis on "blocking and tackling" before taking on more sophisticated supply management endeavors. An absence of these capabilities correlates highly with an absence of global excellence. We know this to be true.

Prediction: The pressure to improve costs will remain relentless and severe, leading to a search for innovative and aggressive ways to reduce supply chain costs. In the world of predictions, and given the uncertainty that surrounds the world's economic systems, predicting that the pressure to reduce costs will remain relentless and severe comes with a high degree of certainty. It is unlikely that there will ever be a point in our lifetimes when companies are not under pressure to control costs. This pressure, brought about by intense competition, demanding customers, and government regulators, will encourage companies to pursue activities that are part of a global supply model. And for companies that are well along the global performance curve, the emphasis will be on extending their already advanced capabilities. Giunipero and Handfield support the notion that cost reduction pressures are not going away anytime soon.[3] During their most recent purchasing education and training study, supply managers were asked to predict the likelihood of various trends. Of all the trends evaluated, and there were many, the top three that respondents believed were most likely to occur are:

- The pressure to reduce costs will increase.
- Strategic cost management will increase.
- Supplier selection will focus on total cost analysis.

Other predictions from this study have definite cost implications or support an expected shift toward strategic supply management (their rank order is in parenthesis):

- Sourcing will focus more on strategic issues (5).
- Global sourcing will increase (6).
- Strategic sourcing will increase in importance (7).
- More coordinated buying across operating units will occur (11).
- Two levels of purchasing will evolve: strategic and transactional/day-to-day buying (15).

Each of these predictions is consistent with the themes presented throughout this book.

Prediction: Relentless cost pressures will result in a continuous search for suppliers in emerging and low-cost supply markets. Open almost any supply chain trade journal and there will be a prediction about outsourced jobs coming back to the home market. For example, Sallie Mae, the financial institution that has received attention during the U.S. financial meltdown, announced it will bring 2000 jobs back to the U.S. as it shifts call centers and other operations from overseas.[4] According to some observers, this shifting is the inevitable result of changing economic conditions and an inability to manage worldwide risk. These predictions provide some good sound bites on the home front, but the reality is that outsourced work _will not_ be rushing back into the U.S. or Western Europe anytime soon. As Western suppliers go out of business, there is often no one left to bring the work back to. Worldwide economic conditions will always result in adjustments to supply networks, but large-scale shifting of global buying patterns over the next 3 to 5 years is probably not going to happen. A decline in the volume of goods and services sourced worldwide due to a decline in the demand for finished goods is another story. One thing we can bet on is the constant search by Western supply managers for low-cost sources of supply. This search is almost an obsession, particularly for companies that face intense competitive pressure.

A 2009 news headline announced that IBM was further cutting 5000 U.S. jobs and transferring that work to India. Foreign workers now account for 71% of the IBM workforce, up from 65% several years ago.[5] Supply leaders at IBM have formed a group called the Global Procurement Support Group (GPSG) and assigned to it a single mission: the group is responsible for identifying untapped supply opportunities in emerging supply markets.[6] Moving outside of China and Taiwan, this group travels to Brazil, Belarus, Ukraine, Vietnam, Malaysia, Hungary, and Romania. Software and labor-intensive products, which IBM requires in huge quantities, are the focus of the GPSC. Their search for low-cost suppliers is an ongoing one.

Although economic and risk factors will result in some sourcing shifts across regions, don't expect a mass exodus from the East back to the West. If anything, supply managers will broaden their search to consider a broader mix of countries. For example, other countries will work hard to unseat India as the current destination of choice for business process outsourcing. And other regions will begin to challenge Asia as a low-cost sourcing region.

For example, Africa (a region noted in Chapter 1 as not currently being on the radar screen of most supply managers) has an abundant labor pool at competitive rates as well as other important resources. Africa's potential advantages become more obvious when examining the length of global supply chains. Many African ports have access to shorter supply routes to the European Union and the U.S. compared with Asian countries. Some African nations are already hard at work building the infrastructure necessary to become part of the global market.[7] In particular, South Africa is pushing export growth and welcomes foreign buyers and investors. While still maintaining its long tradition of mineral exporting, the country is working hard to develop exports from its automotive, chemical, and pharmaceutical industries. Foreign buyers will find that they can receive attractive purchase incentives provided by the South African government, including export credit insurance and excise duty refunds.[8] The results of a recent presidential election may change this dynamic.

Mexico is a country that will likely receive some benefit from shifting trade patterns. Several things combine to make Mexico the new sourcing hotspot: the desire of an increasing number of U.S. companies to nearshore their operations due to the increased cost and hassle of doing business over great distances; a government/industry collaboration that is producing more highly skilled Mexican workers at a reasonable cost; and a large drop in the value of the peso relative to the dollar.[9] The risk of continued drug violence, however, could lessen the appeal of Mexico.

Prediction: Expect a continued development and refinement of global sourcing and supply management processes. This is a safe prediction. One reason is that a majority of supply organizations do not yet practice the highest levels of global supply management. Therefore we know that they do not have in place company-wide processes to guide their global efforts. Because most organizations expect to elevate their global capabilities, and we know that the presence of well-defined processes is a critical global success factor, it is almost a given that continued development and refinement of global supply processes will occur. Another reason that this is a safe prediction is that most supply managers recognize the need for continuous improvement, which means the improvement of any global processes that are in place.

Prediction: Expect major industrial customers to place greater emphasis on being treated as a single global customer by suppliers. Expecting to be treated as

Global Customer Demands

Global Customers	
	❏ Expect suppliers to provide global standards, specifications, pricing, product and service availability, and uniform service and delivery to all worldwide locations
	❏ Expect consistent worldwide electronic linkages with suppliers
	❏ Expect suppliers to support the customer's worldwide expansion strategies
Global Suppliers	❏ Expect suppliers to grow globally with the buying company

Figure 14.1. Global Customer Expectations.

a single global customer will place an emphasis on searching for suppliers with true global capabilities. But a lack of suppliers with global capabilities can be a constraint for any supply organization that expects to develop global rather than regional contracts. (Recall that Chapter 11 identified the availability of suppliers with true global capabilities as a factor that correlates directly with effective global supply management.) Focus group research with leading supply organizations has helped identify a set of requirements that industrial buyers have when engaging in global sourcing and supply. A conclusion from this research is that industrial customers often have a clear set of global expectations that suppliers must meet or exceed (Figure 14.1 summarizes these expectations).

The pressure to become a global supplier is partly responsible for a wave of mergers and acquisitions across certain industries, including the automotive, aerospace, and electronic industries. These mergers and acquisitions are occurring primarily for two reasons:

- To broaden a supplier's geographic reach (A supplier that is North American-centric could find itself at a disadvantage when it competes for contracts against suppliers that have a global reach.)
- To be in a better position to satisfy the growing pressure from customers to provide an expanded set of capabilities and services globally

We have been aware for some time of the need to evolve from simply providing a product to providing a full product-service package. Services that suppliers might be expected to provide globally include providing worldwide engineering support or managing a customer's inventories.

Prediction: The shift toward centrally led supply management will continue.
It's difficult to see what might reverse the trend toward a centrally led global

Supply/Supply Chain Area	Related Finance Area
Evaluating and selecting world-class suppliers	Analyzing supplier financial statements and ratios
Managing inventory investment effectively	Financial techniques for measuring working capital improvements
Managing costs across the supply chain, including how to create a lean supply chain	Using return on assets to evaluate the financial impact of supply chain activities
International sourcing	Hedging currencies and materials
Developing supplier performance capabilities	Calculating internal rate of return, payback, ROI, and NPV

Figure 14.2. Merging Supply, Supply Chain, and Financial Management.

supply model. Too many companies have experienced firsthand the value of taking a coordinated approach to sourcing and supply to begin shifting back toward a decentralized organizational structure. The challenge that remains will be creating an organizational model that captures the benefits of taking a centrally led view of supply management while still being responsive to the needs of internal customers located at different buying and operating sites.

Activities that are part of a centralized or centrally led supply organization will increasingly include developing purchase family strategies; locating potential supply sources; evaluating and selecting suppliers; negotiating and establishing contracts; managing supplier relationships; managing supplier development activities; establishing specifications; developing supplier performance measurement systems; and providing supplier performance feedback. Expect these activities to increasingly play out at a global level rather than regional level. It is reasonable to conclude that maintaining a centrally controlled or centrally led perspective over global supply activities enhances the probability of achieving improved sourcing outcomes.

Prediction: Supply managers and finance managers will become better acquainted. If you have not done so already, it is probably time to get up from your chair, walk down the hall or over to the next building, and become better acquainted with the group called finance. Closer interaction between supply, supply chain, and financial managers is inevitable over the next 3 to 5 years. After all, a big part of global supply management is about managing the amount and flow of funds.

Moving beyond the general statement that supply, supply chain, and financial groups need to work more closely together, what are some areas where this could occur? Figure 14.2 provides some supply chain areas and some financial applications that will help us understand each area. We expect that financial analysts will increasingly be assigned to work within supply and supply chain groups as a support resource. The supply and finance side of your business must become more familiar with the interrelationships between them.

Prediction: Global supply management will shift from component sourcing to subsystem and system sourcing. Two conclusions became clear several years ago as leading companies began their journey toward global supply management. The first conclusion was that early global efforts centered primarily on global contracting. A focus on worldwide consistency in terms of processes and practices usually came about later, if at all. Early global emphasis was, in the words of one supply executive, to "do the deal." The second conclusion was that these initial global contracts covered almost exclusively direct materials involving components. The items covered by these contracts usually did not include anything as complex as subsystems or systems. Most supply organizations wanted to learn how to walk before they learned how to run.

A strict emphasis on global contracts that feature the sourcing of components should gradually evolve toward subsystem and system sourcing, which will involve relying on global suppliers for greater design and engineering support—something that simply was not going to happen during the initial stages of globalization. This evolution to subsystem and system sourcing is a natural extension of global supply management, particularly as leading companies gain confidence in their supply management abilities.

Perhaps one of the most visible examples of a shift from component to subsystem and system sourcing is the Boeing 787 Dreamliner aircraft. Boeing relies on a network of worldwide suppliers to design, manufacture, and assemble major systems on the 787. Unfortunately, Dreamliner production is several years behind schedule, partly due to the inability of certain suppliers to design and deliver very complex systems. (A joint venture between Vought and an Italian supplier performed so poorly that Boeing was forced to step in and assume Vought's role. It's a safe bet that Boeing did not select this newly formed supplier with the intention of becoming so involved.) Boeing has recently announced a review of its global supply chain with the expectation of bringing some system work closer to home.

We expect a gradual shift from component to subsystem and system sourcing over the next 3 to 5 years. But this shift, as Boeing has discovered, will not be quick and easy.

Prediction: Supply managers will increasingly develop global supply strategies for indirect items and services. Just as we expect a greater emphasis on global subsystem and system sourcing, we also expect a greater emphasis on the global sourcing of indirect items and services. Whether a manufacturer takes a regional or global perspective, direct items almost always receive the first and the most attention of any purchase category. There is logic behind why this is true. For most companies that make a tangible product rather than provide a service, the bulk of their external spending goes toward direct materials. Furthermore, it is easier for a supplier to ship direct material around the world than it is to provide a service that requires a physical presence. As supplier capabilities expand, and as supply managers continuously search for cost reduction opportunities, expect indirect items and services to receive greater attention. And, increasingly this attention will occur at a global rather than at a local, country, or even regional level.

Prediction: Global supply management will move beyond an emphasis on contracting to include an emphasis on process and practice consistency across worldwide locations. Growth in the percentage of companies practicing Level V global supply management is expected to continue. Remember that a defining characteristic of Level V is a movement beyond global contracting to an emphasis on developing global processes and practices. We are already witnessing this transition for supply organizations that are proficient at Level IV global supply management, a level that emphasizes global contracting. (Chapter 13 presented some excellent examples of companies that are taking their global supply game to more sophisticated levels by developing processes and practices that provide consistency, perhaps even standardization, across worldwide operating locations.) In 5 to 10 years, global consistency will be expected for companies that compete globally.

Prediction: The use of global supply teams will increase, making cross-cultural and communication issues more challenging. We see no evidence that the use of teams to manage global commodities and supply networks will diminish. In fact, we expect continued growth in the use of global supply teams, which will create pressure to develop state-of-the art communication systems that allow global teams to share information seamlessly. Global teams will increasingly consist of personnel from different geographic regions. It is unreasonable to expect team members from geographically dispersed teams to meet face-to-face on a regular basis. Although face-to-face strategy coordination sessions will periodically occur, time and budget constraints, not to mention physical exhaustion, almost guarantee that supply organizations will pursue other ways to support routine or day-to-day communication requirements.

Geographic dispersion will elevate other issues beside communication. We expect supply leaders to address, and perhaps even struggle with, how to evaluate and reward team members. These supply leaders will increasingly feel pressure to develop metrics that clearly define the success of global supply teams and the effectiveness of individual members. Geographic dispersion and communication requirements will not be a concern for supply organizations whose team members are located in close proximity.

Cross-cultural issues, including issues associated with time zone differences, will also make the use of global supply team increasingly challenging. It is safe to conclude that a supply model that features geographically dispersed team members will become more common over the next 5 years. It is also safe to conclude that a supply model that features geographically dispersed teams will be exponentially more complex to manage compared with one that features co-located participants. This is an issue that supply organizations must proactively address.

The predictions that relate directly to global supply management, while certainly not an exhaustive set, highlight what we feel will be the future state of global supply management. Only time will tell how close these predictions are to reality.

PREDICTIONS RELATED TO GLOBAL RISK MANAGEMENT

When companies operate globally, a variety of topics we have raised are associated with various risks, including economic, political, logistical, contractual/legal, competitive, cultural, and environmental and infrastructure concerns. The following sections present some predictions, trends, and future areas of focus in risk management as we envision them.

Prediction: Global supply strategies will increasingly include global risk management strategies. An evolving trend is the integration of risk management strategies with global commodity strategies. In fact, some leading companies now make the development of risk management plans a required part of their global commodity strategies. We predict that more supply groups will be combined with their counterparts in transportation and logistics. After all, once something is sourced offshore, it is usually up to the transportation and logistics group to manage the shipping and in-transit risks. Why not integrate at least some elements of the supply and logistics groups?

Most observers think that a good part of the world, while seemingly attractive from a low-cost sourcing perspective, will continue to pose a risk to continuity of supply. Instability of governments and a lack of law and order also have supply risk implications. Companies that source globally will need to be increasingly flexible and adjust their strategies to account for any instability. For example, a major U.S. company recently decided to source cotton products in Ethiopia, but switched quickly to Egypt due to instability within Ethiopia.

Supply managers need to be attuned to global risks as they select suppliers. Approaches such as dual country sourcing; additional inventory in the supply chain; building adaptability and flexibility into supply chains; and the capability to switch relatively quickly to alternate sources of supply are all possible risk management approaches. We predict that in several years, a commodity team will not be likely to propose a global supply strategy without having a global risk management plan attached.

Prediction: Expect a shift toward the greater use of cost-based models to support global risk management. The pressure to pursue more sophisticated approaches to cost management, especially given the relentless pressure to reduce costs, is a primary driver behind this prediction. Total cost analysis is a powerful risk management technique. And integration between global supply management and global risk management is likely to increase over the next 5 years. It is logical to conclude that cost-based modeling will increase.

Supply leaders will increasingly demand that global commodity teams make major sourcing decisions only after developing total cost of ownership models. Furthermore, risk management decisions will increasingly rely on total cost models as a source of insight. We also expect that sophisticated customers will help their suppliers develop life cycle cost models. These customers will want to ensure that major buying decisions are based on total cost or value rather than price. Shifting toward a total cost perspective will be a major adjustment for many supply organizations.

Information will continue to be the "currency" of the supply chain. In the future, information about fluctuations in national currencies, inflation rates among countries, and changing material and labor costs must be incorporated quickly into total cost models. The ability to gather supply market intelligence will become a major enabler of effective total costs systems as well as an enabler of effective risk management.

Prediction: Supply organizations will increasingly rely on international purchasing offices as a means for managing global supply risk. Few global supply features receive such rave reviews regarding their effectiveness as international purchasing offices (IPOs). This consensus ensures that companies will increasingly look to foreign offices as a way to support their global strategies and manage supply chain risk. Expecting domestic supply managers to continuously travel the globe to perform the types of duties that IPO personnel routinely perform simply is not feasible. Establishing IPOs is a logical maturation within the global supply management framework, a progression that should continue as long as supply managers pursue global strategies. And let's be clear about something here: the word is already out about what these offices can do for your company.

Something that might change in the future is how global supply organizations structure and manage their IPOs. The predominant IPO model has been to own an IPO, sometimes as a separate legal structure, which is staffed with managers who are expatriates. The high fixed costs associated with owning an IPO, however, will deter some supply organizations from pursuing this type of model. We might see a shift from a fixed-cost model of ownership to a variable-cost model of ownership. The variable-cost model features a supply organization contracting and paying for IPO services as they are requested. The supply organization does not own the foreign office. This might be a good option for companies that are reluctant or unable to take on additional fixed assets. Whatever model is used, supply organizations will take a close look at what is the right mix and number of IPOs to maintain.

Prediction: As smaller companies increasingly pursue international purchasing, they will expose themselves to greater supply chain risk. Most knowledgeable observers expect smaller companies to try to benefit from a worldwide view of sourcing and supply, particularly those companies that differentiate themselves on price. Unfortunately, searching offshore will increase their risk exposure. A multinational risk survey of chief executive operating and financial officers and risk managers found that small and midsize companies were more likely to experience losses from doing business outside the U.S. or Canada compared with larger companies. Compared to companies with annual revenues of more than $1 billion, smaller companies had at least a 50% higher frequency of foreign losses due to liability lawsuits, theft of intellectual property, and the theft of goods in transit.[10] It is safe to conclude that smaller companies will expose themselves to greater risks as they ramp up their international efforts. Smaller companies face several hurdles that larger companies do not:

- A smaller talent pool that limits their ability to perform the due diligence necessary to identify the best foreign suppliers[11]
- A lack of resources to make sense of the global patchwork of different laws and languages, currencies, and styles of conducting business[12]
- A lack of resources required to manage an extended supply chain
- Underestimating the effort involved when sourcing offshore (Many smaller companies fall into the trap of underestimating the effort involved when sourcing offshore. But we have also seen this happen over and over even in larger companies.)

Prediction: Companies will increasingly recognize the interdependencies between global events and global risk management. Events such as the SARS epidemic in 2002, the September 11, 2001 terrorist attacks, and more recently Hurricanes Rita and Katrina have demonstrated that events affecting one part of the supply chain often interrupt the operations of other supply chain members. Increasingly important is reviewing the entire supply chain, across all countries, and across all tiers of supply, when developing risk management strategies. The days are gone when supply managers can focus on one country or region or only on first- and second-tier suppliers. Unless trade protectionism takes over, the world will become more interconnected, making the need to link global supply management and global risk management even greater.[13]

Prediction: Global supply managers will elevate the importance of supplier quality when making selection decisions. From lead in children's toys, to tainted baby milk formula, to poisoned pet food, horror stories abound concerning supply from foreign countries. As supply managers expand their supply networks globally, they will need to be aware of the social, legal, and economic risks of poor-quality goods from foreign suppliers. Supply organizations will need to ensure that they have stringent risk management strategies in place with current and new suppliers to ensure quality of supply. We predict that the evaluation of supplier quality during the selection process will take on added importance as a way to manage the risk of poor quality. And, hopefully, supplier selection decisions will not be based as often on product samples. Supply managers are becoming acutely aware of the connection between supplier quality lapses and the resulting erosion to their company's standing in the marketplace. Poor supplier quality is not just a supply management issue. It is a corporate issue.

Prediction: Environmental performance and compliance to rigorous standards will become a more important issue during worldwide supplier evaluation. It would be surprising not to have a prediction related to the environment. Environmental risk from foreign suppliers will continue to be a major source of concern as the importance of this topic increases worldwide. The trend by governments and companies toward greater environmental protection and ensuring that environmentally safe practices are in place is expected to gain momentum among developed and emerging countries. Greater environmental protection and environmentally safe practice regulations will likely raise the cost of doing business with emerging country suppliers. After all, these suppliers often have lower costs because of lax environmental standards. A buying company places itself at risk when it does business with suppliers that are flagrant environmental abusers. These same suppliers might also be less than ideal in terms of how they manage their labor force or product quality. Arguing that how a supplier treats the environment or its workers is not a buyer's concern sounds naïve in an era when information and disinformation travel over the Internet at the speed of light.

CONCLUDING THOUGHTS

Global risk and supply management involves having a set of continuously maturing processes that, if managed properly, should provide a steady stream of benefits. From a global perspective, even relatively mature companies can *never* stop improving or extending their processes. A company that has done an effective job coordinating the purchase of its direct materials globally will want to extend its efforts into indirect materials, services, and capital equipment. Or, a company that is good at developing global contracts will want to ensure that it is applying a consistent set of best practices across its buying locations and centers. Underlying this global view must be a total appreciation of risk management. As John Steinbeck once wrote, "The best laid plans of mice and men often go astray." As it pertains to global business today, going astray is not that hard to do.

A fact of life is that the need for improvement is never ending. Another fact of life might be that beyond death and taxes, change and uncertainty are about the only things we can count on right now. No one is immune from change. And no one lives in a predictable and static environment. The day we think that we have "arrived" in terms of performance or that improvement is no longer a necessity is the day that we start a backward performance trip.

The search for new and innovative ways to compete, including within the domain of global supply management, is never ending. And the need to combine global supply management and risk prevention within this domain has never been greater.

REFERENCES

1. R.J. Trent. *Strategic Supply Management: Creating the Next Source of Competitive Advantage* 2007. Ft. Lauderdale, FL: J. Ross Publishing; 35–106.

2. R.M. Monczka, R.J. Trent, and K.J. Petersen. *Effective Global Sourcing and Supply for Superior Results* 2006. Tempe, AZ: CAPS Research; 70–71.

3. L. Giunipero and R. Handfield. *Purchasing Education and Training II* 2004. Tempe, AZ: CAPS Research; 64.

4. Associated Press. Sallie Mae to Shift Jobs to the U.S. Reported in *The Wall Street Journal* 2009 Apr 7; B5.

5. W. Bulkeley. IBM to Cut Jobs, Expand in India. Reported in *The Wall Street Journal* 2009 Mar 26; B1.

6. Anon. Searching for New Suppliers. Reported in *Purchasing Magazine Online* 2005 Feb 17; www.purchasing.com.

7. S. Welch. Offering Much, Africa Looks to Compete with China for Manufacturing. *Supply Chain Brain.com* 2006 Feb 1. Retrieved from http://www.supplychainbrain.com/content/nc/world-regions/middle-eastafrica/single-article-page/article/offering-much-africa-looks-to-compete-with-china-for-manufacturing/.

8. C. Coetzer. Transformation Occurring in South Africa. *Inside Supply Management* 2009 Mar; 20(3): 26.

9. P. Engardio and G. Smith. Business Is Standing Its Ground. *Business Week* 2009 Apr 20; 4127: 36.

10. C. MacDonald. Small U.S. Businesses Face Bigger Risks Abroad. *National Underwriter, P&C* 2008 May 5; 112(7): 10.

11. R. Wery. What Smaller Companies Need to Consider When They Go Offshore. *World Trade* 2005 Jul; 18(7): 19.

12. MacDonald, C. Small U.S. Businesses Face Bigger Risks Abroad. *National Underwriter, P&C* 2008 May 5; 112(7): 32.

13. I. Manuj and J.T. Mentzer. Global Supply Chain Risk Management. *Journal of Business Logistics* 2008; 29(8): 133.

INDEX